The BIG BLACK BOOK *of*

INCOME SECRETS

Tom Dyson
Publisher, Palm Beach Research Group

PALM BEACH RESEARCH GROUP

What Some of Our Readers Are Saying About Palm Beach Research's "Black Book" Income Strategies

- The Palm Beach Research Group gives a fresh new perspective to providing income for retirement. Keep up the good work. **–John C.**

- Finally, an approach that I can follow and still sleep at night. **–Jim K.**

- The Palm Beach Research Group has given me a different perspective on investing. I enjoy the education and suggestions for income. **–John A.**

- I think you are doing a great job with the alternative investments because it is broadening my horizon. **–Josh L.**

- The Palm Beach Research Group has opened my mind to new and creative ways of income creation and preservation. It is inspiring to receive detailed financial information with real world actionable content.

- Am very impressed by the common sense, no nonsense approach to building wealth. I am looking forward to the new Palm Beach Research Group income strategies. **–D.W.**

- The Palm Beach Research Group has given me a new perspective on how to look at the market and the various ways outside of the market to generate income. Learning from those that have already done it and continue to do it is just super... thank YOU! –**Ken C.**

- I appreciate your level-headed investment advice. Best of all is how you offer both wealth preservation and income generating strategies. –**Michael D.**

- I needed to improve long-term income. I have listened to and applied your recommendations with much success. I read and apply the teachings you share and greatly appreciate the work you do for my financial well-being. I look forward to many years of partnership. Many thanks. –**Terry B.**

- Information is useless unless you use it. The Palm Beach Research Group not only provides a practical approach to investing, it also provides its readers with multiple opportunities to create income. –**Angelo G.**

- Let me start by saying thank you. The Palm Beach Research Group has changed my mindset, and my income. My life is great. I've started my own staffing agency, and now have become depended on myself. Thanks for encouraging me to think outside the box. –**Dustin A.**

The BIG BLACK BOOK *of*

INCOME
SECRETS

Tom Dyson
Publisher, Palm Beach Research Group

ISBN 978-0-9963632-1-1

Published by:
The Palm Beach Research Group
Delray Beach, Florida

www.palmbeachgroup.com

Edited by:
Jeff Remsburg

PALM BEACH RESEARCH GROUP

About the Palm Beach Research Group

The Palm Beach Research Group is an independent financial publishing company based in Delray Beach, Florida. It publishes various advisories that provide stock, options, and income recommendations—as well as non-market wealth-building advice—to more than 75,000 subscribers.

When founders Mark Ford and Tom Dyson launched the Palm Beach Research Group in 2011, they wanted to create a publishing company unlike any other.

Most financial advisories are little more than stock "tip sheets." Mark and Tom had a different vision for their company. They wanted to provide subscribers a comprehensive wealth-building plan; one that would guide readers along the path to real, sustained financial prosperity.

To this end, Mark and Tom focused the Palm Beach Research Group on three key areas... safe income, safe growth, and comprehensive 360-degree wealth building.

Specifically, they've combined Tom's experience in the financial markets with Mark's success as a serial entrepreneur and real estate investor to achieve their goal—a holistic, wealth-building publishing company.

Services now include:

- Stock market investments (long term and trading)
- Cash-generating options strategies
- Rental real estate investing strategies

- "Outside the market" ideas for generating additional active income
- Credit repair strategies
- Entrepreneurial guidelines on starting your own business
- Retirement lifestyle guidelines.

And much more...

Each service supports the central mission of the Palm Beach Research Group:

Help readers get richer every single year.

To learn more about the Palm Beach Research Group, visit www.palmbeachgroup.com/about.

About the Authors:

- **Tom Dyson** is the publisher of the Palm Beach Research Group. Tom bought his first stock when he was 11 years old, and he has been studying the art of investing and speculating ever since.

  Tom graduated from the University of Nottingham, in the United Kingdom. He's a member of the Chartered Institute of Management Accountants, one of Britain's top accounting bodies. He went on to work for bond trading desks at Salomon Brothers and Citigroup.

  Tom then spent six years researching and writing about conservative income investments at Stansberry Research. His income-focused newsletter, *The 12% Letter*, was one of the most popular advisories in America. He still holds several of the "top 10" spots in Stansberry's hall of fame for highest gains on his recommendations.

  Today, Tom leads the Palm Beach Research Group, which is not just a stock market investment advisory, but a holistic, 360-degree wealth-building service.

- **Mark Ford** is the editor of *Creating Wealth* and co-founder of the Palm Beach Research Group. Mark started his first business when he was 11 years old. In the decades since, he's started hundreds more.

  Mark grew up in Brooklyn and Long Island, New York. He has a bachelor's degree from Queens College, CUNY, a master's degree from the University of Michigan, and did Ph.D. work at Catholic

University. After college, Mark joined the Peace Corps and spent two years teaching at the University of Chad in Africa.

In 1982, Mark moved to Palm Beach County and took a job with a small publishing company. He worked as an apprentice to a well-known businessman in South Florida. He helped that company grow to $135 million in annual revenues, became a multimillionaire himself, and retired at age 39.

After a year of writing poetry, he became a consultant to the health and investment publishing industries. He was involved in the development of dozens of multimillion-dollar businesses, including one whose revenues recently exceeded the $400 million mark.

He has also written a dozen books on entrepreneurship, personal productivity, and wealth building. Three of these were *New York Times* and *Wall Street Journal* best-sellers.

After turning 60 years old, Mark "retired" again. He now focuses on growing his investments and writing for the Palm Beach Research Group.

Mark currently lives in Palm Beach with his wife, Kathy.

- **Grant Wasylik** is the chief analyst for *The Palm Beach Letter*. Originally from Pennsylvania, Grant graduated from Juniata College with a degree in economics.

His previous experience includes working as a trading supervisor for a discount broker, an elite trading specialist for Charles Schwab, and a lead research analyst for a billion-dollar wealth manager.

Grant moved to Florida in 2013. He lives in Palm Beach County with his wife, two children, and two dogs.

- **Stan Haithcock**, aka Stan The Annuity Man, is a nationally recognized expert on annuities known for his transparency, honesty, and endless research. He has spoken at every major financial trade show in the United States. He is rigorously independent, representing all major carriers that meet his uncompromisingly high standards.

  With a financial background that spans some of the major wirehouse organizations such as Dean Witter, Morgan Stanley, Paine Webber, and UBS, Stan brings to his clients an informed clarity and "insider" wisdom that makes him extra careful and cognizant of risks and how to avoid them.

  In 2005, when Stan became Stan The Annuity Man, he determined that each client deserved his undivided personal attention and that his mission was to become a trusted member of each client's financial team. That meant he would be known for fly-to-your-home, coast-to-coast service. Today, Stan does indeed have clients nationwide.

  Stan and his wife, Christine, reside in Ponte Vedra Beach, Florida with their two daughters and their Shih Tzu, Cutie the Wonder Dog.

Contents

Part 4: Safe Stock Market Income

Part 5: Bet on Yourself

Introduction

Dear Reader,

Seven years ago, my father—like many retirees—lost nearly all his retirement savings in the Great Recession.

My dad thought he was safe. He had saved and invested wisely over the years, amassing a large retirement nest egg. But he hadn't allocated it wisely—too large a percentage of his savings was in Lehman Brothers and Citigroup stock (where he had worked). When Lehman went bankrupt in 2008, he lost hundreds of thousands of dollars.

One minute, he was preparing for a leisurely retirement of golf, travel, and relaxation. The next, he found himself forced back into the labor pool, working as a piano teacher to pay his bills.

It was an unthinkable situation: suddenly needing tens of thousands of dollars in extra income... and without any idea of how to find it.

I couldn't just stand by watching, so I set out to help him...

I'd spent my entire professional life helping folks grow their money in the financial markets. Surely I could help my own father, right?

But the landscape had changed...

As any retiree is now all too aware, finding safe income has become a daunting challenge.

Thanks to the Federal Reserve's zero-interest-rate policy, living off of fixed-income investments doesn't seem likely... or even possible... anymore.

Bank accounts used to pay more than 5% interest. Today, they pay less than 1%... and in many cases, they pay nothing.

You won't find any help from CDs. In 2007, you could find a 1-year CD paying about 4%. As I write this, the average one-year CD pays 0.27%.

It's no better with corporate bonds. You used to be able to get nearly 10% from bonds and bond funds, even the safe ones. Today, there's nothing of quality paying much more than about 5%.

You used to be able to find high yields in the stock market, as well. When I first started looking at high-yield stock investments 10 years ago, the safe investments paid 10%, and the risky ones paid 20%. Today, even the riskiest high-yield stocks pay less than 10%.

All of this pointed me toward one conclusion...

I wouldn't find the solution to my father's problem in traditional places.

The markets and investments that had once held the promise of a safe, comfortable retirement had failed my father and so many other retirees just like him.

So I began a new journey... a research experiment that would take me to the "fringes" of American finance...

I began looking in places they don't teach you about it business school or on Wall Street—the "nooks and crannies" of the U.S. markets, if you will.

To my relief—and surprise—the answers I found were not only safe, but they represented a REAL solution to my father's crisis.

They can do the same for you.

Now, you won't find these ideas written about in investing newsletters, pushed by the mainstream financial media, or discussed at cocktail parties. They're simply too off the radar.

But it's for this reason they're so powerful... and hold the promise of safe income.

Today, I'm proud to present to you *The Big Black Book of Income Secrets*. It's the culmination of seven years of research. May the contents prove as valuable to you as they have to my own father.

Good investing,

Tom Dyson

PART 1:

Income for Life Uncovered

CHAPTER 1

Income for Life: How to Fund Your Own Worry-Free, 100% Tax-Free Retirement

This super-safe "off the IRS grid" account can't go down in value, has paid uninterrupted dividends for over 100 years, and currently earns five times more than your bank savings account and CDs.

By Tom Dyson

I thought I'd seen it all...

Over the past 10 years, I've examined almost every type of safe income investment in existence.

I've studied utilities, municipal bonds, real estate, and real estate investment trusts. I've researched MLPs, BDCs, and royalty trusts. I've dug into CDs and bank deposits. And I've analyzed almost every well-known dividend-paying stock in America.

And before that, I worked for two of the world's largest banks— Salomon Brothers and Citibank—in London.

So I must admit, when I discovered a secret, high-yield account used by more than 4,000 banks, I was a little shocked.

For example:

- Bank of America has $18.5 billion tucked away in these accounts

---

- Citibank has $4.5 billion hidden in its own secret accounts
- And JPMorgan Chase conceals $9.8 billion in this type of account.

They'd put more of their money in these accounts if they could, but regulators restrict them from putting more than 25% of their Tier 1 capital there.

You see, just like IRAs, Roth IRAs, and 401(k)s, Income for Life lets you grow your money tax-free.

That's why top bankers and Fortune 500 executives in the know have quietly been taking advantage of opportunities like these for years now... Safely earning generous yields on their money—up to 5% on average—while everyone else has been stuck chasing low-paying CDs, bonds, and dividends.

[Tax-free returns of 5% may not sound like much, but if you're in a 35% tax bracket, that's the equivalent of earning close to 8% in your regular taxable brokerage account.]

The Most Underground Income Investment I've Ever Seen

At first, when I first learned of this secret from my friend Tim several years ago, I was a little skeptical...

But I knew Tim was a smart guy... and I couldn't ignore it.

Tim recommended an obscure book that explained the account and this strategy in more detail.

How obscure?

There are 136,450 books for sale on Amazon with the words "real estate" in the title.

There are 65,137 books on Amazon with the words "stock market" in the title.

But there are fewer than 15 books I know of that discuss this idea...

I looked up the book Tim recommended. Amazon didn't have it in stock, but I was able to buy a 10-year-old used edition for $5.

A few weeks later, I sat down and read it...

I was intrigued, so I didn't stop there. I tracked down a few other books on the subject and read those.

Then I wrote to five or six of my contacts in the finance business to get their opinions on this idea.

None of them had heard of this particular idea.

I couldn't find any articles about this in the newspapers and magazines. And I couldn't find any advertisements for it.

In short, this idea is so underground, the only way you'd ever hear about it is if you stumbled onto it by accident. Even then, you'd be unlikely to get involved unless you invested the time to understand its full power. (There are no glossy brochures with bullet-points to explain how it works.)

So I contacted Tim again. He had been using this account himself. And he shared everything he knew. He also put me in touch with an expert who has helped some of the wealthiest people in America set up and use this account.

Within a few weeks, this expert flew to Delray Beach, Fla., and spent the afternoon in my conference room explaining the details and answering all of my questions.

Finally, I was convinced. And excited. I made two decisions. To do it myself, for the benefit of my family. And to share it with Palm Beach Research Group readers...

Why was I so convinced? Why was I so excited about what I learned?

The "Swiss Army" Knife of Financial Accounts

The Swiss Army Knife is arguably the world's most popular pocketknife. You likely own one. The red casing. The white cross. The various tools and mechanisms.

The knife originated in the 1880s when the Swiss army decided to purchase a new folding pocketknife for its foot soldiers. The original Swiss Army Knife had a blade, reamer, can opener, and screwdriver.

Soldiers could open their canned food. They could repair their rifles. Or they could use the knife blade for dozens of other tasks.

Today, the Swiss Army Knife is robust and versatile. Possible tools include multiple blades, tweezers, toothpick, saw, magnifying glass, screwdriver, pliers, corkscrew, and ballpoint pen to name a few.

A dozen tools; three dozen applications. All in a compact pocketknife. An all-in-one solution in case you need it for the random task or situation that pops up.

Now, as I studied this underground account, I compiled a list of its many benefits. Its multiple uses and versatility left me with one conclusion: This account is the financial equivalent of the Swiss Army Knife. With this account you can...

- Grow your money at up to 5% over the long term
- Have a contractual guaranteed minimum growth rate of 4%
- Compound your money tax deferred (pay no taxes on gains each year)

- Completely avoid risk of principal loss—meaning you can sleep at night knowing your account balance won't go down in value (even if the stock market crashes 50% tomorrow)
- Safeguard your money in a place with a century-long track record of safety
- Protect your money from creditors or lawsuits (in most states)
- Contribute unlimited amounts to it (unlike an IRA or 401(k))
- Avoid reporting it to the IRS come tax time
- Access your money anytime without penalty or withholding taxes
- Build a line of credit to use for any reason—no questions asked.

As you can see, there are so many benefits to this account. Two different people might choose to open this account for totally different reasons. That's one of the things that make it such a powerful financial tool.

I'm not going to get into the details of each benefit here. That will come later. Instead, right now, I'd just like to focus on two of my favorite benefits. One, this account's safety. And two, the way it enables me to maintain 100% control over my money—accessing it whenever I want.

It's important we review these benefits before talking about Income for Life.

Let's talk about safety first.

The Huge Risks Retirees Take Today

At the Palm Beach Research Group, we place an enormous emphasis on teaching our readers to avoid risk and keep their money safe.

A big part of that is making sure people know the difference between saving and investing. Most financial planners use the terms

---

synonymously. But that's not accurate. Saving and investing have distinct differences.

The primary purpose of investing is to *grow* your capital. The primary purpose of saving is to *preserve* it. As any stock market crash will illustrate, preserving your capital doesn't always happen when you're investing.

Understanding this distinction could mean the difference between financial success and failure over your investing career.

Take my dad, for example. He learned this lesson the hard way.

My father retired on New Year's Eve, 1999. As an investment banker on Wall Street during an economic boom, he'd spent the previous 10 years working harder than he'd ever thought possible... and getting paid more than he'd ever imagined.

At the age of 52, with several million dollars in "savings," he decided it was time for a new, more leisurely lifestyle. He hung up his suits, threw out his alarm clock, and began composing poetry and oil paintings.

But his money wasn't in "savings" at all. He'd put all of his money in the stock market... and concentrated it in several bank stocks, including Lehman Brothers.

Think back to when you were a teenager saving for your first car. Did you give the money you were saving to a friend so he could start a new business? No! You put it in a safe place, like a bank account or a sock drawer.

You put it in a place where there was no chance you would lose any of it, where you could add to it when you needed to, and where you could access it whenever you wanted it.

Well, my dad didn't do this. Turns out, he had his "savings" invested in the worst possible place—a company that was about to go bankrupt.

In the crash of '08, Lehman Brothers folded, and Dad lost almost everything. Most of his life savings vanished.

He has had to go back to work... as a piano teacher. If he'd put that money into true savings vehicles, where there was no risk of loss, he'd probably still be retired.

As you can see, the distinction between savings and investing is a distinction of purpose. Savings is money earmarked for certain future expenses. Investing is extra money set aside simply to build wealth... after you've taken care of your saving and spending.

These different purposes demand different strategies. Saving requires a very low degree of risk. Investing allows for some—but not too much—risk.

As an investor, you can put your money into a wider range of stocks—including some that you believe will "outperform" the market, such as some of the recommendations you get in *The Palm Beach Letter*'s Performance Portfolio. Or you can buy real estate that you believe will appreciate in value. Or you could fund a private business that you believe in. Or you can trade options and so on. (We cover all these strategies.)

But here's the thing... Investments will always be subject to loss. The business you invest in could fail (as nine out of 10 startups do). The stock you invest in could go belly up. The stock market could crash, just like it did in 2008.

Your savings, on the other hand, should be very safe. It should be trusted to only the sturdiest possible financial vehicles. There should be no risk that you'll lose it.

It wasn't just my dad who made this mistake. Tens, even hundreds of thousands of retirees worldwide made the same one.

In fact, I'll bet many of you reading this haven't yet distinguished between saving and investing—you may have ALL your retirement money invested in vehicles such as 401(k)s and IRAs or ALL your children's education expenses in Coverdell or 529 plans.

Almost all of these vehicles are in stock market-related investments like mutual funds or stocks. But this money should also be in savings vehicles.

This is one of the reasons why I was so drawn to this account—my money is totally safe. That's because this account has no exposure to the stock market. If the Dow crashes 50% tomorrow, my account balance won't drop a single dime.

With this strategy, there is virtually no risk of principal loss. Like a bank account, your money will never go down in value.

Many of the companies that administer these accounts have safely grown investors' savings for over a century without default.

I'll give you far more detail later on.

100% Control and Access to My Money

The second benefit I'd like to briefly touch on involves my ability to access my money.

I'm 38. I've got three young kids and a full life ahead of me. I'm thinking a lot about my financial future. Saving for retirement. Buying a new house. Generally, I don't believe in college, but I'm considering setting aside some money for my kids if they want to go.

If I follow mainstream financial advice, how do I plan for these life events? Well, I should have a 401(k) and maybe an IRA to save for retirement. If I'm considering savings for my kids' college, I'll open a Coverdell or 529 plan. A new house, I better save up for a down payment and make sure my credit is up to par for my future mortgage.

But there's always been something very unsettling to me about these options.

What if I wanted to retire when I was 50? I'd have to pay steep penalties to access my 401(k) or IRA funds before 59-and-a-half. What if I didn't want to retire or need to access the money in my retirement accounts? It wouldn't matter, the government would force me to take that money at age 70 so it could get its taxes.

What if my kids didn't want to go to college? I'd have to pay penalties to access the funds in those 529 accounts.

What if I had an unexpected medical emergency expense? Same thing, I'd have to pay penalties to access my money to handle that.

Though I have some of these accounts, I've never liked the lack of control. I've never liked all the rules and restrictions that come with them. And I've never liked having all my money scattered amongst these separate accounts.

As I dug deeper into the details of Income for Life, I discovered that it offered me complete control of my money. Because of a special set of features, it could act as a central warehouse for my money. Using the strategies I read about, this account gives me the flexibility to use it for any financial life event... virtually anything I could imagine.

It could act as my retirement plan. Meaning I could get the bulk of my retirement income from it in the future.

It could act as a college savings plan for my kids.

I could use it to pay for any big-ticket expense. A vacation. A down payment on a house. A new car.

I could leverage its funds to invest in anything... rental real estate, stocks, options, or precious metals.

I could use the funds to start a business. Or loan money to a friend or family member.

I love this kind of control. I can let my money sit—or I can access it at any point, no questions asked, in less than three days.

This Has Become My Single-Largest Investment...

Today, my wife and I have more than 75% of our total net worth allocated to the Income for Life strategy... and we're still adding money to it. We have made it the foundation of our retirement strategy.

I've even opened up accounts for each of my three children, and because of this decision, they'll now be financially set for life. (My oldest son, for example, will have about $4 million in his account by the time he retires.)

Today, I'm going to share with you everything I know about this strategy... and explain how you can set one up for yourself.

With this strategy, there is virtually no risk of principal loss. Like a bank account, your money will never go down in value.

The Safest Place on the Planet for Your Money

We're putting our money into a special type of dividend-paying company. You've probably never heard of these companies, even though they're among the oldest in America. Most financial professionals haven't heard of them, either.

I made a list of 35 of these special companies doing business in America today. The oldest company on the list is 177 years old. The average age of these companies is 106 years. Nineteen of them have been in business for more than a century.

These companies are rare. No one has formed one in a very long time (worldwide), and no new ones are likely to ever be formed again.

These companies do NOT trade on the stock market. Their values don't fluctuate like traded stocks.

They don't use debt.

Acquiring one of these companies is illegal. This is why Wall Street has no business with them. And it's why you've probably never heard of them.

And, of course, they generate tons of cash and they pay large dividends to their owners every year.

The World's Safest Industry

The companies I'm describing are a special breed of life insurance company. Now, I know what you're thinking. Most financial gurus say life insurance is a bad place for your money.

But please bear with me.

What we discovered are not your run-of-the-mill insurance companies. (I'll explain why they're different from regular life insurance companies in a moment.) In fact, these companies behave much more like savings or investment accounts than insurance companies. However, the government restricts the advertising these companies can use.

Okay, so first let me explain why life insurance is such a great industry for safety-conscious investors...

Life insurance is one of the oldest financial products in existence. The sale of life insurance in the U.S. began in the late 1760s. Life insurance has proven itself through two world wars, a revolution, a civil war, the Great Depression, and numerous other recessions.

There hasn't been a single life insurance contract default in the last 300 years in America.

Can you think of any other product that has proved itself like this? Popular investment products today include mutual funds, ETFs (exchange trades funds), 401(k)s, and IRAs. None of these products has been around longer than a few decades.

Life insurance is a recession-proof business. People need it regardless of what's going on in the economy. It's also a mathematical business, like running a casino, but with even better odds. As long as you price your risk correctly and you don't do anything stupid with the premiums you collect, you won't lose money over the long term.

Of all of the different types of insurance companies, life insurance companies are the safest.

Consider common insurable events, such as fires, earthquakes, or hurricanes. They're rare. So scientists have few examples to study. The damage claims can be astronomical. And you can't predict when these types of events will occur.

Now consider life insurance. A person's death is certain. Life expectancy is predictable for large groups. There's plenty of data. And the insurance company knows what the payout for death claims will be.

Demand for life insurance never changes. Even in a depression or an economic boom. This industry doesn't have a business cycle.

Statistics drive profits in this industry. As long as their equations are accurate—which they are, because they've been using them successfully for decades—they make predictable profits.

Insurance companies hire data-crunching experts called "actuaries." Actuaries study this data. Then they create life insurance policies for the companies' customers. As long as the actuaries do their jobs and the insurance companies have enough customers, you can virtually guarantee they'll be profitable.

During the Great Depression, more than 9,000 banks went bankrupt. According to a hearing of the Temporary National Economic Committee in 1940, only 2% of the total assets of all life insurance companies in the U.S. became impaired during the Great Depression (1929 to 1938).

Because the life insurance industry was so strong, it played a big part in keeping the country afloat and helping many troubled businesses get back on their feet.

One example is department store mogul James Cash Penney. The great stock market crash of 1929 almost wiped out J.C. Penney. He was able to borrow funds against his life insurance policy to keep his small department store chain in business through the Depression. Today, JCPenney has 1,000 stores and is worth $3.4 billion.

The same pattern appeared after the stock market crash of 2008-2009. We examined several of the safest insurance companies and found that less than 1% of their investments were listed as "nonperforming" during the financial crisis.

Not only did the recent financial crisis not affect these insurance companies, but they also continued their century-long track records of paying dividends. If I had to bet on a group of companies being around 100 years from now, I'd choose these.

But, as anyone who invested in MetLife stock knows, not all insurance companies are equal. MetLife's stock crashed 80% between 2008 and 2009.

For our Income for Life strategy, we're interested in only a tiny—much safer—subset of the life insurance industry.

STOP: READ THIS—Your Top Objections Answered

I know you may be shocked to hear this account is associated with a type of life insurance.

But it's not about life insurance at all—it's about the foundation it's built on. We use this special type of insurance like a car frame. You can build an average car or a sports car on the same frame.

We take the same life insurance framework and use it to build a financial vehicle with qualities we want. We design it in a special way to compound our money at up to 5% per year, tax-free. This unique type of life insurance account is the best vehicle we know of to guarantee growth and provide safety.

We've spent endless time, energy, and money to research this topic.

We've disproved many of the common myths and overcome many objections.

Read the rest of this report, and you will see the answers to the top objections answered shortly.

An Elite Subclass of Life Insurance Companies

There are two types of life insurance companies: stock life insurance companies and mutual life insurance companies.

Stock life insurance companies are life insurance companies that trade on the stock market. They issue stock, and they trade like any other public company. Hartford, MetLife, and Prudential are all examples of stock life insurance companies. So are some previously recommended *Palm Beach Letter* stocks such as American National Insurance Company, Kansas City Life Insurance, and National Western Life Insurance.

Mutual life insurance companies do not trade on the stock market. They don't have shares, and you can't buy into them through the stock market. They're like credit unions, except the policyholder is an owner in the insurance company.

Mutual life insurance companies are much safer than their "stock-issuing" cousins.

For one thing, because mutual companies have no shareholders, Wall Street analysts and money managers cannot pressure management to make short-term decisions. The companies are free to pursue long-term strategies. As a result, these corporations are known to be among the most conservatively managed companies in the world.

Stock life insurance companies have millions of shareholders. Many of these shareholders are powerful money managers. They want higher returns on their investments. It encourages the management of stock life insurance companies to take risks.

Mutual life insurance companies serve only one master... the policyholder. There are no outside shareholders to split profits with. No Wall Street. No quarterly earnings estimates. No conference calls. No insider trading. No takeovers. No message board gossip. No stock options.

Think of mutual life insurance companies as cooperatives... or not-for-profit clubs. A bunch of people have come together and pooled their money to provide life insurance for themselves.

Safety, stability, and good service are the only goals of the insurance company. Mutual insurance companies still generate profits. But those profits get distributed back to all of the members each year as dividends. (We'll get to dividends in a minute.)

You're more likely to see stock insurance companies borrowing money, advertising, and using other aggressive growth strategies.

They'll invest in riskier assets to appease hedge funds or large shareholders with higher returns.

They're also more likely to fudge their quarterly earnings releases to make their results seem better.

In sum, mutual insurance companies are one of the safest places on the planet to put your money. And some of the highest-paying places as well.

In the rest of this report, I'm going to explain how you can use mutuals as "secret savings accounts" that offer the guaranteed growth of our money for the REST OF OUR LIVES.

Right now, they're paying rates of up to 5% per year tax-free. (These rates could be lower depending on one's age and health rating.)

Most Life Insurance Is a Bet on Your Life

The life insurance business started as a wager.

On June 18, 1583, a London man named Richard Martin placed a bet with a group of merchants. The bet was on the life of another man, William Gybbon. Martin put up 30 pounds.

If Gybbon died within one year, Martin would make 400 pounds. But if Gybbon did not die, Martin would lose his 30-pound stake.

Gybbon died just before the end of the year. But the merchants refused to pay Martin his winnings. So Martin took them to court. The court ruled in favor of Martin. And the merchants' payment to Martin became the first official life insurance payout.

The modern name for this type of life insurance agreement is a "term" policy.

Putting the above example into contemporary terms, Richard Martin was the "policyholder" and "beneficiary" of the policy. The

30 pounds he paid in was his "premium payment." The merchants were the "insurance company." And we'd call William Gybbon the "insured."

Term insurance is just a simple bet. It's the policyholder betting against the insurance company. The policyholder is betting on a death, usually his own. And the insurance company is betting on survival.

If the insured person dies in the allotted time or "term," the policyholder wins the bet (and the beneficiary gets the money). If the insured survives, the insurance company wins the bet and the policyholder loses his stream of payments.

Please note, buying term life insurance is a bet the policyholder expects to lose, but it's still a bet. And he's willing to take this bet. That's because it's cheap. And he can provide his family with financial protection if he dies.

Today, term policies are the most popular type of insurance policy, representing just fewer than 40% of all life insurance premiums paid out in America each year. (Today, it's most common to buy 10- or 20-year term policies.)

But here's a fact that may shock you.

Only 3% of the term insurance contracts conclude with a payout. What that means is the insurance company "wins" the bet 97% of the time!

The Savings Account No One Knows Exists

Early in the 19th century, insurance companies developed a new type of insurance policy. They called it permanent insurance.

Permanent insurance is an insurance contract that remains in force until the insured dies. It has no term. It's permanent.

Because there is a 100% chance that the insured will die, permanent life insurance is NOT a gamble; it's a certainty. You buy $1 million of permanent life insurance. As long as you don't cancel the policy and you make your premium payments, the insurance company is going to pay out $1 million someday.

To pay out $1 million when you die, the insurance company must accumulate at least $1 million while you're living in order to make the payout and not go out of business.

It accumulates this money by collecting premiums from you each year. These premiums build up over time, and they generate interest—which also builds up and compounds. By the time of your death, you've built up enough money with the insurance company that it can pay your policy off.

To reinforce this point:

In order for the insurance company to pay out your life insurance policy when you die, it must first accumulate this money while you're alive. It does this by collecting premiums from you and investing them each year.

When you boil permanent life insurance down to its basic cash flows, first you make a series of payments to the insurance company while you're alive. The insurance company collects these payments, grows them, and then gives them back to you at the end of your life.

In other words, permanent life insurance has almost nothing to do with life insurance. It's a way while you're alive to save money that you get back when you die.

Do you see that?

Permanent life insurance is a certain payment to you from the insurance company in the future. This money exists because you've saved it up— and the insurance company has grown it—over many years.

In this way, permanent life insurance has nothing to do with life insurance. It's about saving money. It's a glorified bank savings account with a much higher interest rate.

In contrast, term life insurance is a wager with the insurance company whether or not you'll die in a given period. Term life insurance is not a vehicle for saving money. It's a way to protect your family in case you die unexpectedly.

The Opportunity

As you can see, a permanent life insurance contract is really a strategy for saving up money over time so that the insurance company can pay out the full amount when you die.

Here's the beautiful part:

While you're accumulating money with the insurance company, your money earns interest.

Due to special tax provisions for insurance companies, this return is tax-free.

When you buy your policy through a mutual life insurance company, you become an owner of the company. As an owner, you receive a share of the profits the company generates via dividends.

In fact, we studied eight companies that provide these policies, and they have now paid out, on average, for 121 years in a row.

When I add it up right now, the money I have in Income for Life is generating a return of 5% per year, tax-free, after dividends and interest. If long-term interest rates rise, my dividend will also rise.

Your Big Objection

I know you have one major objection to this plan. If you're like me, you're probably thinking:

"Why would I put my money into an account that pays only when I die?"

This is a great question. And the answer is very simple. The way permanent life insurance works is that you can use the money you're accumulating at the life insurance company anytime you want. You can do this through something the experts call a "policy loan."

Not one in 100 people know this, but you can use your Income for Life policy to pay for just about anything...

I'm using these policy loans to pay for all of my vacations, cars, houses, and medical expenses. I'll also use these loans to finance any future investments I make in stocks, real estate, or small businesses.

By running these expenses through my Income for Life policy, I'll generate an enormous positive cash flow, and no one in my family will ever have to borrow money from a bank or financing firm again.

I won't get into the details of this strategy here. For now, all you need to know is that you can use the money you've saved anytime you want. You can do this with no penalty, and no fees, as if it were sitting in a bank account.

And even while you're using it, it keeps growing up to 5% per year.

The Only Life Insurance That's "Palm Beach Worthy"

Three years ago, my wife and I met with a life insurance salesman in Jacksonville, Fla. He was trying to sell us a permanent life insurance policy.

We spent two hours in his office. He spent the first hour asking us dozens of personal questions about our finances. This made us uncomfortable.

He spent the second hour pitching us on a life insurance product involving the stock market. It was so complex that he used a thick binder and several glossy brochures to explain it to us.

The Big Black Book of Income Secrets

My wife and I left the meeting annoyed and confused. We decided we would never buy permanent life insurance. "We'll never understand it," we said.

I'm certain complexity is the biggest reason people hate permanent life insurance.

Insurance companies have sold permanent life insurance for centuries. But over the last three decades, they've made "innovations" to the original model. This has hurt its reputation.

For example, today, insurance companies sell policies in which you can adjust how much money you get when you die. Or when you pay the premiums. You can buy policies that pay interest based on the stock market's performance... or the bond market's performance.

You may have heard of some of these innovations. They have names like universal life, variable life, equity indexed universal life, etc.

In short, these innovations have introduced hundreds of variables into permanent life insurance policies. The customer can't understand them. Most agents don't understand them. And most important of all, they have shifted the risk away from the insurance company and back to the policyholder.

Plus, the complexity makes it easy for the insurance companies to hide the fees and commissions they're charging.

This was a big reason my wife and I wouldn't buy life insurance. I couldn't understand the fees the company wanted to charge me.

I'm not saying you couldn't structure an Income for Life strategy with a universal, variable, or equity indexed life insurance policy. But I'd advise you not to. They're too complicated.

Here at the Palm Beach Research Group, we hate complexity. One of the rules Mark and I established when we first started was we'd never recommend anything we couldn't understand and explain in simple terms.

Our Income for Life strategy uses the most ordinary type of permanent life insurance. It's the Coca-Cola Classic of the insurance industry. Its design hasn't changed in over 100 years.

Here's how it works:

First, you agree with the insurance company how much money you want your beneficiaries to receive when you die.

Then you pay a minimum amount every year into your policy. They call these payments "premiums." You agree to these amounts up front with the insurance company. They never change.

While you're alive, these payments build up a cash value in your policy. And you earn interest and dividends, tax-free, on this cash. Meanwhile, you can also use this money whenever you need it.

That's it.

There are no fancy customizations. And it has nothing to do with the stock market. But it's easy to understand. It's been tried and tested for over two centuries. And it comes with some of the lowest commissions of any permanent life insurance product on the market.

In the industry, they call it "whole life insurance." Whole life insurance is a common insurance product. You can buy it from almost any insurance agent in the country... or around the world.

Our Income for Life strategy uses a "participating" or "dividend-paying" whole life insurance policy...

Becoming a Part Owner to Share in the Profits

When you own a participating whole life insurance policy, you become a part owner of the insurance company. That means you're entitled to a share of the profits. Profits come from two places, underwriting and investments.

Now, most insurance companies have several lines of business. They'll issue term policies. Or they'll offer employee benefit programs that offer medical, dental, and disability insurance.

They might issue auto policies. And most have retirement divisions that offer things such as 401(k)s, annuities, or long-term care solutions.

If insurance companies underwrite and manage these programs the right way, they'll pour money into the insurance companies' coffers. And the only customers of the life insurance companies who share in the underwriting profits—the ones these multiple lines of businesses generate—are the ones with "participating" whole life policies.

The second way insurance companies generate profits is from their investing activities. Think of the hundreds of thousands of customers an insurance company has. All of these customers make annual, quarterly, or monthly payments to the insurance company for all of the policies they have.

That means there's a steady stream of cash pouring into the company each day. The insurance company won't need to pay many of its claims immediately. It takes years, sometimes decades, for people to collect.

Instead of sitting on this cash, insurance companies conservatively invest and grow it. They know with exact precision when they'll need the money to pay claims.

At the end of each year, the insurance company tallies the profits from its investing and underwriting activities. It pays expenses and claims, then sets aside a little into a reserve account for extra safety. What happens to the rest of the profits?

They're dispersed to "participating" policyholders as a dividend each year.

The top mutual insurance companies we recommend are so prudent at managing their investments and insurance businesses that they've managed to pay dividends to their participating policyholders for more than 100 years in a row.

There's one final twist we'll add to a dividend-paying whole life insurance policy. This twist makes it different from any other type of life insurance policy, including most of the whole life policies the industry sells today.

[When a mutual insurance company issues a whole life policy, it calls it "participating" or "dividend-paying" whole life insurance. Policyholders own the mutual company and "participate" in the profits by earning interest and dividends.]

The Secret Ingredient That Makes Income for Life

Call up your local life insurance agent. Ask him for a whole life insurance policy. He'll sell you the life insurance coverage that comes with a savings component.

But we've established that Income for Life is NOT about the life insurance coverage.

What do I mean by this?

Most people think of life insurance as something you buy to protect your family in case you die. It's a precaution. But our Income for Life strategy has nothing to do with estate planning, protection, or life insurance.

It's a program to save money and build wealth *while you're still living*. We structure our whole life policy to emphasize the savings aspect and minimize the life insurance aspect.

In the insurance industry, they'd say we were trying to "maximize the cash value of the policy and minimize the life insurance coverage."

We do this by stuffing as much money into our whole life policy as we can, as fast as possible, keeping our life insurance coverage as low as possible.

For example, a typical term life insurance buyer might pay $1,000 per year for a $2 million policy.

But we would prefer to pay $20,000 per year for a $500,000 whole life policy. This way, we get much more money earning interest and dividends in our policy, and we give much less money to the insurance company for life coverage.

Do you see this?

Most people want as MUCH life insurance coverage as possible by spending as LITTLE money as possible.

With our Income for Life strategy, we want to get as LITTLE life insurance coverage as possible, by putting as MUCH money as possible into our policy.

Income for Life uses a special tool to make this happen. It's called a paid-up additions (PUA) rider. Most life insurance companies offer this rider. But few insurance agents know it exists.

A PUA rider is a way to stuff as much money into your policy as is legally possible. This way, you're earning more interest and more dividends in your account, without increasing the amount you spend on life insurance protection.

I'm not going to get into all of the details of the PUA rider just yet.

For now, all you need to know is that the PUA rider changes an ordinary whole life insurance policy into a wealth-building machine.

What do I mean by stuffing as much money in your policy as is "legally possible"?

Insurance policies confer enormous tax benefits. In the '70s and '80s, investors and corporations plowed billions into permanent life insurance policies to take advantage of the tax benefits. In 1986, the IRS clamped down. It set a limit on how much cash you could put into permanent life insurance.

If you exceed this limit, your life insurance policy turns into what the IRS calls a modified endowment contract, or MEC. And it won't qualify for the tax benefits.

The illustration to the right shows the relationships of insurance types to this MEC line.

At the top of the scale, you have insurance policies that offer 100% savings with the least amount of life insurance. These are MECs.

At the bottom of the chart, you have term insurance. It offers just insurance, and it's the cheapest. There is no savings component with term insurance.

In between, you have other types of permanent life insurance.

The thick dotted line shows where an insurance policy turns into an MEC and loses its tax benefits (tax-free growth).

Income for Life uses a participating/dividend-paying whole life insurance policy from a mutual insurance company. It uses a PUA rider to put as much money into your whole life policy as possible WITHOUT crossing the MEC line.

The fact that the government limits how much money you can put into your insurance policy should show you how powerful this strategy is.

Wealth Building or Life Insurance Coverage?

Income for Life uses as little life insurance coverage as possible,
without breaching the IRS's MEC rule

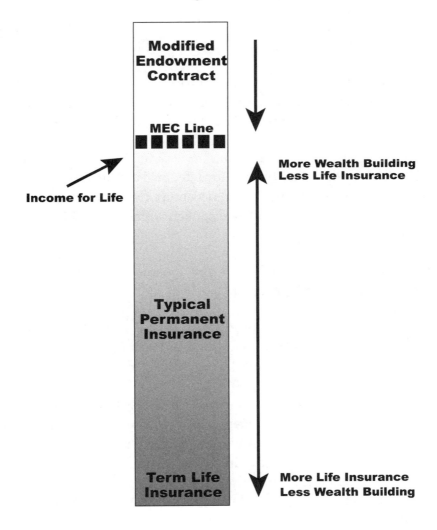

How to Open an Income for Life Policy

In 2011, the Palm Beach Research Group hired a life insurance investigator.

We paid him to investigate the Income for Life industry and figure out which Income for Life experts, if any, we could recommend to you.

"Not only should our experts have the experience," I said, "but they should also have perfect reputations. And, most important of all, they must use the Income for Life strategy with their own money."

This investigator was already familiar with the industry. Plus, he'd read all of the books on Income for Life, he'd attended both major Income for Life conferences, he knew more than a dozen of the top Income for Life experts, and he'd spoken with dozens of Income for Life customers.

He'd also taken out several of his own Income for Life policies on himself and his family members.

Our investigator was Tim Mittelstaedt. He did such a thorough investigation that I hired him to work for Palm Beach Research Group full time. And he's now the editorial director here.

Tim and I chose the best Income for Life agency to help serve our readers. It has hundreds of clients. Its agents have set up thousands of Income for Life policies. And these agents have more than 53 years of combined experience in the industry.

Most importantly, they all put their own money... lots of it... into Income for Life policies.

We know them, we like them, and we trust them. And we recommend them to you because they understand how to set up and use our Income for Life strategy better than anyone else. It's as simple as that.

An Important Warning about Scammers

Before we get to our experts, we need to pause for a second. Before you move any further, we need to ask you to please be aware: 95% of the information you'll find online about Income for Life is published by opportunistic salespeople using the movement to generate sales for their own life insurance businesses.

These scammers post free information online (sometimes using the terms Income for Life, 770 account, or Infinite Banking) and try to convert the traffic Google sends their way.

The Income for Life strategy is very specific. If you don't set it up right, it won't work as well. You'll waste thousands of dollars and end up with a horrible mess.

Some of these agents are good guys, and they mean well. They understand the Income for Life concept and they'll take good care of you.

Most are NOT good guys. They don't understand Income for Life at all. They'll sell you a garbage product not compatible with this strategy and give you terrible service. Or worse, they'll set up your policy and then disappear. Later in life, when you have questions or want to use your policy, they're nowhere to be found.

We know of several Palm Beach Research Group readers who've been duped this way.

So why take the risk?

Below, we've provided the names of some of the most widely recognized, most knowledgeable Income for Life professionals in the industry. As with any recommendation we make in *The Palm Beach Letter* or any of the other Palm Beach Research Group services, we don't receive commissions, fees, kickbacks, or compensation of any kind for recommending these experts.

They'll take great care of you. And they won't cost you any more than an online agent in terms of commissions.

[Life insurance commissions are state regulated, so there's no competing on price. An agent cannot charge any more or any less than any other agent.]

This is your livelihood we're talking about. And your retirement. Don't throw it away by working with an unqualified agent. Better to sleep well at night knowing your policy was set up correctly by an agency that'll be there for you for the rest of your life.

Preferred Income for Life Agency—Paradigm Life

Our preferred Income for Life agency is Paradigm Life, based in Salt Lake City, Utah. Patrick Donohoe is the founder of Paradigm Life. He formed his company in 2007. Patrick is my personal life insurance expert. He's set up six policies for me so far. And he owns 11 policies of his own.

Patrick understands Income for Life better than anyone we've met. He and his team of agents are on the cutting edge of education, training, and implementation of Income for Life. That's why we've listed them as our preferred agency.

Getting Started

To schedule a free, no-strings-attached meeting with one of Paradigm's Income for Life experts, email them at incomeforlife@paradigmlife.net.

You can also meet and contact the nine experts we've picked to help our readers.

You should hear from someone on the Paradigm Life team within 24 hours.

Paradigm Life
132 W. Pierpont Ave., Suite 250
Salt Lake City, Utah 84101

Phone: (855) 801-6306

www.paradigmlife.net

incomeforlife@paradigmlife.net

Note: When I hired Tim in 2011, I tasked him with understanding everything he could about insurance. He got licensed with Paradigm Life as an agent.

Why?

I wanted him to have access to all the data directly from the insurance companies that regular consumers like you and me can't access. Patrick agreed to license him. It's how we've been able to research Income for Life so thoroughly.

That said, you should know that neither Tim nor the Palm Beach Research Group make a dime from recommending Paradigm Life to you.

Tips on Working with Our Income for Life Experts

To open an Income for Life policy, the first thing you must do is contact one of our recommended Income for Life experts.

Life insurance policies require lots of setup, customization, and a fair bit of paperwork. Plus, there is a health exam and some other stuff you have to do.

It can take up to a month to set up your policy. Sometimes longer.

Income for Life is a lifelong strategy you'll have in place for decades. There's no rush. A few days or weeks won't matter in the big picture.

So be patient.

Keep these general tips in mind as you consider opening an Income for Life policy.

1. Pick an expert you connect with.

The government regulates the fees life insurance agents can charge you. So from a cost perspective, it doesn't matter whom you choose. You'll pay the same.

You'll have your Income for Life policy for the rest of your life. And you're going to work with your agent for many years. It's important that you like working with and connect with him or her.

If—for whatever reason—you aren't connecting with the expert you request or are assigned, don't be afraid to ask for someone different.

2. Determine how much money you intend to put into Income for Life.

You don't need to have an exact number at this point. You may not have even made up your mind about starting an Income for Life policy yet.

But before you call one of our experts, please have a rough number in mind that could make sense for you. For example:

"I could afford to save $100 per month" or "I'm considering starting with $10,000 per year."

Also if you have some cash saved up, think about how much of that cash you'd like to put into a policy, in addition to a monthly or annual commitment.

Why?

Using this number, our experts will create an example policy for you. They call it a "policy illustration." It'll show you how your money will grow over time. And your expert can talk you through real-life examples of how you could use your Income for Life policy.

3. Be prepared for tons of personal questions.

Our Income for Life experts are going to ask you dozens of personal questions about your income, your savings, your health, and your family situation.

They need this information to make sure Income for Life is right for you, and to figure out the best way to structure your policy. When you first contact our experts by email, you'll be asked to fill out a financial questionnaire.

You might be as uncomfortable talking about these personal details as we are. But in order to set up your policy correctly, your expert needs to understand your personal financial situation.

4. Be prepared to take a medical exam.

Unless you're insuring a newborn baby, you will need to take a medical exam.

Think of the medical exam like a pre-approval for a mortgage. It won't cost you any money. And it's easy.

The insurance company will send a nurse to your house at a time that's convenient for you. The nurse will take urine and blood samples, your blood pressure, and some basic measurements. Then he'll ask you questions about your health and your family's medical history.

If you're older and you have a longer medical history, expect delays as the insurance company's underwriting department verifies your health conditions.

If you're concerned you may not qualify because of an existing or past condition, and you don't want to waste the time filling out an application, tell your expert. In some cases, they can gather some basic information about your health problems and do a preliminary check with the insurance company to see if you're still insurable.

5.   Don't be afraid to start small.

When I invest in a new investment class I'm not familiar with, I start small.

Then, when I'm satisfied that my investment is acting the way I expected it to, I add to my position.

With Income for Life, I started with one small policy. A year later, I took out four more—much larger—policies.

There's no financial cost to adding policies in this way. And there are no flat fees or minimum amounts.

6.   Raise your questions and concerns up front.

Do you have concerns that you are too old? Are you considering getting rid of your term insurance policy and putting the money into a whole life insurance policy? Do you want to use Income for Life to save for retirement, pay for your kids' college expenses, or finance your vehicles?

Please raise these questions and concerns the first time you speak with our Income for Life experts. This way, they'll be able to give you more focused advice and better service.

PART 2:

Off-the-Grid Income

CHAPTER 2

Using Peer-to-Peer Lending as a Fixed Income Platform

Get Safe 6-8% Returns... Without Buying a Stock or Bond

By Grant Wasylik and Tom Dyson

Simon Cunningham didn't trust the risky stock market or the low-yielding bond market in 2011.

He wanted solid, passive income... double-digit returns, preferably.

So he began exploring other ways to put his savings to work—safely.

After his research revealed a budding platform, he became an early adopter, putting his excess cash to work.

Soon, Simon moved his entire Roth IRA to this platform.

For the next three-plus years, he achieved an impressive 11.8% annualized return.

As a result, Simon now thinks this method is "the greatest thing since sliced bread."

And he proclaims, "I found the love of my (financial) life."

Other "early adopter" investors—unhappy with today's low-yielding

---

traditional investments—have joined Simon...

Bob has been investing on the same platform since November 2009. He's invested almost $40,000. And has enjoyed 15% net annualized returns.

Tom has been using this technique for three years. He's funded over 7,000 different investments courtesy of this new vehicle. These investments have outperformed his other stock and bond investments. Tom's booked a steady net return of 6.8%.

Joe used the income he received from this method to pay off student loans, and even buy an engagement ring. He's been using it since August 2009, averaging 8% returns each year.

Now, we must warn you—these returns aren't going to last forever. In fact, they may disappear soon...

Even Simon earned "only" a 10.4% return in the fourth quarter of 2014. That's down from the 19.8% he earned in the fourth quarter of 2012.

The problem is this "little-known market" is quickly becoming more well known. New investment dollars are flooding in.

This fresh cash is pushing down returns... as the demand to invest exceeds the supply of investments.

Eventually, this market should find equilibrium... most likely at lower return levels than we're seeing today.

But right now, this opportunity is still very profitable for participants...

So we recommend that you act quickly if it interests you.

Now it's not a stock, bond, or fund. And you can't buy it in your existing brokerage account.

In fact, it legality wasn't settled until 2008... when SEC regulators finally gave their blessing.

But we think you'll agree it's worth the wait... as well as the little bit of extra time it will take to set up.

Remember, here at the Palm Beach Research Group, we're always going the extra mile. We log hundreds of hours of research every month to uncover these income opportunities. We aren't afraid of unconventional ideas—as long as they pass our strict tests for safety and income.

In this chapter, we have another one.

We won't promise the double-digit returns that Simon and Bob have enjoyed. Yet we believe you'll make 6-8% returns like Tom and Joe—with very limited risk.

And we'll also pinpoint the returns you can make, show you why it's safe, and walk you through step-by-step instructions on how to set yourself up on this investment platform.

You'll be able to take advantage of this opportunity from the comfort of your own home.

So let's get started... with a little background on how this all began...

From Temples to Big Banks... to Anyone's Computer

The very first banks in ancient Greece and Egypt were actually temples.

Priests and temple workers were trusted individuals. Wealthy people felt secure storing their money there. Temples not only took deposits, they also loaned money out.

Then the Romans came along. They weren't as pious. And they

eventually moved their banks from humble temples to district buildings. The industry continued to consolidate...

Large merchant banks were created (Barclays (1690), JPMorgan Chase (1799), Goldman Sachs (1869), to name a few)... the Federal Reserve Bank was formed in 1913... and the FDIC was created in 1933.

These big banks loaned more and more money... until the 2008 financial crisis. Then, they sharply pulled back their lending... which still hasn't recovered to pre-crisis levels...

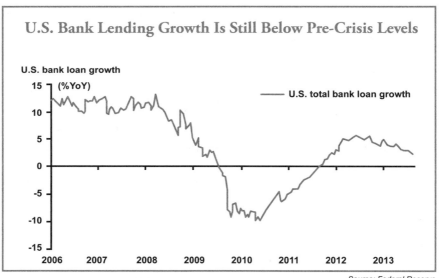

U.S. Bank Lending Growth Is Still Below Pre-Crisis Levels

U.S. bank loan growth
(%YoY)

—— U.S. total bank loan growth

Source: Federal Reserve

But individuals and businesses still need to borrow money. And they're now starting to get that cash somewhere else.

Non-bank lending is growing around 10% per year. And today's recommendation—a small subset of non-bank lenders—grew 166% in 2014.

We're talking about peer-to-peer lending—the fast-growing industry that Simon Cunningham uncovered in 2011.

Peer-to-Peer Lending: A Primer

Peer-to-peer lending is simply people with money (investors) lending directly to people who need money (borrowers).

They both cut out the "middleman"—such as a bank—to do business directly with each other.

With the rapid growth of the Internet and social networking, this practice is thriving online. It's increasingly filling the gap left by the banks when they pulled back consumer lending...

P2P Loans Skyrocket as
Standard Consumer-Finance Loans Decline

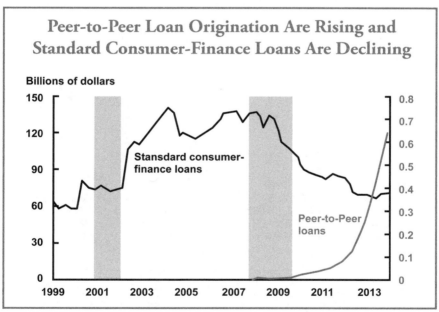

Source: Federal Reserve Bank of Cleveland

Peer-to-peer (P2P) lending works like this:

1. Borrower applies for a loan on a major P2P lending platform.

---

2. The platform verifies each borrower.

3. Approved loans are added to the platform and given loan grades (higher grade loans offer lower yields).

4. Investors choose the loans they want to invest in.

Borrowers can borrow money from people they've never met before. And investors can lend money to borrowers based on their credit information—without having to know them personally.

And all without any bank involvement.

Here's an illustration:

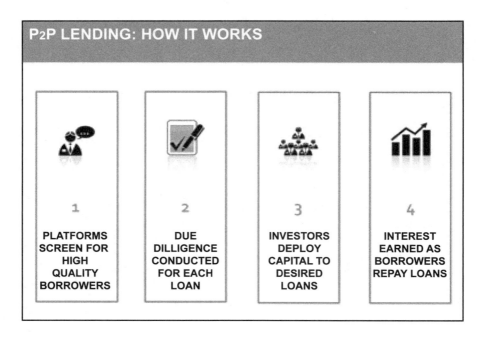

P2P LENDING: HOW IT WORKS

1	2	3	4
PLATFORMS SCREEN FOR HIGH QUALITY BORROWERS	DUE DILLIGENCE CONDUCTED FOR EACH LOAN	INVESTORS DEPLOY CAPITAL TO DESIRED LOANS	INTEREST EARNED AS BORROWERS REPAY LOANS

Also called social lending and person-to-person lending, here's how it all got started...

In 2005, U.K. company Zopa launched the world's first online P2P lender. Zopa has lent more than $814 million in P2P loans over the last decade. It's Europe's largest P2P lending service.

In the U.S., there are two established companies: Prosper and Lending Club.

Prosper started in February 2006. It's America's first P2P lending marketplace. With over $2 billion in funded loans, Prosper is the world's No. 2 player in the market.

Lending Club began operations in May 2007 as a Facebook application. Within months, it became the main U.S. competitor to Prosper. Lending Club is now the world's largest P2P lending platform with more than $7.6 billion in funded loans.

Lending Club vs. Prosper... Who Do We Prefer?

We've chosen Lending Club for these five reasons...

No. 1: Lending Club has four times as many loans for us to choose from...

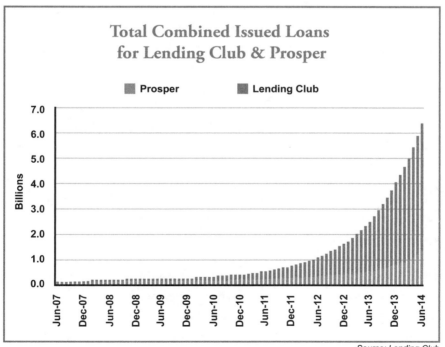

Source: Lending Club

Lending Club has close to $8 billion in funded loans. Prosper has $2 billion.

No. 2: Lending Club is the most reputable. Not only does it attract the most members in the P2P lending universe, it has received some high-profile endorsements:

- Google, Alibaba, and BankAlliance (a pool of 200 community banks) have recently announced partnerships...

- Former U.S. Treasury Secretary Larry Summers, ex-Morgan Stanley CEO John Mack, and venture capitalist Mary Meeker (Forbes' 77th most-powerful woman in the world) are on the company's board...

- Venture capitalist Charles Moldow owns 11% of its outstanding stock (he sold previous startups to Microsoft and Yahoo).

In fact, we spoke with Peter Renton, founder of Lend Academy Media and one of the leading educators on P2P lending. Peter is also recognized as the "expert on all things Lending Club." He told us that part of the reason Lending Club did its initial public offering (IPO) less than three months ago... was to create more awareness around the industry and their platform.

No. 3: Lending Club has a convenient "one-click" investment method that we're recommending (more on that later). And a better website overall.

No. 4: For borrowers, Lending Club requires a higher minimum credit score (660) than Prosper (640). We're going to be lenders, so we prefer higher-credit borrowers.

No. 5: Lending Club vets its borrowers more thoroughly. It looks at over 100 variables when reviewing a borrower's profile—such as FICO score, income, revolving credit balances, monthly payments, past bankruptcies, and debt-to-income ratio. Prosper, meanwhile, only requires a 640 credit score from Experian.

We like the returns offered, as well.

The Expected Yields are 12 to 130 Times the Yields of CDs and Savings Accounts

As we write, P2P lending yields are 100 to 130 times the average savings account yield. And 12 to 17 times the yield of a three-year CD...

Our preferred P2P investments (first three bars below) all yield more than traditional fixed-income assets.

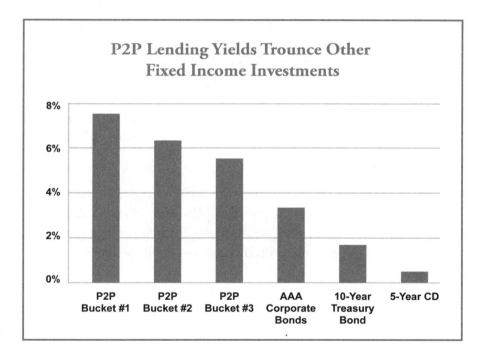

The three "one-click" investment options we have for you earn 7.85%, 6.66%, and 5.83%, respectively. We'll highlight each of them shortly.

And best of all, these returns are net of fees and net of charge-offs (defaults).

For investors, there's no fee for opening an account. Lending Club charges borrowers a 1% service fee. The company makes its

---

real money on origination. It charges 1-5% in origination fees to borrowers. We're lenders, though. Our fees are much less.

Now, 6-8% returns may sound great. But to be a *PBL*-worthy investment, we also require significant safety...

And Here's Why Lending Club Is a Safe Place for Your Money

First, as we write this, the U.S. consumer is improving...

The Federal Reserve reports total household debt (mortgage debt, auto loans, credit card debt, and student loans) totaled $11.8 trillion as of December 31, 2014. Household debt peaked at $12.7 trillion on September 30, 2008. About 7% shaved off in six years.

And the job market is getting better. The economy is generating more than 200,000 new jobs per month, consistently. Non-farm payroll employment has been over 200,000 for 11 months in a row. The long-term average is 120,000.

Second, more and more consumers are turning to P2P lending. Banks have high overhead costs, inflexible underwriting criteria, limited access to capital after 2008, multiple layers of costs and fees that dilute investor returns, and tiny returns for depositors.

The process of getting a loan from a bank is time-consuming and inefficient. More and more consumers will become familiar with P2P lending. This should continue to supply an ample amount of borrowers as they realize it's possible to bypass the banking system.

In other words, it's safe to say: P2P lending is here to stay.

Third, it adds diversification to an investor's overall portfolio. Diversification lowers risk. You're investing in "consumer credit"—a different asset class than other typical investments.

Fourth, low default rates. From 2007 to 2014, Lending Club

averaged a default rate of just 6.9% for 36-month loans. If we ignore 2007 and 2008—when Lending Club only issued about 3,000 loans—the average default rate for the last six years is 4.8%. With improving U.S. consumer balance sheets, default rates should remain low.

Fifth, you're loaning money to quality borrowers that have been pre-screened. And about *90% of potential borrower applicants are rejected* by Lending Club. That's right, Lending Club turns away nine out of every 10 potential borrowers. That's a lot of business the company is turning away... so that its lenders can invest with confidence.

Which means the borrowers that do make the cut have A-1 characteristics. As of December 31, 2014, the average Lending Club borrower had: a 700 FICO score... a 17.2% debt-to-income ratio... a 15.9 year credit history... a $73,278 personal income (top 10% of U.S. population)... and an average loan size of $14,292.

And last, 84% of Lending Club borrowers use their loans to refinance existing loans or pay off credit cards. These people are just lowering their debt service payments. They're not taking on more debt.

They're folks like Chanda Lugere—a 30-something banker who was paying double-digit rates on her credit card debt.

Despite her balances, she had an excellent credit score. But her bank wouldn't give her a loan to pay off her debt. Nor would the other banks she asked.

So she turned to Lending Club. And cut her interest rate in half.

Lugere described her experience:

> *I went ahead and applied for the loan and I was able to get it funded in one week. My rate was 6%. So it's half of what I had*

been paying. I thought it was a really great experience from beginning to end—really easy, you apply online and they gave you status updates.

Many indebted U.S. consumers are improving their personal balance sheets like Lugere. They're turning to Lending Club to consolidate their debt and lower interest-rate payments.

But remember, we still have 16% of borrowers using Lending Club for other purposes. Are they safe?

People like entrepreneur Cris Zukowski, who owns Renaissance Fine Wines & Spirits—a Manhattan-based wine shop.

Zukowski's store has a 12-year track record of stable ownership, consistent profits, and happy customers.

Last year, he wanted to expand his offerings and launch an online "wine school" for his customers.

To do it, he needed extra capital.

A traditional bank loan was, unfortunately, out of the question. That's the reality of our post-2008 banking world.

So, Zukowski turned to P2P lending. He had the money he

IRA Eligible

You can open a traditional IRA, Roth IRA, SEP IRA, and Simple IRA account with Lending Club.

Their platform also accepts IRA transfers, Roth conversions, and 401(k) rollovers.

If you have any of these options available, you should consider them...

Taxable accounts are taxed at ordinary income rates. You can avoid this tax burden by using non-taxable accounts, which grow tax-deferred.

Please consult your accountant or tax adviser if you're unsure of which type of account is best for you.

wanted within a month, and launched his wine school soon thereafter.

He now earns $59 per month in recurring revenue from each customer, in exchange for two bottles of wine that the student sips and studies along with the video instructor.

Becoming an investor at Lending Club will provide you with attractive risk-adjusted returns. Here's how you can join this fast-growing market...

How to Open Your Account in Less Than Five Minutes...

I (Grant) opened an account for my mother several weeks ago. She's 69 years old, widowed, and works two part-time jobs.

I handle all her investments.

She expects me to generate safe mid-to-high single-digit returns for her. And the last thing she wants is risk.

My mother doesn't follow the stock or bond market. But when I told her about Lending Club and the available returns, she was excited. She knows what her savings account is paying!

I signed her up with her looking over my shoulder. But she could have easily done it herself.

The sign-up process took less than five minutes.

Note: There are two things you'll need here that you may not have memorized. First, your bank's routing number; second, the account number where you'll want to transfer money from. Get that ready before you begin to save some time.

Also, we recommend having at least $2,500 when opening an account. This way, you can spread your money across 100 loans ($25 minimum investment per loan).

<u>According to Lending Club, 99.9% of investors that own 100-plus notes of relatively equal size have seen positive returns</u>.

The more loans you can make… the more diversification and safety you'll get.

And keep in mind, your return on investment will come in the form of steady, monthly cash flows. After the borrower sends his or her monthly payment to Lending Club, you'll see the credit hit your account in a couple days.

This isn't a stock, with lots of "return" left unrealized (in the form of capital gains, for example). With Lending Club, you get your entire return in cash. And you get it monthly.

You can withdraw that cash if you like. Or reinvest the principal and interest payments you receive into more loans.

Now, let's discuss why <u>"Automated Investing" is the way to go</u>…

No Need to Pick Loans Yourself: Just Use "Automated Investing"

There are two ways to invest your cash at Lending Club…

First, you can browse the loans listed on the website one by one.

Lending Club gives a "credit grade" of each loan… from "A" for the safest borrowers, to "G" for the riskiest.

This is based on the borrower's credit score… and other risk factors as determined by Lending Club.

Higher Risk Borrowers Pay Higher Rates

Reward / Risk

A Grade	B Grade	C Grade	D Grade	E Grade	F Grade	G Grade
7.58%	11.50%	14.70%	17.58%	20.60%	23.59%	25.01%

Average borrower interest rates as of December 31, 2014

Lower interest payments	**Higher interest payments**
Lower expected loan losses	**Higher expected loan losses**
(fewer charge offs)	(more charge offs)
Lower expected returns	**Higher expected returns**
Lower expected volatility	**Higher expected volatility**

The riskier the borrower, the higher the interest payment you'll get.

From here, you can evaluate each borrower one at a time, and lend money to the people you like. Lending Club posts loans four times per day. This creates a competitive market that rewards rapid execution. Approximately 90% of "A" and "B" grade loans are snapped up in the first 30 seconds of each of the four daily listings.

Don't worry. You can skip all the legwork by using Lending Club's "Automated Investing" option...

Think of this as the "Index Fund" investing option for Lending Club. You simply give Lending Club your investment criteria, and it deploys your cash accordingly.

It's less work. And most likely, your returns will be just as good.

Popular finance blogger Mr. Money Mustache documented his Lending Club experience earlier this year—and verified the automated option is just as good.

He achieved an impressive 10.6% long-term return picking his own investments.

Yet he determined that he couldn't "beat the market" himself. That is, he noticed his manual lone selection didn't do any better at increasing returns or decreasing defaults.

Lending Club posts the returns of its "Automated Investing" funds. These are all projected returns: net of 1% lender fees... net of assumed defaults... and clear of any legwork on the investor's part.

So, Mr. Money Mustache moved his account over to the "Automated Investing" option.

There are three options we like here. They don't yield what they used to a few years ago... but they still outpace other fixed income options handily...

Three "Automated Investing" Options
With Yields From 5.83% to 7.85%

Here's our advice on selecting an automated investing option:

If you're worried about another 2008 crash, you may want to go with the "A & B Weighted" option (selected in the image above). Or, if you're not a risk taker and near 6% returns are good enough, this is the option for you. For example: I signed my mom up for the 5.83% projected returns from the "A & B" option.

If you're okay with taking some additional risk and have a well-diversified portfolio, consider the "Platform Mix" option. For example: You're in your mid-40s and have reached your peak earnings potential. So you may be willing to take extra risk for an extra 1% return.

Or let's say you're pretty sure the last financial crisis was an isolated event. You're willing to take on the riskiest of the auto-options,

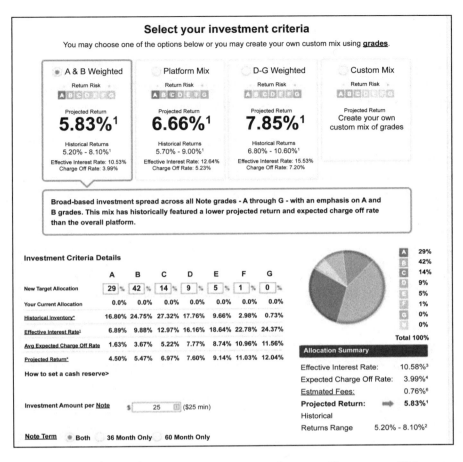

Select your investment criteria

You may choose one of the options below or you may create your own custom mix using **grades**.

○ A & B Weighted	○ Platform Mix	○ D-G Weighted	○ Custom Mix
Return Risk	Return Risk	Return Risk	Return Risk
A B C D E F G	A B C D E F G	A B C D E F G	A B C D E F G
Projected Return	Projected Return	Projected Return	Projected Return
5.83%[1]	**6.66%**[1]	**7.85%**[1]	Create your own custom mix of grades
Historical Returns 5.20% - 8.10%[1]	Historical Returns 5.70% - 9.00%[1]	Historical Returns 6.80% - 10.60%[1]	
Effective Interest Rate: 10.53% Charge Off Rate: 3.99%	Effective Interest Rate: 12.64% Charge Off Rate: 5.23%	Effective Interest Rate: 15.53% Charge Off Rate: 7.20%	

> Broad-based investment spread across all Note grades - A through G - with an emphasis on A and B grades. This mix has historically featured a lower projected return and expected charge off rate than the overall platform.

Investment Criteria Details

	A	B	C	D	E	F	G
New Target Allocation	29 %	42 %	14 %	9 %	5 %	1 %	0 %
Your Current Allocation	0.0%	0.0%	0.0%	0.0%	0.0%	0.0%	0.0%
Historical Inventory*	16.80%	24.75%	27.32%	17.76%	9.66%	2.98%	0.73%
Effective Interest Rate[1]	6.89%	9.88%	12.97%	16.16%	18.64%	22.78%	24.37%
Avg Expected Charge Off Rate	1.63%	3.67%	5.22%	7.77%	8.74%	10.96%	11.56%
Projected Return*	4.50%	5.47%	6.97%	7.60%	9.14%	11.03%	12.04%

How to set a cash reserve>

Investment Amount per **Note** $ [25]   ($25 min)

Note Term   ● Both   ○ 36 Month Only   ○ 60 Month Only

A	29%
B	42%
C	14%
D	9%
E	5%
F	1%
G	0%
	0%
Total	**100%**

Allocation Summary

Effective Interest Rate:	10.58%[3]
Expected Charge Off Rate:	3.99%[4]
Estmated Fees:	0.76%[6]
Projected Return:	**5.83%**[1]
Historical Returns Range	5.20% - 8.10%[2]

knowing that if another 2008 hits, your charge-off rates could jump. Here, you might elect the "D-G Weighted" option. For example: You're a 28-year-old millennial who's willing to take the highest risk option for the highest return.

For most of you, we'd suggest one of the first two options: "A & B Weighted" or "Platform Mix." We don't see a scenario where you'd lose money with either of these two options.

Whichever option you choose, there's an urgency to putting this plan into action...

Time Is Critical: Do It Now

The size of the P2P lending space is $10 to $15 billion. Venture capitalist Charles Moldow issued a report concluding that the total market could hit $1 trillion by 2025.

If Moldow is right, this means P2P lending would have to increase at least 7,000% over the next decade. To put this in perspective, the S&P 500 would have to skyrocket from its current levels to over 140,000 if it saw this same level of growth!

More and more investors are entering the P2P space. And they're not just individuals... hedge funds, banks, and other large institutions are profiting from P2P lending platforms. They're all competing for the same (albeit, growing) pool of loans.

What does this mean for you and me?

Unfortunately, it means yields have come down. According to *PBL* friend and P2P lending expert David Halabu (founder and CEO of Yield Crowd), yields have already dropped 2-3% over the last few years.

Our lending expert, Peter Renton, also confirmed that Lending Club's yields have dropped about 2% over the last two or three years.

And remember, Simon Cunningham's yield dropped from 19.8% to 10.4% over a two-year period as well.

More investors will continue entering this space, drawn by the attractive, safe returns. Until U.S. government, banks, and brokerage money market funds start paying significant yield— or Lending Club's yields decline significantly—it will remain an enticing, alternative option.

This opportunity for safe, diversified 6-8% income won't last forever. In fact, yields may never be this high again if the P2P space continues to attract the capital we believe it will.

So, you should take advantage of this platform now—and start collecting monthly payments from the loans you provide.

You'll earn more than 12-times what you'd get from a three-year CD, and more than 100-times what your savings account will pay you (based on rates as of the time of this writing). And you won't have to buy a stock or a bond...

This safe, fixed-income avenue that's generating sizable returns won't stay underground much longer... so, <u>you need to move now</u>.

Action to Take: Sign up and use Lending Club.

CHAPTER 3

Single Premium Immediate Annuities (SPIAs)

How to Guarantee a 5-7% Payout for the Rest of Your Life

By Grant Wasylik and Tom Dyson

Stan swerved his '94 Ford Expedition off the side of the road and threw it into park...

He had reached his boiling point. And he needed to make a phone call immediately.

Stan was listening to talk radio that Saturday morning. The topic was a unique type of financial product. The show's hosts were promoting this product as a way to make returns from the stock market without any downside risks. And in the meantime, this product would allegedly generate high interest for average investors as well. The hosts were calling it the "greatest investment product on the planet."

But Stan knew the truth about this product from his days working for top Wall Street firms like Dean Witter, Morgan Stanley, and UBS.

It wasn't risk-free... the returns weren't as high as the radio show hosts were promising... and in the end, salesmen would grab big commissions and consumers would be left very disappointed.

So Stan called into the radio show. Live on air, he argued with the radio show hosts about the product they were pitching. From his '94 Ford Expedition parked on the side of the road, Stan picked apart their faulty argument so well that they hung up on him.

What was this "financial product" at the center of the debate? It's actually one of the most controversial products in the investment world—annuities.

Within minutes, Stan's cell started buzzing...

"Stan, heard you on the radio. Will you look at my annuity?"

Another call...

"Stan, caught you on the show. Can I get your opinion on the correct strategy for me and my wife?"

Over the next few hours, Stan received at least two dozen more calls. He didn't realize it at the time... but it was the genesis of "Stan The Annuity Man."

Fast-forward 10 years, and Stan Haithcock is the top annuity expert in the country today... a respected author of two books (with a third on the way)... the most sought-after speaker on this controversial topic (The World Money Show, AAII National Conference, Investment U Conference, Fox Business News, etc.)... and he's the most-read annuity commentator in America (a regular contributor to *The Wall Street Journal*, MarketWatch, *USA Today*, *The New York Times*, and many more).

Because of his ironclad stance on annuities, he's been introduced at various speaking engagements as the "walking middle finger of annuity truth."

We invited Stan to meet with us at Palm Beach Research Group headquarters to give us a thorough, truthful breakdown on annuities.

You see, behind the scenes here at PBRG, we've had different opinions on annuities. Some of us have been skeptical, citing an annuity's reputation for high fees and terrible performance—similar to what we found when researching life insurance.

But others here at PBRG believe annuities can solve a difficult retirement problem: helping people create an "income floor" until they die.

By "income floor," we mean a baseline, guaranteed amount of regular income. You can think of it as the money that will show up in your bank account—100% reliable—no matter what the stock market does. For most people, an income floor comes from Social Security or a pension.

The problem is, for many subscribers, their income floor isn't big enough to cover their basic bills (groceries, cable, water, etc.).

So we invited Stan to our office... and warned him he'd be presenting to an audience with mixed views on annuities.

In this chapter, we present what we learned from Stan. Plus, we'll actually recommend one annuity product that ended up winning over our team... even our most skeptical analysts.

This special type of annuity product will help you fully fund your "income floor."

Here's what you're going to get with today's "peace of mind" recommendation:

1. A guaranteed income stream that lasts for the rest of your life.

---

2. Annual distribution rates of 5-7% (depending on your age, could be lower or higher).

3. Safety.

4. Low commissions (built into the product) averaging around 1%.

Before we get into more details, let's address retirees' biggest concern...

The Biggest Fear Facing Retirees Today

Recently, Tom had this conversation with his mother...

> *Tom: Mum, sell some of your tobacco stocks. You have too much money in tobacco stocks. You're retired. And you have enough money where you don't need to take the risk.*
>
> *Tom's mom: But Tom, I need the income! My tobacco stocks pay good dividends.*
>
> *Tom: Sell those stocks. You don't need that much money in the stock market. Live off your nest egg—that's what it's there for. Don't worry about dividends. You have plenty of money saved up... spend it.*
>
> *Tom's mom: Tom, I don't want to touch my nest egg. I don't want to spend my capital. What if I run out of money before I die? I can't depend on you taking care of me. I'd rather risk my money in the stock market...*

With interest rates around the world so low (as we write), there's never been a harder time to earn interest and dividends than right now. It's creating a huge problem for retirees like Tom's mother.

Most retirees have money... but they need income. They don't want to live off their nest eggs because they're terrified of running out of money before they die.

So, they turn to the stock market to provide that income (in the form of dividends). But, as you know, the stock market has the potential to destroy that nest egg in a 2008-style crash.

Tom knows a retired couple in Florida in a comparable situation.

His friends have $4 million in net worth. They told him...

> *Married couple: Tom, we really need income. We have big medical expenses coming that we must pay.*
>
> *Tom: At your age, with your financial situation, you shouldn't put a large percentage of your money in the stock market. If we get another crisis like 2008, you could lose half of that allocation. You're much better off keeping most of your money in cash and spending what you need.*
>
> *Married couple: We can't spend our savings, Tom. What if we run out of money before both of us die? We want that money to be there for our children, as an inheritance. We can't spend it. Please help us generate safe income with it.*

These examples illustrate the dilemmas retirees face when they quit their jobs. They're scared of running out of money and depleting their nest eggs. They're (rightfully) wary of the stock market because their portfolios may never recover from a crash. But without dividends from stocks, they can't find enough income sources to cover their baseline expenses.

The regular paychecks have stopped (or will soon). So, they turn to Social Security... and a pension, if they are lucky... to replace part of their income.

The rest of the income they need comes from their nest egg... the pile of cash they've saved from their working years.

Both retirees and soon-to-be retirees are in a predicament. Their problem—the same dilemma facing Tom's mother and his friends— is twofold...

1. They're concerned about running out of money before they die.

2. So in hopes of generating income, they expose themselves to future stock market crashes.

By teaming up with Stan The Annuity Man, we came up with a solution to this large-scale, binary retirement problem.

Current and soon-to-be retirees can use this solution to turn a sizable nest egg into a large "stock-market safe" monthly payment... or a modest cash sum into a modest payment that helps pay the bills.

Either way, it will help these folks eliminate concerns of stock market crashes, running out of money, and monthly bill paying... giving them a stress-free and peaceful retirement.

The origin of this solution dates all the way back to Roman times...

When in Rome...

As you probably know, the Romans sent their soldiers away from home for long periods of time. They had to defend the empire, after all... and conquer the lands around it.

To appease the wives of these soldiers, the Roman government cut them regular checks... or pensions.

They were paying the world's first annuity.

Today, this classic and most popular annuity structure is known as the **Single Premium Immediate Annuity (SPIA)**. You contribute a lump sum of money, and in return, you receive regular payments for life, or for a set period of time.

These payments start right away. And they are guaranteed. No matter what the stock market does... or the bond market, for that matter... you get the exact payment you're promised.

As we wrote earlier, here at *The Palm Beach Letter*, we've had some annuity skeptics amongst us. Those of us who didn't like annuities pointed toward their high fees... their complexity... the likelihood of never getting your money back... and the salesmen who are merely peddling products to land the biggest paydays (the same guys Stan dismantled on air).

We weren't alone on our annuity skepticism. Ken Fisher, the largest wealth manager in the U.S., "hates annuities"... Suze Orman, personal finance expert and star of *The Suze Orman Show*, calls them "the worst investment you will ever make"... and Jim Cramer, *Mad Money* host, claims annuities are bad investments in general.

But our eight-hour day with Stan and several follow-up phone conversations gave the skeptics among us a different perspective on annuities. We realized that Stan's extensive knowledge base made Fisher, Orman, and Cramer seem like novices in this arena.

Stan actually agreed with the viewpoint that most annuities are scams. But not all of them. In fact, he said the Romans had it right...

They're Supposed to Be Safe, Independent Fixed-Income Sources

There are two major benefits of traditional annuities:

1. They are not correlated to the financial markets.
2. They are safe sources (contractual guarantees) of income.

Annuities should be assets that do not move with the stock market or the bond market... or any other financial market.

They're meant to pay you regular income... cover your expenses... protect your lifestyle... and give you comfort and peace of mind.

This is what Single Premium Immediate Annuities (SPIAs) provide.

The skeptics here at *The Palm Beach Letter* had overlooked SPIAs until we met with Stan.

When we thought of annuities before, our minds jumped to variable and indexed annuities being sold with false growth promises.

Stan Says, "Watch Out for These Annuity Rip-Offs."

Each year, $250 billion of annuities are peddled and sold. Two types of annuities represent 75% of all sales: variable and indexed annuities. Coincidentally, they're the annuities that pay the highest commissions (5-9% of the premium).

Be wary of these common annuity agent pitches:

Annuity Agent Pitch... aka Rip-Off No. 1: *"I can guarantee you 8% (or more) with my annuity."*

Contractual Reality: With the 10-year Treasury around 2%, it's quite challenging for an annuity company to generate a true yield of 8% or more. Usually, they are juicing their returns with an "Income Rider." The secret? You have to pay more for it... and it's a phantom account that can only be used for income. Income riders are not yield. And you can't "walk away" with the money.

Annuity Agent Pitch... aka Rip-Off No. 2: *"I can get you an upfront bonus on your money."*

Contractual Reality: Many annuity carriers offer "upfront bonuses." Keep in mind, this is not free money. Insurance companies don't give **anything** away for free. If you're getting a bonus... it's coming out of your pocket somehow.

Annuity Agent Pitch... aka Rip-Off No. 3: *"Indexed annuities give you market upside with **no** downside."*

Contractual Reality: Only half of that statement is true. Indexed annuities are fixed annuities—they do protect

---

your principal. Indexed annuities were designed in 1995 to compete with CD (not market) returns. Historically, that's what they've done.

Annuity Agent Pitch... aka Rip-Off No. 4: *"This annuity provides long-term care coverage without any medical exam."*

Contractual Reality: This guaranteed benefit is not long-term care, and does not carry those same tax advantages. It can only be looked at as supplemental coverage at best. Never replace traditional long-term care coverage with this agent-advertised benefit.

Annuity Agent Pitch... aka Rip-Off No. 5: *"This annuity will increase your income stream every year the S&P 500 index rises to combat inflation."*

Contractual Reality: Remember, insurance companies know what they're doing when it comes to math. If a variable or indexed annuity promoter comes to you with this claim, know that the annuity carrier will simply lower the initial payment for this potential increase in income. If you're retired, you already own the best inflation annuity... Social Security.

Your mind may have jumped that way when you started reading this, also.

But SPIAs are different... they're contractual realities. Most agents don't pitch them because the commissions are too low. But, for investors, they're the best annuity products out there—and they do a great job of helping retirees fully fund their income floor.

SPIAs: A Safe Way to Never Run Out of Money and Avoid Stock Market Risks

The benefit of a SPIA is that you can turn over a chunk of your money... like $100,000... to an insurance company, and that annuity contract will pay you a guaranteed amount of money regularly... say, $500 per month, for the rest of your life.

You'll get that $500 every month no matter what the stock market does. Any market crash won't affect your payments. The burden is on the insurance company to pay you.

Meanwhile, they'll invest your $100,000, and you won't have to worry about it. You can sleep well every night while your friends sweat out market gyrations.

And that $500 per month is higher than regular interest payments. That's because these monthly payments are a combination of interest and return of principal (some of your $100,000).

So, if you're managing your money wisely, a SPIA is a great tool to help you fund an income floor that enables you to pay your base expenses for as long as you live...

Plus, SPIAs have low commissions and no annual fees. They are instant pensions starting 30 days from the contract date. And they're very simple to understand and set up.

How SPIAs Work... and Can Build Your "Income Floor"

A SPIA works in a very simple way. You provide the insurance company with a single lump sum of money... and they, in turn, promise to pay you guaranteed income each month.

How much will that company promise to pay you?

It depends.

SPIAs, and annuities in general, are a statistical bet with the insurance company about how long you're going to live.

The older you are when you open a policy, the higher a guaranteed payment the insurance company will offer you.

Let's say you take their offer. If you "die too soon" (before your life expectancy), you will likely get back <u>less</u> than the amount you paid in. However, if you "live too long" (outlive your life expectancy), you'll likely get back more than the lump-sum cost of your annuity.

SPIAs are a simple and fair wager on life expectancy. As such, they counter the typical problems of most other types of annuities by providing:

- A guaranteed contractual income that you can never outlive.
- A "gap-filler." Meaning, they provide a guaranteed income stream for a needed gap in your monthly payment total.
- Tax benefits (in a non-IRA account, the majority of the income stream is non-taxable).
- Full protection of principal when structured accordingly.

If you're old enough to receive Social Security, this is one "layer" of your income floor. And if you're fortunate enough to have a pension, that's another layer.

These secure income sources "layer" on top of each other to form your guaranteed income floor.

For example, let's say you get $1,300 per month from Social Security... and $1,000 per month from your pension. You have a guaranteed income floor of $2,300 per month to pay your basic living expenses.

But for some people, this may not be enough to cover all their basic expenses.

So a SPIA can boost this monthly number even higher.

Let's see how it can help a recently retired man supplement his income...

Case Study: Three Example SPIAs for a 65-Year-Old Male

Plan 1: A 65-Year-Old Married Man

Leo is a retired 65-year-old man living in Florida with his wife, Mona. They've paid off their house and plan on living a simple retirement. They have $2,600 of monthly income coming in from Social Security. Leo needs to generate another $400 in monthly income to cover his remaining fixed expenses.

They've got $100,000 in cash.

Leo believes he can expect a 6% cash yield. That'd get him $500 per month in income ($100 more than he needs).

But Leo is hesitant to actively manage his $100,000. He remembers the 2008 financial crisis. Back then, he was fully invested and his retirement portfolio was cut in half. He's been sitting in cash ever since.

Leo would much rather put his $100,000 into a SPIA. That way, he'd get fixed, stable income. He could enjoy his retirement without having to track the markets and actively manage his account.

We had Stan The Annuity Man obtain SPIA quotes for Leo from 18 high-quality insurance companies. Here are the top seven...

Financial Institution	Premium	Monthly Income	Monthly Taxable Portion	Year 1 Yield (Pre-Tax)	Credit Rating
Principal Financial	$100,000.00	$547.03	$130.19	6.56%	A+
Guardian	$100,000.00	$544.82	$128.03	6.54%	A++
American National	$100,000.00	$543.45	$126.62	6.52%	A
MetLife	$100,000.00	$542.12	$125.23	6.51%	A+
Voya	$100,000.00	$537.87	$121.02	6.45%	A
American General	$100,000.00	$535.95	$119.52	6.43%	A
Minnesota Life	$100,000.00	$535.90	$118.97	6.43%	A+

The highest quote came from Principal Financial Group. If Leo forked over $100,000 to the insurance company, they'd promise to pay Leo **$547.03 in monthly income**. And only **$130.19 of that monthly income would be taxable**. That's a 6.56% distribution rate.

The $547.03 monthly sum would be paid out to Leo for the rest of his life.

But, there's one problem...

This is a "**Single Life**" annuity. That means the annuity and its monthly payments stop when Leo passes away. If Leo passed away at 70, his wife, Mona, would now be short $547 in monthly income.

There's a simple fix to this. And that is making sure your SPIA is "**Joint Life**."

Plan 2: A 65-Year-Old Married Couple

Leo suspects he'll be the first one to pass away. He wants to ensure Mona can continue to pay the bills after he passes. So this time, Leo includes Mona's life on his SPIA. This means, if Leo passes away before Mona, she will continue to receive these payments for the rest of her life (or vice versa, if Mona dies first).

Again, we had Stan obtain a "**Joint Life**" SPIA quote for Leo and Mona from 18 insurance companies. Here are the top seven...

Financial Institution	Premium	Monthly Income	Monthly Taxable Portion	Year 1 Yield (Pre-Tax)	Credit Rating
Principal Financial	$100,000.00	$459.91	$126.48	5.52%	A+
MetLife	$100,000.00	$458.84	$125.72	5.51%	A+
Voya	$100,000.00	$451.05	$117.72	5.41%	A
Integrity	$100,000.00	$450.40	$117.10	5.40%	A+
Nationwide	$100,000.00	$446.19	$112.86	5.35%	A+
Guardian	$100,000.00	$445.77	$112.33	5.35%	A++
Penn Mutual	$100,000.00	$441.16	$107.64	5.29%	A+

Once again, the highest quote came from Principal Financial Group. They offered to pay Leo and Mona **$459.91 in monthly income**... of which **$126.48 would be taxable**.

Why is the insurance company paying them 15% less income? Remember, in this scenario, Principal Financial Group is on the hook to pay out as long as Leo <u>and</u> Mona are around to receive it. There's a much higher chance the insurance company is going to have to make more payments from its coffers.

So there is a cost to get a SPIA based on both lives. That cost is a lower monthly or annual amount of income. But it comes with added comfort. Both spouses can count on the income to last as long as either of them lives.

That makes a joint life SPIA the most logical choice for most married couples.

Plan 3: A 65-Year-Old Married Couple with an Existing Income for Life Policy

There's one problem or concern some may have with Leo and Mona's joint life SPIA...

When both spouses pass away, the insurance company keeps the remaining money.

Now remember, that's the deal Leo made with the insurance company. He gave them $100,000 in exchange for lifetime payments for Mona and him.

While this provided secure income for the couple, it wasn't a "risk-free" deal for the insurance company. If Leo and/or Mona live into their 80s or 90s, the insurance company could pay out more (potentially much more) money to the couple than it actually collected.

Taking Leo's lump sum of money up front—and keeping that money—helps the insurance company reduce its risk on the deal.

You may be fine with letting the insurance company keep your lump sum if you're only concerned about having income while you're alive.

But if you want to pass on an inheritance to your children or charity, putting money into a SPIA (without extra provisions) is not going to sit well with you.

What if there were a way for you to put money into a SPIA and also be able to pass along an inheritance when both of you are gone? What if there were a way to get more income?

Enter **Income for Life (IFL).**

Income for Life is a great place to put your money to get up to 5% returns, tax-free, over the long term. Using a special rider, we stuff as much cash into the policy as possible.

In this scenario, Leo and Mona started Income for Life policies back when they were 55. They made their payments regularly. And 10 years later, each policy has around $150,000 of death benefit.

Both Income for Life policies could also be put on autopilot. That means Leo and Mona do not have to make another life insurance premium payment ever again. But their policies will continue to be intact until they pass.

Leo knows he can put $100,000 into his single life SPIA. He'll get the higher $547 in monthly income.

Why is he able to do this?

He knows that whenever he passes, Mona will receive $150,000 in death benefit... whether he passes at age 68 or 88.

Mona can then take the death benefit proceeds from Leo's Income for Life policy and put it in a new single life SPIA on her life.

And she's able to put it into a single life SPIA because she also has an Income for Life policy. Her new SPIA will now pay her monthly income for the rest of her life.

When she passes away, the insurance company she has the SPIA with keeps the unpaid amount of the original $100,000. But, the insurance company she has her policy with will pay out $150,000 to her kids.

In summary, if leaving a legacy... if leaving some money to your kids is important to you... it's worth it to consider a SPIA/IFL combo.

Be Smart... and Safe

Remember, we don't have any stock market risk here. But that doesn't mean we have zero risk.

Annuities are contractual guarantees with the insurance company itself.

They are unattached to the stock market, so they'll hold up in worst-case, Armageddon scenarios... as long as the insurance company stays in business.

Insurance companies don't fail often. There were only two notable failures in the last 25 years... a period that includes the Great Recession.

A company called Executive Life went bankrupt about 25 years ago. And Standard Life of Indiana was the only insurance company to be absorbed by its state insurance department in 2008.

That's not a bad quarter-century... but we want to be 100% sure that our contractual guarantor will be around.

So, you should only use high-rated, safe insurance companies. Reputable carriers include New York Life, MetLife, Principal, Guardian, Lincoln, Mass Mutual, and Northwestern Mutual (we'll talk about safety rankings in a bit).

New York Life, for example, has $1.7 trillion in assets. That's "too big to fail" as far as the Federal government is concerned. (When the Feds bailed out AIG in 2008, it had "only" $1.1 trillion in assets.)

Annuity and SPIA Secrets You May Not Know...

Creditor Protection

In some states (like Florida & Texas), creditors can't touch annuities.

If you buy an annuity and someone runs into your car and tries to sue you... you can rest easy, because they can't touch your annuity. Annuities are safe havens in some states... if someone is trying to sue you, they can't get to them. That's the reason lots of surgeons buy SPIAs. They also have the ability to lower their malpractice insurance.

Even O.J. Simpson's annuities couldn't be touched by the Goldman family. There's documentation of the Goldmans trying to go get his variable annuities, and they couldn't. He was living in Florida at the time. And Florida statutes section 222.14 protected his annuity contracts.

Life Expectancy Table Risk

Stan believes the possibility of the life expectancy tables changing is a bigger risk for SPIA buyers than the current focus on interest rates.

People are focused on interest rates, but they should be focused on life expectancy. Life expectancy is the primary pricing mechanism on an annuity. Eventually, insurance companies will reevaluate life expectancy tables. People are living longer... with each passing year, newborns live about three months longer than those born the prior year.

The Society of Actuaries says the average 65-year-old male has a life expectancy of 21.6 years (to 86.6 years of age). That's an increase in life expectancy of 24 months in the last 15 years. The average 65-year-old female has gained 29 months of life expectancy over the same period.

If you're projected to live longer, then insurance companies are going to pay you less dollars per payment. If the average 65-year-old male picks up an extra 2 years of life expectancy, his monthly payments have to stretch another 24 months. Insurance company's business is to adjust for increasing longevity... so you may be getting a better annuity deal than you think.

Life With Installment Refund

This is the most popular way to structure a SPIA for maximizing the lifetime income stream. With this option, you assure that 100% of the initial premium will go to someone in your family (i.e., listed beneficiaries). If you pass away before receiving an income benefit equal to your premiums paid, your beneficiaries will receive the difference in installment payments. This optionality results in lower payments, but it compensates the annuitant's beneficiaries.

COLAs and CPI-U Increases

At the time of application, some SPIAs offer contractual and annual increases of the income stream for life by using a COLA or CPI-U. For example, a 3% COLA (Cost of Living Adjustment) increases the income stream by 3% for the life of the policy. The annuity carrier does lower the initial payout if you choose this option, but if longevity is in your family genes, this might make sense. If you're worried about inflation, this is one method to help counter it.

<u>Laddering Strategies</u>

If you think that rates will move in the near future, then laddering the purchase date of your SPIA might make sense. For example, if you have $400,000 allocated for a SPIA-guaranteed income stream... it might be prudent to buy a $100,000 SPIA every year for four consecutive years. This is another approach to combat inflation.

<u>Start at the Finish Line</u>

Annuities should only be owned for their contractual guarantees. Because of this, it is important to always start at the finish line with your decision. What that means is to figure out what you want the money to do, and when you want that to happen. From those two "finish line" answers, go find the best contractual guarantees to back up those specific goals.

SPIAs, by nature, are safe. But by picking top carriers, you're adding another layer of safety.

Next, let's go over the final SPIA game plan...

How to Get Your Own SPIA

It's easy to set up a SPIA because everything is customizable to your specific situation. There are two ways you can approach it...

Approach No. 1: Plug Your Income Floor Shortfall (Recommended)

We recommend you start at the finish line and identify the "income floor" you want. Remember, an "income floor" is payments you know you'll receive (Social Security, pension, even dividend and interest income). Tally your bills and expenses that you want your SPIA to cover.

In our example, Leo and Mona had $2,600 of monthly income from Social Security. Assuming no pension, Mona and Leo needed another $400 of guaranteed income to cover their monthly bills. Instead of plunking down $100,000, they could have gone to their agent with a different request: What is the dollar amount they'd need to deposit to ensure monthly payments of $400?

If solving for your income floor need, here's the simple calculation:

(Social Security + Pensions + Other Guaranteed Income Sources)—Monthly Expenses = Surplus (+) or Shortfall (−)

In this case, you'll just **tell your broker your specific income need**... your **income floor shortfall**... and he'll figure out the contract needed to guarantee that amount.

Approach No. 2: Find the Highest Monthly Payment

Alternatively, you may prefer to determine the largest amount of cash you're willing to put in a SPIA and check your payment quotes that way—just like how Leo and Mona put down $100,000 in exchange for a monthly payment.

Here, you'll **tell your broker the "lump sum" you have to invest**... and he'll tell you what the highest SPIA guarantees are.

While we believe that the right use of a SPIA is to plug an income floor shortfall, we fully understand if you want to enjoy your retirement without ever checking another stock ticker again.

You'll also want to consider these three SPIA options before speaking to your agent...

1. **Payment period**—You don't have to commit to a lifetime payment. You can choose a "period-certain" contract. That is, you can say, "I want a 5-year payment"... or "I want a 20-year payment."

2. **Payment frequency**—You can get paid monthly, quarterly, semiannually, or annually.

3. **Payment method**—You can opt to receive a check or go with direct deposit.

Okay, you've done your homework. And you are ready to pick up the phone to obtain a SPIA quote. Our annuity guru says to make sure to mention these five things...

The top five SPIA requests you should ask your agent:

1. "Please show me 'Life Only' (or 'Joint Life Only' with spouse) and 'Life with Installment Refund' so I can compare these top two quotes." If you want your beneficiaries to receive unused money (if you die early in the contract), you'll want to see a "Life with Installment Refund" quote, as well.

2. "Please show me the same quotes with a 3% COLA (Cost of Living Adjustment) annual increase for comparison purposes."

3. "Please show me at least five different carriers that have a COMDEX ranking (average score a company receives based on all four ratings services: AM Best, Moody's, S&P, and Fitch) of at least 80 or above."

4. "Please quote numbers that reflect my specific [IRA or non-IRA] funds."

5. [For non-IRA funds] "Please provide my tax bracket so I can see the effect of the annuitized 'exclusion ratio' on your income stream."

Remember, a Single Premium Immediate Annuity (SPIA) is the best product in the financial universe that will guarantee to pay you for life... regardless of how long you live, and no matter what the stock market does.

You are transferring that risk of payment to the annuity carrier... and they have a fiduciary responsibility to pay you the regular income you were promised.

Your Social Security payments and pension payments are, in essence, annuities that form the foundation of your "guaranteed income floor."

And a SPIA is a tool that allows you to build that floor higher if you want...

If you're a retiree or soon becoming one... have a savings stockpile that's yielding nothing... and want to lock in guaranteed future income to cover your expenses (giving you some peace of mind)... then, you may want to consider a SPIA as a piece of your "retirement puzzle" solution.

Action to Take: Call Stan The Annuity Man at (800) 509-6473 or your agent to learn if a SPIA would work for you.

CHAPTER 4

Qualified Longevity Annuity Contracts (QLACs)

Lock in Another Guaranteed Income Stream at a Future Date

By Stan Haithcock

Editor's note: *We introduced you to our colleague and friend Stan Haithcock (Stan the Annuity Man) in our last chapter featuring Single Premium Immediate Annuities (SPIAs). Stan knows more about annuities than anyone on the planet. In this chapter, he is going to share with you his "other" favorite annuity structure—the QLAC.*

Guess What?

You already own a QLAC.

You probably didn't even know that you already own a QLAC structure. That future annuity payment is called Social Security. Yes, that's an annuity. When you choose to delay your Social Security payment, then that is in essence a longevity annuity structure. Congratulations! After reading this chapter, you might need to consider adding another QLAC to your portfolio. By then, you will know if it fits your specific situation.

QLAC Specifics: July 1st, 2014—
The Day Annuities Changed Forever

On this date of annuity infamy, the world of annuities was turned upside down when the IRS and the Department of the Treasury approved the use of QLACs in qualified plans—like a 401(k) or traditional IRA.

What Is a QLAC?

QLAC stands for Qualified Longevity Annuity Contract. Within the actual statute, it is also called a Qualifying Longevity Annuity Contract. A QLAC is a unique type of longevity annuity that can be used in qualified plans like a 401(k) or traditional IRA.

What Is a Longevity Annuity?

A Longevity Annuity is a fixed annuity that guarantees a future income stream at a date you specify. It is also called commonly referred to as a Deferred Income Annuity (DIA). Some DIA contracts allow you to defer as short as 2 years, and as long as 45 years. Originally introduced in 2004, Longevity Annuities have started to become popular in the last few years as a simplistic alternative to income riders attached to variable and indexed annuities.

Not All Longevity Annuities Are QLACs

Longevity Annuities have been around and sold in both IRA and non-IRA accounts. A ton of my clients already own them for future guaranteed income needs. However, they do not own a QLAC. Just because it is called a Longevity Annuity doesn't mean that it is recognized as a QLAC. This is very important to know, and it will be a center of confusion as the QLAC strategy starts being offered by carriers. If you already own a Longevity Annuity, it CANNOT be re-classified as a QLAC. If you owned a Longevity Annuity contract within an IRA, most carriers required you to turn on the income stream before 70 ½, and would not even run proposals past that age.

Treasury & IRS Working Together!

In a pensionless world, people need to create their own pension, and the QLAC strategy provides a good start in that direction.

Traditional IRA holders are also being encouraged to plan for lifetime income needs using the QLAC strategy. The big deal here is that people can lessen the RMD (Required Minimum Distribution) on their IRAs and, in turn, potentially reduce taxes on their overall taxable income by using the QLAC. Anytime the government agrees that it's going to get less tax revenue, it's worth paying attention to why.

QLAC Ruling Summary & Premium Limits

QLAC Ruling Summary

- Can be used in participating 401(k), 403(b), and governmental 457(b) plans

- Can be used in traditional IRAs (non-Roth IRAs)

- CANNOT be used in Defined Benefit Plans (i.e. pension plans), Roth IRAs, and Inherited IRAs

- Can defer to a specific age, but no later than age 85

QLAC Premium Limits

- 25% of total amount of all qualified accounts or $125,000 (whichever is less)

- The $125,000 limit is an aggregate amount of all IRAs and plans for one individual

- The $125,000 limit will be indexed for inflation and adjusted in $10,000 increments

- The 25% limit on IRAs applies to as many IRAs as you may have. The IRS is looking at the total dollar amount.

- When it comes to 401(k), 403(b), and governmental 457(b) plans, the 25% limitation applies to each participating plan with the $125,000 rule still in place.

Death Benefits—ROP (Return of Premium)

QLACs can have death benefits, but are limited to specific structuring that can provide survivor annuity payments. If you die before the income stream starts, 100% of the initial premium will be returned to your listed beneficiaries in a lump sum. Even after you start taking income from a QLAC (called ASD–"after start date") the ROP feature applies as long as the death benefit is paid out under specific calendar year guidelines.

A lot of the QLAC death benefit details will be revealed when the contracts are finally available, but the key thing to remember is that the evil annuity company will not keep any of the money. QLACs are pure transfer-of-risk lifetime income guarantees with principal protection of the premium. Sounds like a pretty good deal because it is.

This ROP feature is available for both spouse and non-spouse beneficiaries. In addition to return of premium, you can also have a spousal QLAC beneficiary receive lifetime payments under specific provisions in lieu of ROP.

Spousal Benefits

A benefit that I'm not hearing anyone (but me) talk about is that both you and your spouse can take advantage of the QLAC rules. Obviously, your spouse would have to possess their own qualifying IRA, but could also contribute 25% or $125,000 (whichever is less) into a QLAC contract. That's potentially as high as $250,000 per household (husband & wife) that can be allocated to QLAC strategies.

QLACs will allow you to add your spouse as a joint annuitant to the contract. What that means is the lifetime income guarantee is for both lives, regardless of how long either of you live. The contractually guaranteed payment will be lower because the carrier will be covering 2 lives, but I personally think it's worth it.

Beneficiary/Non-Spousal Benefits

QLACs allow you to list as many beneficiaries to the policy as needed. These beneficiary listings are revocable, and can be changed at the contract owner's discretion. Non-spouse QLAC benefits are a little more complex than spousal. You do have an option to guarantee payments to a non-spouse beneficiary, but the rules are a tad more complicated and will also depend on the specific QLAC product and carrier you choose.

Cash Value Rules

One of the limitations of the QLAC strategy is that there is no cash value once the policy is purchased. In other words, you can't get to the principal except in payment form.

How Payments are Calculated

All annuity payments, including QLACs, are primarily based on your life expectancy at the time you start taking the payments. In actuarial speak, it's a combination of interest rates and mortality credits. In essence, it's a bet between you and the issuing annuity carrier that you think you will live longer than they think you will live. What sets annuities apart from ALL other products, is that the annuity company is on the hook to pay you regardless of how long you live. That's the benefit proposition of an income annuity, and the QLAC product offers that same transfer-of-risk security of knowing that you will never outlive your money.

In addition to your life expectancy, interest rates do play a complementary role in the pricing of your lifetime payment. The 10-

---

year Treasury is typically the bogey for annuity pricing.

Structuring the Payment

One of the common misconceptions with annuity lifetime income streams is that if you die, the evil annuity company keeps the money. That is definitely not true with QLACs, or even with other annuities that provide a guaranteed lifetime income stream. It all comes down to how you structure the payment, and payments must start by age 85.

Like other annuity product offerings, QLAC issuers will have their own specific choices of how to structure the future incomes stream, and they will allow you to customize the contract for both spousal and non-spousal guaranteed benefits.

QLAC Account Valuation Rules

According to the QLAC ruling, you calculate the 25% or $125,000 amount on the date of the payment into the QLAC policy using the prior year-end total of your qualifying IRAs. This rule seems to apply to the traditional IRA owner.

For a qualified plan participant utilizing a QLAC, the limit "is applied with respect to an employee's account balance under a qualified plan as of the last valuation date preceding the date of the premium payment."

QLACs in 401(k)s

For people who are still working and are participating in a 401(k)-type defined contribution plan, you need to urge your administrator to offer QLACs within your specific plan. Defined benefit plans are not approved to use the QLAC strategy.

A potential issue for 401(k) participants is that the QLAC product is optional for plan sponsors to include in their plan.

QLACs in Traditional IRAs

Qualified Longevity Annuity Contracts can be used in traditional IRAs for lifetime income needs starting at a future date. QLACs in a Roth IRA make no sense, because all money coming out of a Roth is tax free. QLACs are not approved for use in Roth IRAs. However, a traditional longevity annuity (DIA) could work in a Roth for future income needs.

QLACs Can Potentially Help Reduce Your Taxes

Under the QLAC ruling, if you have a traditional IRA, you can defer 25% of the total of all of your IRAs or $125,000 (whichever is less) using a Qualified Longevity Annuity Contract. That dollar amount can be deferred to age 85, and is not included when calculating RMDs (Required Minimum Distributions). For example, if you have a $500,000 IRA, you could defer $125,000 under QLAC rules, and then be able to calculate your Required Minimum Distributions on $375,000 instead of $500,000.

A quick reminder concerning RMD rules, just in case you are not clear. Distribution payments have to begin by April 1st of the year following the year the IRA owner turns 70 1/2. In addition, those payments have to be structured so that they will be completely paid out over the life expectancies of the owner and their beneficiaries. For you research types out there, the Internal Revenue Code, section 401(a)(9) covers the taxation of RMDs, and was the primary hurdle for the QLAC strategy to be approved.

QLACs could potentially help reduce those taxes you have to pay because your Required Minimum Distribution calculations will be based on a smaller dollar amount. The only QLAC requirement is that payments have to start from the QLAC total at a specified date that is no later than age 85. Paying less in taxes is always a good thing, and QLACs could help with this goal, depending on your specific situation.

Defer Past 70 1/2

RMDs are the equivalent of the IRS tapping you on the shoulder to "remind" you that it's time to start paying taxes on all of that money you have been deferring. With the QLAC strategy, you get to defer a little longer. QLACs allow you to defer 25% of your IRA total or $125,000 (whichever is less) up to age 85.

Longevity Annuities in Non-IRA Accounts

Longevity Annuities, not classified as QLACs, can be purchased in non-IRA (i.e. non-qualified) and Roth IRA accounts. The strategy is the same, which means you can plan for lifetime income needs starting at a future date that you choose. I predict that as the QLAC strategy grows in qualified plans, a correlating growth will happen with Longevity Annuities in non-qualified accounts as well. The Longevity Annuity strategy is so transparent and easy to understand that it will eventually be the gold standard of the annuity world.

QLAC Benefits

- Principal protection via a fixed annuity structure

- Lifetime income guarantee regardless of how long you live

- No annual fees

- Simple and easy to understand

- Transparent contractually guaranteed proposal

- You can structure the policy to provide a legacy to your beneficiaries

- Younger workers in a participating 401(k) can plan for future income needs

- Traditional IRA holders can plan for future income needs

- You can defer up to 15 years, or age 85, with a traditional IRA

- COLAs (Cost of Living Adjustments) can be added to the QLAC policy to contractually increase the income stream

- You can ladder QLAC contracts so you have income starting at different dates

- Money can be added to the QLAC contract (specific rules apply)

- Traditional IRAs, 401(k)s, 403(b)s, and eligible governmental deferred compensation plans can offer QLACs

QLAC Limitations

- Lack of liquidity

- No growth component during deferral years

- Rigid contract

- No cash surrender value

- Premium limits of 25% of your total IRA or $125,000 (whichever is less)

- QLACs are optional for 401(k)-type plan sponsors

- Roth IRAs, Defined Benefit Plans, and non-governmental 457 plans cannot house QLACs (but you can buy a traditional Longevity Annuity (DIA) in non-qualified accounts)

No Annual Fees

There are many annuity types that have no annual fees, and QLACs are one of them. No fees for the life of the policy. Yes, the agent gets paid a small commission that is paid out of the carrier's reserves, but buying a QLAC is a net transaction to you.

Adding Money to Your Existing QLAC

QLACs do allow you to add money to your existing policy, but the funding rules still apply. Just to remind you again, that premium limitation is 25% of your qualified account or $125,000 (whichever is the lesser amount). The primary reason that QLACs allow money to be added is for the benefit of those participating in an employer retirement plan offering the QLAC option. This feature allows money to be added to the QLAC, just like money is added to mutual funds within a 401(k).

What Happens If You "Overfund" Your QLAC?

The QLAC ruling actually covers the possibility of mistakenly exceeding the funding limitations of the lessor of 25% or $125,000. This provision will take the excess amount out of the QLAC and back into your general account. Once again, I think this will primarily apply to QLACs within employer retirement plans. There is a one-year window to correct QLACs that are overfunded.

Similar to a SPIA

Longevity Annuities and their QLAC cousin are structured very similarly to a Single Premium Immediate Annuity (SPIA). SPIAs provide what I call "income now," whereas a QLAC will provide "income later." Both are simple transfer-of-risk strategies that solve for lifetime income needs. QLACs and SPIAs have no fees, no moving parts, no market attachments, are both fixed annuities, and pay the agent a very low commission.

You Can Drink the COLA

COLA refers to Cost of Living Adjustment annual increases that can be attached to a policy. It's important to know and understand the basics of how a COLA works.

At the time of application, you can choose a percentage that you would like the income to increase on an annual basis. For example, if you chose a 3% COLA, this means the income would increase by 3% every year for the life of the policy. Sounds like a no brainer, right? One of the reasons that insurance companies have the big buildings is that they don't give anything away for free. If you add a COLA to a policy, the carrier will simply lower the initial payout compared to the same annuity without a COLA. It all comes down to math, and your life expectancy.

No Money Left on the Table

One of the most common misconceptions concerning annuities is that when you die, the evil insurance company keeps all of the money. This is totally untrue. What people are referring to with this broad-brush comment is a "Life Only" payout structure, which is one of over 15 different ways to set up the payout. Your QLAC can be structured so that 100% of the money will go to you, your spouse, or your listed beneficiaries. The annuity company will NOT keep a penny.

Potential QLAC Speed Bumps

Because the QLAC structure is new for the carriers, I do predict that there will be some initial growing pains. In addition, because the IRS and the Treasury Department are majorly involved, government's track record for efficiency is not very good. Hopefully, these potential issues will not arise, and if they do, they will be temporary.

In the future, I think that the QLAC could be used to lure the best employees by offering this strategy within their retirement plan. Even though QLACs will be portable from plan to plan according to the ruling, the portability issue is another potential administrative hurdle if not handled properly.

Why You Should Consider a QLAC

Qualified Longevity Annuity Contracts should be used primarily for lifetime income needs starting at a future date that you specify at the time of application. If you are a younger worker and your 401(k) offers a QLAC choice, then you should definitely consider adding that to your asset allocation so you will have a guaranteed income stream in the future. If you are retired or have a traditional IRA, then you have two strategies where a QLAC can benefit your current plans. The obvious QLAC solution is for guaranteed future income, but another popular QLAC strategy will be to potentially lessen taxes on RMDs (Required Minimum Distributions) and defer income past age 70 1/2 in your traditional IRA (up to age 85).

Another positive that also should be considered is that adding a QLAC policy to your portfolio shortens the time horizon on your other IRA investments because of the contractual guarantees and specific time horizon of the income stream. This allows you to potentially invest more aggressively because of the 100% contractual certainty of the QLAC policy. The QLAC also balances out the volatility of any other investment type future income streams.

Why the QLAC Ruling Is a Game Changer: Bought Not Sold

With the introduction of the QLAC version of the traditional longevity annuity, the annuity industry will transition from a product category that is sold to one that is actually purchased by the consumer.

No VAs or FIAs Allowed in QLAC Building

One of the key rulings from the Department of the Treasury and the IRS was that variable annuities and fixed index annuities (aka: indexed or "hybrid" annuities") CANNOT be classified as a QLAC. This is fantastic news for the consumer, because agents will not be able to "juice" proposal numbers with QLACs like they do to sell variable or indexed annuities.

The indexed-and-variable cult members will definitely keep fighting for QLAC inclusion, but let's hope that the Department of the Treasury and IRS hold strong and only allow the Longevity Annuity structure to be deemed a QLAC. It's in the consumer's best interest.

The Interest Rate Conundrum

No one can predict interest rate movements—that's been proven. Annuities and their subsequent pricing are affected by interest rates. The 10-year Treasury is the primary benchmark for most annuity carriers, so it's common sense that if interest rates are higher, then annuity pricing will be better. I encourage you to not fall into the trap of cavalierly believing that interest rates "have to" go up. Just ask Japan about that, and check out its interest rate history over the past two decades. It could be a long time until you see the rates you desire, whatever number that is. I want interest rates to go up just like everyone else, but am not sure when that will happen.

Laddering Strategies

Just like you can ladder CDs or bonds, you can also ladder annuity income. For example, you can have guaranteed incomes streams turning on at different ages. As a basic example, under the QLAC funding rules of 25% or $125,000 (whichever is less), you could have different QLAC policies turning on at age 75, 80, and 85. Because annuity payments are primarily based on your life expectancy at the time you take the payments, the older you are, the higher the payment.

Also, it's important to point out that you can buy a traditional Longevity Annuity (DIA) in non-IRA accounts (i.e. non-qualified) to complement the QLAC. With the $125,000 or 25% limitation, your overall longevity annuity strategy might involve both IRA and non-IRA accounts.

No ROI Till You Die

Return on Investment (ROI) is a required obsession with investors, regardless of what they are investing in. With the QLAC strategy, you'll need to leave ROI calculations at the door. With lifetime income stream payments, there is no way to calculate ROI until you pass away. Yes, you can figure out what would happen if you lived to 95, but you'd just be guessing.

QLACs should be positioned in your mind and in your portfolio as a non- correlated (i.e. non-market) asset, and right beside your Social Security payment and your pension (if you are so fortunate). QLACs are pure transfer-of-risk strategies that contractually guarantee that you will never outlive your money. Always remember that annuities are not investments. They are contractually guaranteed risk transfer strategies.

The Gorilla in the Room... Inflation

Inflation is the "nailing Jell-O to the wall" concern for most informed investors. There is no annuity on the planet that perfectly solves for inflation, regardless of what eager agents might tell you. With QLACs, you do have the ability to attach a COLA (Cost of Living Adjustment) annual increase at the time of application, and choose the percentage increase for the life of the policy. For example, you could attach a 3% COLA to your QLAC policy, which means that your income stream will increase by 3% per year for the life of the policy. Sounds great, right? It can be, adding a COLA will lower your initial payment when compared to the same QLAC without a COLA. Remember that annuities are never too good to be true, but they can be pretty darn good when fully understood and placed properly within a portfolio.

The good news with the QLAC is that the $125,000 funding limit will be indexed to inflation and adjusted in $10,000 increments. If you project inflation at 3%+ per year, then the increase will probably happen every 3 to 4 years.

The Other "IRS"—Implied Return Scenarios

Implied Longevity Yield (ILY) calculations are used to try to make the decision whether it makes sense to purchase an annuity right now or wait until a later date. Developed and trademarked by annuity industry icon Moshe Milevsky ILY calculates what yield you would have to achieve from a non-annuity product that would match the lifetime income guarantees of an income annuity like a QLAC.

The bottom line is that all of us know it is impossible to "time" interest rates. Because there is no growth component during the deferral years with a QLAC, an ILY type calculation could be used to make somewhat of an apples-to-oranges comparison.

Carrier Competition = Better QLACs

As more and more carriers enter the QLAC arena, the offerings will get better because these annuity companies will be directly competing for your business. This is why I love the United States, and why I think our capitalistic system is so fantastic. You are the winner here, and I encourage you to shop all of the carriers that offer QLACs to see which offering best fits your specific goals.

IRAs in Play... Not Sure About the 401(k)

The QLAC ruling was put in place primarily for pre-retirement workers to be able to add another guaranteed income stream other than Social Security. I personally believe that it will take a while, and a lot of education, for employer plan participants to understand and fully utilize the QLAC strategy. It will eventually happen, but it won't be immediate.

The QLAC will hit full speed very quickly with consumers who are traditional IRA owners. When people figure out that they can potentially reduce their RMDs (Required Minimum Distributions), the annuity floodgates will open up. QLACs will contractually protect your principal, and also allow spousal benefits, non-spousal benefits, and the ability to add a COLA to the policy. These attractive features will just add fuel to the popularity fire.

I predict that in the very near future, having a QLAC in a traditional IRA will be commonplace. Of course the annuity industry doesn't agree with me on this, and still wants to focus on complex, high-fee products. Once again, I will prove them wrong.

QLAC-Specific Example: Traditional IRA With $500,000 for a 70-Year-Old Male

In this situation, the client is 70 years old, which means he will have to start taking RMDs (Required Minimum Distributions) from his IRA at age 70 ½. With a QLAC strategy, he can take 25% or $125,000 (whichever is less) and defer the income stream to start as far out as age 85.

So when he calculates his RMDs, the amount would be based on $375,000 instead of $500,000. Because it is a lesser amount, his RMDs will be lower. In essence, the value of the QLAC is ignored when calculating the RMD.

With the $500,000 example above, RMDs before implementing a QLAC strategy would be $18,250. After implementing a $125,000 QLAC, the RMDs would be $13,688. That's $4,562 less in taxable income.

The QLAC is principal protected in case he passes away before the income starts—and when he reaches age 85, the lifetime income stream will start. He can also choose to add his spouse as a joint life payout.

2% Becomes the Majority

The longevity annuity product type was actually introduced in 2004, but has just become popular within the last three years. Most of those were sold outside of IRA structures, and before the QLAC ruling was approved. Currently, longevity annuities represent less than 2% of all annuities sold annually in the U.S. With over $250 billion annuities sold every year, longevity annuities are a blip on the screen right now. With the QLAC ruling, my prediction is that the longevity annuity strategy will become the most popular annuity within the next five years because of its simple structure and lifetime income benefit.

Multiple Names... One Strategy

QLAC is a specific type of longevity annuity, and not all longevity annuities are classified as QLACs. As proof that the annuity industry has no consistent message with any of their 15 different product types, longevity annuities are called many things, but all are one in the same.

Below are the names used for longevity annuities:

> • Longevity Annuities • Longevity Insurance • Deferred Income Annuities (DIAs) • Advanced Delayed Annuities (my favorite!) • Advanced Life Deferred Annuities (ALDAs) • Qualified Plan Longevity Annuity Contract • Qualifying Longevity Annuity Contract • QLAC (Qualified Longevity Annuity Contract)

QLAC Carriers and Availability

The carriers that will offer the QLAC product will primarily be those you are already familiar with. This is a good thing for the consumer, because annuity guarantees are only as good as the company backing up those guarantees.

Transfer the Risk

Annuities should be positioned in your portfolio as "transfer-of-risk" solutions. With the QLAC strategy, you are transferring the risk to the carrier to provide an income stream that you will never outlive. Regardless of how long you live, the annuity carrier is on the hook to pay. That's the pure definition of risk transfer.

"Will Do," Not "Might Do"

I always tell people that you should "own an annuity for what it *will* do, not what it *might* do." What that means is that you should only purchase an annuity for the contractual guarantees. QLACs are really just pension-type income guarantees that will start at a future date of your choice. QLACs are a pure transfer-of-risk solution that will solve for longevity risk, which means never outliving your money.

Don't Be Limited by the Limit

The biggest negative to the QLAC ruling is the limitation of how much money you can place in the strategy. $125,000 or 25% of your IRA isn't "enough" for many people, but rules are rules. I encourage you to not be handcuffed by the QLAC premium ruling if you like the overall longevity annuity strategy.

So if you max out your QLAC contribution, then switch gears and focus on the same future income strategy in your non-IRA accounts. Contractually guaranteed transfer-of-risk future income works anywhere!

Remember that longevity annuities (aka: deferred income annuities) have been around since 2004, and have just become popular in the last few years as an efficient target date income strategy. Consider using the efficient, no fee longevity annuity (DIA) strategy in your non-IRA (i.e. non-qualified) accounts to contractually guarantee a future income at a specified date. Whether you want to ladder start dates or contractually add COLA increases, longevity annuities in non-IRA accounts can also provide a tax-favorable income stream using the annuitization exclusion ratio.

Laddering longevity transfer-of-risk income strategies could utilize the QLAC strategy as the anchor, or at the top or bottom range of your specific ladder strategy. The rest of the ladder would utilize your non-IRA accounts to achieve your desired income goals.

Action to Take: Contact me (Stan The Annuity Man) personally for a specific QLAC quote, which will list the best contractual guaranteed numbers from top carriers based on your specific situation. If you have a traditional IRA, you will be able to purchase a QLAC directly from me. If you would like to buy a QLAC from your current 401(k) plan, please contact your administrator and urge them to offer QLACs in their specific plan.

CHAPTER 5

A Guaranteed Income Stream With Upside

Get Paid Every Month for Life... and Even More If Stocks Go Up

By Grant Wasylik and Tom Dyson

If you're an average 65-year-old male, and you don't have 20 years' worth of savings, odds are you're going to die broke...

That's according to the Society of Actuaries, which recently amended its mortality tables. A 65-year-old male now has a life expectancy to age 86.6—an increase of 24 months in the 15 years since the last amendment.

If you're a female, you're going to live even longer. The average 65-year-old female now has a life expectancy to age 88.8.

These longevity increases mean your money needs a similar longevity increase. Otherwise, you're in danger of outliving your savings.

Traditionally, the best way to boost retirement savings has been to buy stocks. They've historically outperformed all other asset classes over long periods. Wharton professor Jeremy Siegel calculated that the long-run (200+ years) return on stocks is between 6.5% and 7% per year after inflation.

Here's a chart he showed to a value-investing audience in a 2012 presentation:

Stocks Whip Other Major Asset Classes Over the Long Haul

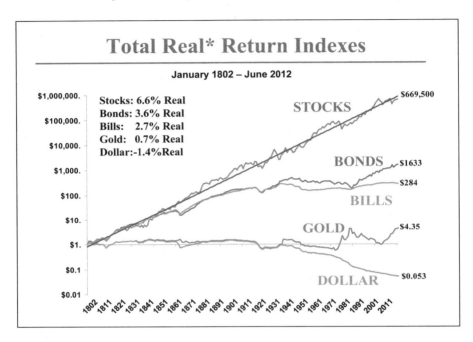

Fast-forward to more recent years, and stocks are still outperforming...

Over the last 10, 20, and 30 years, stocks gained 7.7% per year, 9.9% per year, and 11.3% per year, respectively, on a nominal basis. They beat bonds solidly—which only returned 4.7% per year, 6.2% per year, and 7.4% per year over the same time.

Siegel argues that stocks are actually less risky than bonds. They're more likely to protect your purchasing power and provide you with the best return—**if** you're considering a holding period of 20 years or more.

And that's the major criticism of Siegel's research...

Who has 20 years to hold an investment?

Well, as you can see from the actuarial tables above, it turns out that if you're 65-years-old, <u>you will</u>. And that means you may be leaving big money on the table by selling your stocks in favor of "safeguarding" your wealth in a 100% fixed-income portfolio.

The big money in stocks is made during secular bull markets. By "secular," we mean multi-year to multi-decade periods in which stocks, in aggregate, increase in value.

Over the last century, secular bull markets have returned between 152% and 857% cumulatively...

Secular Bull Markets Return at Least 152% Cumulatively

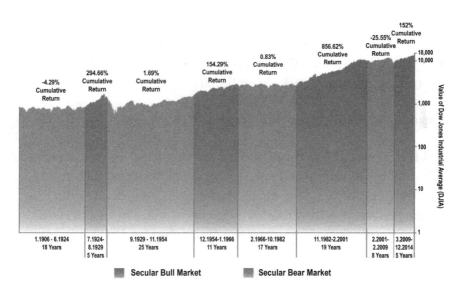

Cashing out of stocks in favor of "safe" fixed income may mean you're giving up the chance at triple-digit gains.

Of course, the rebuttal is that within these long-term averages are shorter bear-market years. And by staying in stocks, you're potentially exposing yourself to big losses.

The most recent bear market drained investors between October 2007 and March 2009. The S&P 500 lost 57% of its value in a year and a half.

If you had been an investor nearing retirement then, the "long-term average gains of stocks" would have been of no value to you.

Had your portfolio lost 50% during the financial crisis, a subsequent gain of 50% would not have gotten you back to even. You actually need a 100% gain to recoup a 50% drop.

And if you're withdrawing money from your brokerage account to pay your living expenses (which many retirees do), your portfolio may not have enough time to get back on its feet.

That leads many retirees to an unsatisfactory trade-off...

Choose the upside of stocks—along with the risk of a bear market. Or choose the safety of fixed income—along with its smaller returns and potential opportunity cost of a bull market.

Fortunately, there's a new option...

In this chapter, we'll tell you about a new solution we've discovered. It's a way in which you can keep a portion of your portfolio fully invested in stocks while insuring it against any downside risk. Plus you can safely withdraw money every year (or every month) to pay your living expenses.

We've never seen a legitimate investment that offers upside potential with zero downside.

If you're a nervous investor nearing retirement—or even a retiree— who wants the best of both worlds (upside and safety), then this chapter is for you.

We're going to show you a solution that'll let you safely withdraw 4-8% of your stock portfolio's "all-time high" value each year. And it will guarantee that you can keep withdrawing *at least this amount for the rest of your life*—regardless of what actually happens to your portfolio.

It all began as the brainchild of a high-profile financial executive back in 2009...

A Lifetime Guaranteed Pension That Lets You Stay Invested

David Stone was senior annuity counsel at Charles Schwab. He and his colleagues helped build the company's annuity platform from nothing to $1.7 billion in annuities under management. Schwab's clients were investors who appreciated the guaranteed income provided by traditional annuities, but they were equity investors at heart.

Many didn't like the actual structure of the product. Sure, they liked the guaranteed lifetime income... but they didn't always want to "cash out" of their investments to get it. They knew that over the long haul, equities historically provided the best returns. So they hated the idea of missing out on those returns. Because they knew that even though they were retired or nearing retirement, there were still decades' worth of stock market gains to be had.

Stone calculated that insurance companies were missing the chance to make money from the $1-2 trillion of investable assets that don't have any sort of income guarantee (such as bonds).

He envisioned a solution where insurance companies would insure existing equity accounts. This would let investors keep their investments. Yet they'd receive the lifetime income of an annuity. Call it the best of both worlds.

On the other side, insurance companies would get to insure a big chunk of assets that they'd otherwise have no access to.

It sounds like a no-brainer. A huge amount of potential business at stake. But insurance companies have traditionally been slow

---

to change and adopt new products. And they had never been comfortable insuring brokerage accounts full of stock positions.

Classic annuities are one thing—insurance companies are good at betting on how long somebody is going to live. But they hadn't placed bets on equity market investments.

But Stone and his team were determined. Schwab's chief technology officer created technology that'd help them insure existing accounts. His model accounted for risk, with riskier funds being more expensive to insure.

In 2009, Stone and a small group of Schwab employees left the company to pursue this new solution for retirees. Their solution would guarantee income while allowing clients to participate in stock market upside.

Then in 2012, they struck a deal with insurance carrier Transamerica. The insurance company agreed to become the first carrier to insure these accounts. Transamerica jumped on board thanks to the system that Schwab's former CTO had developed. (This system monitors each individual account and sends the insurer portfolio snapshots every minute. This way, Transamerica can effectively update its risk models.)

Together, they launched a new solution called **RetireOne**. It became the flagship product of their new company, Aria Retirement Solutions.

The SEC approved RetireOne in 2013. Here's a quick overview of how it works...

1. You purchase insurance on your portfolio with RetireOne. Their exclusive carrier, Transamerica, provides the insurance.

2. You can withdraw a certain amount of money each year from your account.

3. The amount of money you're allowed to withdraw depends on your age, current interest rates, and the highest all-time value of your account.

4. If your account goes up in value (thanks to your investments increasing), your payouts will also increase.

5. If your account goes down in value, your payouts will remain steady—based off the previous "high-water mark" of your account.

6. If you completely deplete your account, Transamerica will still pay you the same payout amount you had been receiving. This money comes out of Transamerica's coffers.

Unlike traditional annuities, RetireOne doesn't make you hand over a lump sum of cash to an insurance company. You can keep your investments right where they are—meaning they stay in your possession. You can even withdraw your entire portfolio from RetireOne at any time with no termination fee.

The only requirement is that you invest your money in pre-approved investments (currently 194 mutual fund and ETF choices).

Now, let's touch back on points 4 and 5 from above to make sure you understand them. They're huge benefits to you...

If your investments rise in value, Transamerica will reappraise your plan and let you withdraw more money. No annuity would ever let you do this.

On the other hand, if your investments go down in value, the payments you receive from Transamerica won't drop by even one dime. You essentially "lock in" payments from Transamerica based on the highest value of your investment account at the end of a given quarter.

It's a bit like refinancing a home, in which you secure lower payments based on the lowest all-time interest rate you locked in. But in this case, you're securing higher cash payouts based on the highest all-time value of your account achieved.

Your Payouts Are Based on Your Account's Highest Value

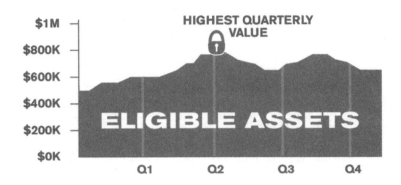

Summing up... you get exposure to market's upside, without <u>any</u> exposure to market downside.

There's simply no other financial product we're aware of that offers this same opportunity.

Step-By-Step Guide: How RetireOne Works

Here's an image to show you how RetireOne works. We'll explain each step in more detail to the right...

HOW THE RETIREONE TRANSAMERICA II SOLUTION WORKS

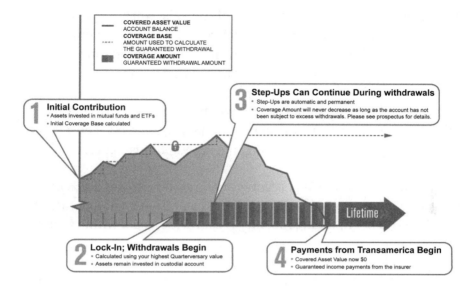

COVERED ASSET VALUE
ACCOUNT BALANCE
COVERAGE BASE
AMOUNT USED TO CALCULATE
THE GUARANTEED WITHDRAWAL
COVERAGE AMOUNT
GUARANTEED WITHDRAWAL AMOUNT

1 Initial Contribution
- Assets invested in mutual funds and ETFs
- Initial Coverage Base calculated

3 Step-Ups Can Continue During withdrawals
- Step-Ups are automatic and permanent
- Coverage Amount will never decrease as long as the account has not been subject to excess withdrawals. Please see prospectus for details.

2 Lock-In; Withdrawals Begin
- Calculated using your highest Quarterversary value
- Assets remain invested in custodial account

4 Payments from Transamerica Begin
- Covered Asset Value now $0
- Guaranteed income payments from the insurer

Lifetime

Step 1—Your "Initial Coverage Base" Is Calculated

You move the assets that you want covered by your new RetireOne plan into pre-approved mutual funds and ETFs (exchange trades funds). There are almost 200 choices. We'll highlight them in the next section.

The total value of these investments forms your Initial Coverage Base. This is what Transamerica is insuring for you.

Step 2 (Optional)—You Can Deposit More Funds Into Your Account and Get a Pay Raise

You can deposit more money into your account anytime before you begin taking withdrawals. By doing this, you'll increase the value of your account and benefit base by $1 for every $1 you deposit—even if you make the deposit after your initial high-water mark is set.

Step 3–You Begin Taking Withdrawals

When you're ready to start taking withdrawals—turning your guaranteed income stream "on"—RetireOne will lock in your coverage base from the highest quarterly value your account has attained since you moved your account to RetireOne.

Your coverage base can never be lower than this level. No matter what happens to your investments—including large market selloffs—you're always going to receive income based on this figure.

Your annual withdrawal percentage will range between 4-8% per year, depending on your age and the 10-year Treasury Note rate at the time you begin taking income. We'll review exact withdrawal ranges later.

Step 4–If Your Account Value Increases, or Interest Rates Increase, You're Eligible for "Step-Ups"

While you'll never receive a pay cut if your account balance decreases, you will enjoy a pay raise if your account goes up. This is called a "Step-Up."

If your account is worth more at the end of the year than your previous all-time high, you'll receive a "Step-Up." This means that your coverage amount will increase—as will your payments.

You can also get a pay raise if interest rates go up. We'll highlight the specific pay raises you'll receive for interest rate increases in a bit.

Step 5 (If Needed)–If Your Account Value Falls to $0, Transamerica Will Still Pay You

You don't have to worry about depleting your account from withdrawals (or from investment losses). If your account hits $0, you'll still receive your guaranteed income payments. That's the benefit of this annuity hybrid.

Your Investment Options

As we mentioned earlier, in order for Transamerica to insure your account, you'll need to move the portion of your funds that you want insured into pre-approved mutual funds and ETFs (exchange trades funds).

There are almost 200 options, and they're vehicles from the best investment companies in the world, such as PIMCO, DFA (Dimensional Fund Advisors), Schwab, Vanguard, Fidelity, and WisdomTree.

Here are some of the major asset classes offered, along with a few sample investment options from each class:

- **Investment-grade debt funds** such as **PIMCO Total Return ETF (BOND)**, **DFA Inflation-Protected Securities Fund (DIPSX)**, and **SPDR Nuveen Barclays Capital Municipal Bond ETF (TFI)**. There are nearly 50 bond funds choices.

- **Large-cap stock funds** such as **Vanguard S&P 500 ETF (VOO)**, **Vanguard Dividend Appreciation ETF (VIG)**, and **Schwab Total Stock Market Index Fund (SWTSX)**. These are just three examples out of more than 35 available options.

- **U.S. small-cap stock funds** such as **Vanguard Small Cap ETF (VB)** and **iShares S&P SmallCap 600 Value ETF (US)**.

- **International stock funds** such as **MSCI Canada (EWC)**, **iShares MSCI EAFE Index (EFA)**, and **WisdomTree International SmallCap Dividend ETF (DLS)**.

- **Emerging market stock funds** such as **iShares MSCI Emerging Markets ETF (EEM)**, **Schwab**

Fundamental Emerging Markets Index Fund (SFENX), and **SPDR S&P China ETF (GXC)**.

- **Real estate funds** such as **Vanguard REIT Index ETF (VNQ), iShares Cohen & Steers Realty Majors ETF, and SPDR Dow Jones Global Real Estate ETF (RWO)**.

- **Commodity funds** such as **iShares Gold Trust (IAU)** and **PowerShares DB Commodity Index Tracking (DBC)**.

- **Alternative funds** such as **ALPS Alerian MLP (AMLP)** and **Nuveen Preferred Securities (NPSAX)**.

There are more categories than just the ones listed above. For example, RetireOne also has balanced funds, foreign bond funds, high-yield bond funds (U.S. or non-U.S.), and more. Please see the Appendix at the end of this report for the full list of current investment options.

Fees and Taxes

Your fees to RetireOne will range from 0.70% to 1.80% annually, depending on the make-up of your portfolio. Basically, the riskier the assets you hold, the higher your fees. So if you own a high percentage of stock-based funds, you'll be on the high end with fees.

When we spoke with Stone at RetireOne, he told us that accounts with less than 60% equity (stock) exposure will generally pay less than 1% in annual fees. This is the cost of the insurance on your portfolio.

Remember, the mutual funds and ETFs you select will charge their own fees independently of RetireOne. In 2014, the average mutual fund charged 1.02% in fees. And currently, the average ETF has an expense ratio of 0.44%.

Regarding taxes... As long as you're withdrawing your own money, you don't have to pay ordinary income taxes on your withdrawals from a RetireOne account. It's considered a return of principal.

You only pay capital gains taxes on your investment gains as long as your account has a positive balance.

If it does go to zero, you would then have to pay income taxes on the majority of the income you receive from Transamerica. That's because those payments would be considered "gains."

Historical Case Study:
RetireOne for a 65-Year-Old Male (2004–2015)

Scenario: Opened a RetireOne Account in July 2004

Carl, a 65-year-old, was set to retire on July 31, 2004. He had $500,000 in a Scottrade account that he'd wanted to keep safe from a stock market crash. And he wanted to turn it into a reliable stream of income to supplement his Social Security checks.

Let's say that Stone and his team had split from Schwab a decade earlier. Suppose the SEC approved RetireOne in 2003, and it was an option for Carl. So he went for it.

Carl insured his account with RetireOne. And he decided he didn't need to start drawing cash right away. In fact, he waited six years to begin taking withdrawals. This was 100% his choice, as is the benefit with RetireOne. You decide when to insure your account. And you also decide when you want to start withdrawing money.

When Carl starting taking money in 2009, RetireOne would have **provided him with 4% annual withdrawals, or $26,878.10 annually**. This is derived from the all-time highest value of his account, which was $671,952.43 in 2007, at the peak of the market.

Of course, the stock market crashed in 2008. But it didn't matter to Carl. His account did fine. That's because his insurance locked in this highest value for his coverage amount.

Many investors sold in a panic in 2008 and 2009, and missed the ensuing bull market that's sent the S&P 500 250% (and counting) higher. Carl didn't sell, because he wasn't terror-stricken. Thanks to his RetireOne insurance.

As a result, his account has bounced back nicely. His asset value is not yet back to its peak, but that's because **Carl has taken $152,309.22 in withdrawals to-date**.

His covered asset value, as of March 31, 2015, would have been $609,846.61. Which means that, before fees, he's **already showing a profit of more than $262,155.83 on his RetireOne account—a 52.4% gain**. And he was completely insulated from the 2008 crash.

A "Back Test" of RetireOne from July 2004 Through March 2015

Date	Age	Historical Rate of Return	Covered Asset Value	Highest Quarterversary Value[2]	Coverage Base Value	10-Year Treasury Bond Yield[3]	Coverage %	Coverage Amount	Total Withdrawals
07/31/04	60	-	$500,000.00	-	$500,000.00	4.47%	-	-	-
07/31/05	61	12.98%	$564,915.76	-	$564,915.76 ↑	4.28%	-	-	-
07/31/06	62	3.33%	$583,746.28	$586,223.98	$586,223.98 ↑	4.98%	-	-	-
07/31/07	63	11.88%	$653,121.90	$671,952.43	$671,952.43 ↑	4.74%	-	-	-
07/31/08	64	-9.48%	$591,179.39	-	$671,952.43	3.95%	-	-	-
07/31/09	65	-10.90%	$526,759.17	-	$671,952.43 🔒	3.48%	4.00%	$26,878.10	-
07/31/10	66	10.03%	$553,723.03	-	$671,952.43	2.91%	4.00%	$26,878.10	$26,878.10
07/31/11	67	12.89%	$596,386.27	-	$671,952.43	2.80%	4.00%	$26,878.10	$53,756.19
07/31/12	68	-2.86%	$552,861.02	-	$671,952.43	1.47%	4.00%	$26,878.10	$80,634.29
07/31/13	69	13.78%	$600,191.52	-	$671,952.43	2.58%	4.00%	$26,878.10	$107,512.39
07/31/14	70	8.91%	$625,484.16	-	$671,952.43	2.56%	4.00%	$26,878.10	$134,390.49
03/31/15	70	0.01%	$609,846.61	-	$671,952.43	1.92%	4.00%	$26,878.10	$152,309.22

| Market volatility caused your covered asset value to decrease by more than 20% in two years. | Ten years since purchasing RetireOne, your covered asset value is $609,846.61, a 21.9% increase from the amount you initially invested. This entire amount remains available to you at any time if you wish to cease the guarantee. | In May 2007, you captured your highest Quarterversary and it was applied to your coverage base in July 2007. This was the second year your coverage base received a step up. | In 2009, you initiate the lock-in feature and begin taking withdrawals. Although your investment value stands at $526,759.17, your coverage base — the balance from which your withdrawal amount is based — has maintained its value at $671,952.43. | Five years after lock-in, you have withdrawn $152,309.22. You can continue to withdraw $26,878.10 per year, even if your covered asset value goes to zero. |

Now, here's another great benefit...

We hope that Carl will continue to live a long and prosperous life. But if he passes away tomorrow, his wife Jill will inherit <u>all</u> the assets in his account.

That's different from a single-life SPIA, which essentially expires when the person does.

In fact, Jill receives a "stepped up" cost basis on the account at Carl's death. This means she won't have to pay taxes on her withdrawals, because those are considered principal. She can also choose to "wrap more assets" into her RetireOne account if she wants to receive more monthly income than Carl was previously receiving.

Your Annual Withdrawal Percentage

How much money are you allowed to take out of your account?

It's a straightforward calculation based upon your age and the current yield on the 10-year Treasury Note.

Today, if you're 60 years old, you'll be allowed to withdraw 4% annually. Your withdrawal percentage gradually increases until age 85. When you reach age 85 or older, you'll be able to withdraw 6% annually.

For example, let's say Joe is a 70-year old retired man. He has $1 million sitting in an investment account that he wants to turn into a stream of guaranteed income.

So, Joe moves the investments into a RetireOne account using the pre-approved mutual funds and ETFs. He has RetireOne insure his account and provide him with a guaranteed income stream to boot.

If Joe's account "locks in" today, he'll be able to withdraw 4.5% annually. That's $45,000 on his $1 million account. And Joe can withdraw the money on a monthly basis if he'd like… instead of taking one large withdrawal for the year. It's his choice.

You can find your exact withdrawal percentage in the table below. As we write, the 10-year Treasury Note is yielding much less than 4.5%—so you'll use the left-most column only.

Locate your age, and you'll see your withdrawal percentage one cell to the right.

| Coverage Percentage – Single Life Option[1] | | | | |
| Your Age at Lock-In Date[2] | 10-Year United States Treasury Bond Yield[3] | | | |
	0.00% to less than 4.5%	4.50% to less than 5.00%	5.00% to less than 5.50%	5.50% to less than 7.00%	7.00% +
60	4.0%	4.0%	4.5%	5.0%	5.5%
61	4.0%	4.1%	4.6%	5.1%	5.6%
62	4.0%	4.2%	4.7%	5.2%	5.7%
63	4.0%	4.3%	4.8%	5.3%	5.8%
64	4.0%	4.4%	4.9%	5.4%	5.9%
65	4.0%	4.5%	5.0%	5.5%	6.0%
66	4.1%	4.6%	5.1%	5.6%	6.1%
67	4.2%	4.7%	5.2%	5.7%	6.2%
68	4.3%	4.8%	5.3%	5.8%	6.3%
69	4.4%	4.9%	5.4%	5.9%	6.4%
70	4.5%	5.0%	5.5%	6.0%	6.5%
71	4.6%	5.1%	5.6%	6.1%	6.6%
72	4.7%	5.2%	5.7%	6.2%	6.7%
73	4.8%	5.3%	5.8%	6.3%	6.8%
74	4.9%	5.4%	5.9%	6.4%	6.9%
75	5.0%	5.5%	6.0%	6.5%	7.0%
76	5.1%	5.6%	6.1%	6.6%	7.1%
77	5.2%	5.7%	6.2%	6.7%	7.2%
78	5.3%	5.8%	6.3%	6.8%	7.3%
79	5.4%	5.9%	6.4%	6.9%	7.4%
80	5.5%	6.0%	6.5%	7.0%	7.5%
81	5.6%	6.1%	6.6%	7.1%	7.6%
82	5.7%	6.2%	6.7%	7.2%	7.7%
83	5.8%	6.3%	6.8%	7.3%	7.8%
84	5.9%	6.4%	6.9%	7.4%	7.9%
85 +	6.0%	6.5%	7.0%	7.5%	8.0%

Safety in Transamerica

Our annuity expert, Stan Haithcock ("Stan The Annuity Man"), recommends that you seek a Comdex ranking of 80 or better from any insurance carrier you consider. (Comdex ranking is the average score a company receives based on all four ratings services: AM Best, Moody's, S&P, and Fitch.)

Reason being, you're relying on your insurance carrier to pay you. And they have a fiduciary responsibility to do so. Which means as long as they are in great financial shape, you have nothing to worry about.

Transamerica has a current Comdex score of 93. That means the company ranks among the highest in its industry in financial strength, according to the major ratings agencies. It received an A+ rating from A.M. Best, an A1 rating from Moody's, an AA- rating from S&P, and an AA- rating from Fitch.

You can be confident that Transamerica will hold up its end of the contract as you collect lifetime income.

How to Get Your Own RetireOne Account

Let's say you're approaching retirement or are retired. And you want to earn guaranteed income from your portfolio. But you don't want to "cash it out" and hand it over outright to an insurance company as you might do with an annuity. Then, you may want to consider RetireOne as part of your retirement solution.

Stone told us he recommends that, as an investor, you put this type of "portfolio protection" in place about five to 10 years before you retire (by the way, you must be at least 35 years old to start a RetireOne account). Reason being, you don't want to leave your portfolio exposed to a 2008-style downturn. Remember, a 50% drop in your portfolio balance means you need a subsequent 100% to recover. And you may not have enough time until retirement to wait for that.

Keep in mind, you're insuring your portfolio from downside risk while keeping your portfolio invested in equities as long as possible to maximize upside exposure. If you're 35 years old, and you're going to work for another 20-30 years, your portfolio has a lot of time to recover from a stock market crash. If you're 55, and you're going to retire within the decade, it does not.

It's easy to set up a RetireOne account. You can build a portfolio of

What Financial Advisors Are Saying About RetireOne...

Comments from advisors that are using RetireOne:

> *What advisors and clients like best about RetireOne are the options and flexibility it offers, without being locked in for life. It gives clients choices that they've never had before. RetireOne investors win by having lifelong investment upside that you don't get with typical annuities.*—Craig Morningstar of Dynamic Wealth Advisors

> *If this product can get those certain clients back into equity markets with the discipline to stay there, it will be a valuable retirement income tool for advisor. Especially those who don't want to sell traditional annuities. Now you can say, 'I believe you can take 4.5% a year from this account for the rest of your life, and for an additional 1% or so, I can guarantee it.'*—Helen Modly of Focus Wealth Management

> *The RetireOne platform is very transparent to the end user. It's easy to understand. And the service is outstanding. RetireOne increases trust with clients, knowing they're not going to be stuck with the high costs of similar kinds of income guarantees.*—Rudy Blanchard of Regatta Research and Money Management

> *RetireOne is the only way to address sequence of returns risk, period. What makes it great is the ability to put the guarantee on the account during the 'death zone' years near retirement. And after 3 years or so if the account is in good shape you can drop it without any cost.*—Michael MacDonald of Michael McDonald Financial

* Remember, <u>you don't need a financial advisor to use RetireOne!</u>

approved mutual funds and/or ETFs, or select from prebuilt models. You can either do it yourself, or with the help of your financial advisor.

Action To Take: Call the Concierge Desk at David Stone's company, Aria Retirement Solutions, at (877) 575-2742 to learn if RetireOne would work for you.

Appendix: RetireOne-Eligible Funds

Here are the funds that you can insure with RetireOne. The fund factor is the risk factor that Transamerica assigns to the fund. The lower the fund factor, the lower the risk as far as Transamerica is concerned.

For a bond fund, the baseline is 0. For an equity fund, the baseline is 1.00. Funds with more risk are more expensive to insure. A lower fund factor means lower fees for you.

BALANCED
ASSET CATEGORY CAP = 0 – 100%

TICKER	FUND NAME	FUND FACTOR
DGTSX	DFA Global Allocation 25/75 Instl	0.20
DGSIX	DFA Global Allocation 60/40 Instl	0.50
PAXWX	Pax World Balanced Individual Inv	0.55
PAAIX	PIMCO All Asset Fund Institutional	0.25
VBINX	Vanguard Balanced Index Inv	0.35

CORE INVESTMENT GRADE DEBT*
ASSET CATEGORY CAP = 20 – 100%

TICKER	FUND NAME	FUND FACTOR
DFGBX	DFA Five-Year Global Fixed-Income Instl	0.00
DIPSX	DFA Inflation-Protected Securities Instl	0.10
DFTIX	DFA Intermediate-Term Municipal	0.00
DFAPX	DFA Investment Grade Instl	0.00
DFIHX	DFA One-Year Fixed Income Instl	0.00
DFEQX	DFA Short-Term Extended Quality Instl	0.00
DFFGX	DFA Short-Term Government Instl	0.00
DFGFX	DFA Two-Year Global Fixed Income I	0.00
FDRXX	Fidelity Cash Reserves	0.00
FMIXX	Fidelity Michigan Municipal Money Market Fund	0.00
SHY	iShares Barclays 1-3 Year Treasury Bond	0.00
MBB	iShares Barcap MBS Bond Fund	0.20
CSJ	iShares Barclays 1-3 Yr. Credit	0.00
TLT	iShares Barclays 20+ Year Treasury Bond	0.20
IEF	iShares Barclays 7-10 Year Treasury	0.05
AGG	iShares Barclays Aggregate Bond	0.00
GVI	iShares Barclays Intermediate Govt/Credit Bond	0.00
CIU	iShares Barclays Intermediate Credit Bond	0.00
SHV	iShares Barclays Short Treasury Bond	0.00
TIP	iShares Barclays TIPS Bond	0.05
LQD	iShares iBoxx Investment Grade Corp	0.10
MUB	iShares S&P National AMT-Free Municipal Bond Fund	0.10
PTTDX	PIMCO Total Return D	0.00
BOND	PIMCO Total Return ETF	0.00
PTTRX	PIMCO Total Return Instl	0.00
SWBDX	Schwab Short-Term Bond Market	0.00
SWLBX	Schwab Total Bond Market	0.00
SCHP	Schwab U.S. TIPS ETF	0.10
SHM	SPDR Nuveen Barclays Capital Short Term Municipal Bond ETF	0.10
TFI	SPDR Nuveen Barclays Capital Municipal Bond Fund	0.10
TGCFX	TCW Core Fixed-Income Instl	0.00
TGLMX	TCW Total Return Bond I	0.00
TGMNX	TCW Total Return Bond N	0.00
VFIJX	Vanguard GNMA Admiral	0.00
BIV	Vanguard Intermediate-Term Bond ETF	0.00
BLV	Vanguard Long-Term Bond Index ETF	0.15
VMBS	Vanguard Mortgage Backed Securities ETF	0.20
BSV	Vanguard Short-Term Bond ETF	0.00
VFSUX	Vanguard Short-Term Investment-Grade Admiral	0.00
VFSTX	Vanguard Short-Term Investment-Grade Inv	0.00
VBTLX	Vanguard Total Bond Market Index Fund Admiral Shares	0.00
BND	Vanguard Total Bond Market ETF	0.00
VBMFX	Vanguard Total Bond Market Index Fund Investor Shares	0.00

ALL MONEY MARKET/CASH OPTIONS OFFERED BY THE CUSTODIAN ARE ELIGIBLE ASSETS AND CONSIDERED CORE INVESTMENT GRADE DEBT.

DOMESTIC LARGE EQUITY
ASSET CATEGORY CAP = 0 – 50%

TICKER	FUND NAME	FUND FACTOR
VQT	Barclay's S&P 500 Dynamic Vector	0.80
BRLIX	Bridgeway Blue Chip 35 Index	0.75
GSFTX	Columbia Dividend Income	0.90
DTMEX	DFA Tax-Managed US Eq	0.85
DFEOX	DFA US Core Equity 1 Instl	0.85
DFUEX	DFA US Social Core Equity 2	1.10
DFLVX	DFA US Large Cap Value Instl	1.10
DFUVX	DFA US Large Cap Value III	1.10
DFUSX	DFA US Large Company	0.85
GATEX	Gateway A	0.80
ITOT	iShares Core S&P Total U.S. Stock Market	0.85
IWF	iShares Russell 1000 Growth Index	0.90
IWB	iShares Russell 1000 Index	0.85
IWD	iShares Russell 1000 Value Index	0.80
OEF	iShares S&P 100	0.80
IVV	iShares S&P 500 Index	0.85
USMV	iShares MSCI USA Minimum Volatility	0.85
PSTKX	PIMCO StocksPLUS Instl	1.00
SNXFX	Schwab 1000 Index	0.85
SFLNX	Schwab Fundamental US Lg Co Idx	0.95
SWPPX	Schwab S&P 500 Index	0.85
SWTSX	Schwab Total Stock Market Index	0.85
SCHB	Schwab U.S. Broad Market ETF	0.85
SCHX	Schwab U.S. Large-Cap ETF	0.85
SCHG	Schwab U.S. Large-Cap Growth ETF	0.90
SCHV	Schwab U.S. Large-Cap Value ETF	0.80
TICRX	TIAA-CREF Social Choice Eq Retail	0.85
VFINX	Vanguard 500 Index Investor	0.85
VIG	Vanguard Dividend Appreciation ETF	0.70
VUG	Vanguard Growth ETF	0.85
VIGRX	Vanguard Growth Index Inv	0.85
MGC	Vanguard Mega Cap ETF	0.80
VONG	Vanguard Russell 1000 Growth Index ETF	0.85
VONV	Vanguard Russell 1000 Value Index ETF	0.85
VOO	Vanguard S&P 500 ETF	0.85
VTI	Vanguard Total Stock Market ETF	0.85
VTV	Vanguard Value ETF	0.85

INTL INVESTMENT GRADE DEBT
ASSET CATEGORY CAP = 0 – 50%

TICKER	FUND NAME	FUND FACTOR
BWX	Barcap Intl Treasury	0.40
ITIP	iShares International Inflation-Linked Bond Fund	0.30
PFORX	PIMCO Foreign Bond (U.S. $-Hedged) Fund Instl Class	0.00
PGAIX	PIMCO Global Multi-Asset Instl	0.90
RPIBX	T. Rowe Price International Bond	0.15
TGBAX	Templeton Global Bond Adv	0.15
BNDX	Vanguard Total International Bond Index	0.30

EMERGING MARKETS DEBT
ASSET CATEGORY CAP = 0 – 10%

TICKER	FUND NAME	FUND FACTOR
BSIIX	BlackRock Strategic Income Opportunities Fund Institutional Shares	0.65
EMB	iShares JPMorgan USD Emerging Markets Bond	0.75
PCY	PowerShares Emerging Mkts Sovereign Debt	0.75
VWOB	Vanguard Emerging Markets Government Bond ETF	0.65

INTERNATIONAL LARGE EQUITY — ASSET CATEGORY CAP = 0 – 50%

TICKER	FUND NAME	FUND FACTOR
MALOX	BlackRock Global Allocation Fund Institutional Shares	1.15
BIBDX	BlackRock Global Dividend Fund Institutional Shares	1.00
DGEIX	DFA Global Equity Instl	0.90
DFIEX	DFA International Core Equity Instl	0.95
DSCLX	DFA International Social Core Equity	1.15
DFIVX	DFA International Value Instl	1.10
DFVIX	DFA International Value III	1.05
DFTWX	DFA T.A. World ex US Core Equity Instl	0.95
DTMIX	DFA Tax-Managed International Value	1.05
HAINX	Harbor International Fund Institutional Class	1.10
ABRZX	Invesco Balanced Risk	0.40
EWL	iShares MSCI Switzerland Index Fund	1.05
EFG	iShares MSCI EAFE Growth Index	0.90
EFA	iShares MSCI EAFE Index	0.90
EFV	iShares MSCI EAFE Value Index	1.00
EWC	MSCI Canada	1.20
SCHF	Schwab International Equity ETF	1.05
SWISX	Schwab International Index	0.90
VEU	Vanguard FTSE All World ex US	0.95
VGK	Vanguard MSCI European Stock Index	0.95
VPL	Vanguard Pacific Stock Index	1.00
VEA	Vanguard Tax-Managed International Fund ETF Shares	0.90
VXUS	Vanguard Total Intl Stock Idx ETF	1.05
VGTSX	Vanguard Total Intl Stock Index Inv	1.05

DOMESTIC SMALL CAP EQUITY — ASSET CATEGORY CAP = 0 – 15%

TICKER	FUND NAME	FUND FACTOR
BOSVX	Bridgeway Omni Small-Cap Value N	1.45
DTMMX	DFA Tax-Managed US Marketwide Value	1.10
DFTSX	DFA Tax-Managed US Small Cap Portfolio	1.10
DTMVX	DFA Tax-Managed US Targeted Value	1.15
DFSTX	DFA US Small Cap Instl	1.10
DFSVX	DFA US Small Cap Value Instl	1.20
DFFVX	DFA US Targeted Value Instl	1.25
DFVEX	DFA US Vector Equity Instl	1.05
IWO	iShares Russell 2000 Growth Index	1.10
IWM	iShares Russell 2000 Index	1.10
IWN	iShares Russell 2000 Value Index	1.15
IWC	iShares Russell Microcap Index	1.15
IJT	iShares S&P SmallCap 600 Growth	0.95
IJR	iShares S&P SmallCap 600 Index	1.00
IJS	iShares S&P SmallCap 600 Value Index	1.10
SWSSX	Schwab Small Cap Index	1.10
SCHA	Schwab U.S. Small-Cap ETF	1.15
VXF	Vanguard Extended Market Index ETF	1.00
VB	Vanguard Small Cap ETF	1.05
VBK	Vanguard Small Cap Growth ETF	1.05
VISGX	Vanguard Small Cap Growth Index Inv	1.05
VBR	Vanguard Small Cap Value ETF	1.10
VYSVX	Vencimetry U.S. Small Cap Value	1.45

DOMESTIC MID CAP EQUITY — ASSET CATEGORY CAP = 0 – 25%

TICKER	FUND NAME	FUND FACTOR
DFTCX	DFA T.A. US Core Equity II Instl	0.95
DFQTX	DFA US Core Equity II Instl	0.95
DFSIX	DFA US Sustainability Core I	0.95
FMDCX	Federated Mid-Cap Index Svc	1.00
IWP	iShares Russell Midcap Growth Index	0.90
IJK	iShares S&P MidCap 400 Growth Index	0.95
IJH	iShares S&P MidCap 400 Index	0.95
IJJ	iShares S&P MidCap 400 Value Index	1.00
OFAIX	O'Shaughnessy All-Cap Core	1.05
PQIIX	PIMCO Dividend and Income Builder INSTL	1.05
SCHM	Schwab U.S. Mid-Cap ETF	1.00
VIMSX	Vanguard Mid-Cap Index Inv	1.00
VO	Vanguard Mid-Cap ETF	0.95
VOE	Vanguard Mid-Cap Value ETF	0.95

HIGH YIELD DEBT — ASSET CATEGORY CAP = 0 – 20%

TICKER	FUND NAME	FUND FACTOR
HWHAX	Hotchkis & Wiley High Yield	0.30
HYG	iShares iBoxx $ High Yield Corporate Bond	0.40
PHYDX	PIMCO High Yield Fund Class D	0.30
JNK	SPDR Barclays Capital High Yield Bond	0.45

EMERGING MKTS LARGE EQUITY — ASSET CATEGORY CAP = 0 – 10%

TICKER	FUND NAME	FUND FACTOR
DFEMX	DFA Emerging Markets	1.45
DFCEX	DFA Emerging Markets Core Equity Instl	1.10
DFESX	DFA Emerging Markets Social Core Equity	1.40
DFEVX	DFA Emerging Markets Value Instl	1.20
EEM	iShares MSCI Emerging Markets Index	1.35
SCHE	Schwab Emerging Markets Equity ETF	1.20
SFENX	Schwab Fundamental Emerging Markets Index	1.15
GXC	SPDR S&P China ETF	1.45
VEIEX	Vanguard Emerging Markets Stock Index	1.15
VWO	Vanguard MSCI Emerging Markets ETF	1.25

REAL ESTATE — ASSET CATEGORY CAP = 0 – 10%

TICKER	FUND NAME	FUND FACTOR
DFREX	DFA Real Estate Securities Instl	1.20
RWO	SPDR Dow Jones Global Real Estate ETF	1.85
ICF	iShares Cohen & Steers Realty Majors	1.20
VGRSX	Vanguard REIT Signal	1.20
VNQ	Vanguard REIT Index ETF	1.20
VGSIX	Vanguard REIT Index Inv	1.20

COMMODITIES — ASSET CATEGORY CAP = 0 – 10%

TICKER	FUND NAME	FUND FACTOR
DCMSX	DFA Commodity Strategy Portfolio Fund	1.60
IAU	iShares Gold Trust	0.80
DBC	PowerShares DB Commodity Index Tracking	0.95
VPU	Vanguard Utilities ETF	0.60
VUIAX	Vanguard Utilities Index Admiral	0.60

CHAPTER 6

Reverse Mortgages—
Are They Right for You?

How to "Spend Down" the Equity in Your House

By Mark Morgan Ford

There are really only three ways to finance your retirement:

- By "spending down" the equity you have accumulated
- By living on the income you receive from Social Security and/or pensions
- By depending on the interest you earn from your retirement saving.

The first was the dream my generation dreamed for most of our lives. Thanks to bubbles and bad government, that is no longer a realistic option.

The second is ideal. But again, most baby boomers (and older readers) are poorer now than they expected to be. Their retirement assets won't be enough to generate the income they need. Especially with interest rates at record lows.

The reality is that most people my age or older will have to consider the third option: gradually "spending down" their assets.

This strategy is simple: Sell some portion of your wealth every year to meet your needs. But don't spend so much that you run out of money before you die.

From a financial management perspective, "spending down" your asset base during retirement is a sound policy... *as long as you are conservative in your projections.*

If you are considering this approach, you may be wondering which of your assets you should sell. The bonds? The stocks? Hard assets?

There are no generally accepted rules to help you make this decision. Some argue you should spend down your most volatile assets first, starting with, say, penny or mining stocks. A second theory is that you should spend down the most time-consuming or irksome asset classes first (rental real estate, for example). A third idea is to sell down collectibles—such as art and coins.

Still another option is what some people call a "reverse mortgage." This is a way of spending down the equity in your house.

Reverse mortgages are becoming increasingly popular today. And with good reason. They allow you to spend the savings that are built up in your house without giving up your mortgage. In other words, they can give you the cash you need without worrying about losing your home.

This is what I want to discuss in this chapter: how a reverse mortgage could help fund your retirement, and whether it might be an option you should consider.

Should You Consider a Reverse Mortgage?

If you go online to research reverse mortgages, you will find many stories about retirees who have been "saved" by this strategy. If you are a member of AARP, you've seen such stories many times. One recent AARP article, for example, profiled 73-year-old Robert Lee White of Fort Lauderdale, Florida.

Robert was in a financial hole. He couldn't afford his refinanced mortgage and was about to lose his home of 45 years. Then he heard about reverse mortgages.

He hired an attorney who persuaded the bank to give Robert a reverse mortgage based on the equity he had in his home. This allowed him to settle his first mortgage. It also gave him needed cash.

Robert told AARP that he was grateful. "Believe me, this has really turned my life around."

While reverse mortgages can help some, they might not make sense for everyone.

For example, Platinum Level subscriber Randy S. recently sent us a note. He said that after taking a big hit on his portfolio in 2008, he worries that he may not be able to recover what he and his wife need for retirement:

> My question is whether we should consider taking out a reverse mortgage on our house and property. The assessed value has dropped over the last few years, but it's still well above what we paid.
>
> None of our children would have any interest in moving here, so there's not really a question of leaving it to them. And as I understand reverse mortgages, the bank will settle the reverse mortgage debt by selling my house when I die.
>
> More than likely, the kids would still get a couple hundred thousand out of it. I'm not really too worried about leaving them a lot, since they're all successful in their own rights.

I answered Randy briefly by saying that it could be a good option. But I urged him to wait a while. At 62, he and his wife have lots of years to live. I encouraged him to develop a second stream of income.

I based my hesitation to recommend a reverse mortgage to Randy on his age. But there are other reasons why you should think twice about a reverse mortgage.

What Exactly Is a Reverse Mortgage?

A reverse mortgage is basically a home equity loan. If you're 62 or older, and you're getting the reverse mortgage on the property that's your primary residence, you may qualify.

The lender gives you a sum of money in return for a second mortgage. The mortgage secures his interest in that equity. You keep the title and the right to stay in your home until (a) you die or (b) you stop living in the house.

Let's say, for example, that your house is worth $500,000. You have a $200,000 mortgage on it. That means your equity in the house is $300,000. You find a banker who will give you $250,000 of that equity. You then can take that $250,000 in a lump sum, in monthly payments, as a line of credit, or as a combination of the three.

A nice benefit of a reverse mortgage is that the money you get is tax-free.

[The money is tax-free because the IRS does not consider it to be income. And in fact, it isn't. You are just borrowing money you have saved in your house.]

Another plus: The payments you receive will *not* diminish your Social Security payments or Medicare benefits. You retain the title to your home, and you don't have to make monthly repayments. The bank settles the loan when you or your surviving borrower dies, sells the home, or no longer lives in the home as a principal residence.

[Under certain reverse mortgage situations, a borrower can live in a nursing home or other medical facility for up to 12 consecutive months. But after 12 months of living somewhere other than the home, the reverse mortgage is due.]

And finally: The government guarantees some reverse mortgages.

Potential Drawbacks of a Reverse Mortgage

Reverse mortgages can be a great option for some retirees to add to or supplement their retirement income. But if you're considering a reverse mortgage, be aware of several things.

Fees

You will almost certainly be charged an origination fee, a mortgage insurance premium (for federally insured home equity conversion mortgages, or HECMs, which are one type of reverse mortgage), and other closing costs for a reverse mortgage.

You also might have to pay servicing fees during the term of the mortgage. Except for origination fees (they are set by law), the lender determines these costs.

These numbers can really add up. Let's look at some.

Proprietary mortgages can charge you pretty much whatever they want. But with HECMs, you can expect the following costs:

Mortgage insurance premium (MIP) = 2% of the appraised value

Origination fee, depending on the home's appraised value

- Appraised value under $125,000 = $2,500
- Appraised value over $125,000 = 2% of the first $200,000, plus 1% of the value over $200,000, with a $6,000 cap

Title insurance = varies by location

Title, attorney, and county recording fees = vary by location

Real estate appraisal = $300-500

Survey (may be required) = $300-500

Good news: With HECMs, you can finance all of these costs, except the real estate appraisal, with the proceeds of the loan itself.

Interest Rates

The interest rates on an HECM are determined on a program-by-program basis. Because the home itself secures the loan, and the U.S. Department of Housing and Urban Development (HUD) backs it, the interest rate should always be below any other available interest rate in the standard reverse mortgage marketplace.

Although some reverse mortgages have fixed rates, most have variable rates. Bankers tie these rates to a financial index. They are likely to change with market conditions. For peace of mind, you should use a fixed rate if you can.

The amount you owe on a reverse mortgage grows over time. Your lender charges you interest on the outstanding balance. He/she adds it to the amount you owe each month. That means your total debt increases as the loan funds increase, which increases the interest on the loan.

Reverse mortgages typically use up most, but not all, of the equity in your home. But it is possible that they can use up all of it or even more. To protect yourself, be sure that the reverse mortgage you get has a "nonrecourse" clause.

This prevents you or your estate from owing more than the value of your home when the loan becomes due. This clause means that it's the bank's problem if you owe more than your house is worth.

Add Both Spouses to the Reverse Mortgage

Mentioning "banks" reminds me of a crucial point: Make sure your spouse's name is on the reverse mortgage with your bank lender.

It may be tempting to put only one name on the contract. Doing this would increase the monthly payments you'd receive. The problem is, if the person whose name appears on the contract passes first, the other spouse is homeless unless he/she can repay the loan without selling the house.

You can avoid this simply by making sure both spouses' names are on the reverse mortgage contract.

Inflation

Because you retain the title to your home, you are responsible for property taxes, insurance, utilities, fuel, maintenance, and other expenses. This can be a problem. If you don't pay property taxes, carry homeowner's insurance, or maintain the condition of your home, your loan may become due and payable. This is especially important when you factor in inflation. When you take out a reverse mortgage, you're typically receiving a series of fixed monthly payments.

But over time, rising inflation can eat away at their value. That would mean your reverse mortgage payments wouldn't buy you as much in the future.

In a worst-case scenario, inflation could grow to the point where you can't afford to keep paying your property taxes and home insurance on top of everyday living expenses. That would give your lender the option to boot you out and sell your house.

Because of this risk, you should factor in your current age when considering a reverse mortgage.

For instance, if you're 83 at the time you get a reverse mortgage, you'll have less worry about the effects of inflation over time. But if you're

65? And you're healthy? You have plenty of years ahead of you.

During that time, inflation can leap up. In 15 or 20 years, you might find yourself in a position where those monthly payments from a reverse mortgage aren't covering your expenses.

Meanwhile, in that same 15 or 20 years, your property taxes and maintenance expenses on the house have likely gone up. But you must pay these expenses as part of your reverse mortgage contract. Unless you have money from somewhere else to pay for these costs, you could lose your home.

How's Your Health?

Another question to ask yourself is "Do I truly believe I'll live in this home until I die?" Many people assume the answer is "yes." But what if you have Parkinson's, Alzheimer's, or some other genetic disease in your family? You may need to move into a health care facility at some point.

As I wrote earlier, under certain reverse mortgage conditions, a borrower can live in a nursing home or other medical facility for up to 12 consecutive months and still maintain their reverse mortgage. But if you haven't lived in your home for 12 consecutive months, this voids your reverse mortgage. You must repay the loan. Not good news if you're prone to illness.

I hope you're seeing that there are many reasons to be cautious about a reverse mortgage. But if, given your specific financial situation, the benefits still outweigh the drawbacks, here are the three main types of reverse mortgages.

Types of Reverse Mortgages

If you've determined you want to get a reverse mortgage, you need to know some basic facts. There are basically three kinds of reverse mortgages:

Single-purpose reverse mortgages. These are usually available through local government agencies and nonprofit organizations.

Home equity conversion mortgages. These are backed by the Federal Housing Administration (FHA).

Proprietary reverse mortgages. These are private loans backed by the companies that develop them.

Each has its own benefits and drawbacks.

Single-purpose reverse mortgages are the least expensive option. But they are not available everywhere. Also, they can be used for only one purpose (specified by the government or nonprofit lender).

Most of the time, you can't use such reverse mortgages to finance your retirement lifestyle. They are usually for such things as home repairs, improvements, or property taxes. I do not recommend this sort of reverse mortgage.

The federal government guarantees HECMs. They are also widely available, have no income or medical requirements, and can be used for any purpose.

Proprietary reverse mortgages are private deals. Some are good. Some are bad. And some are awful. If you are going for a proprietary mortgage, you need to have a trusted lawyer help you.

Both HECMs and proprietary reverse mortgages are more expensive than traditional home loans. The up-front costs can be high. Thus, they don't make any sense if you plan to stay in your home for just a short time or if you want to borrow a small amount.

Getting a Good Deal

If you're considering a reverse mortgage, shop around. Compare your options and the terms various lenders offer. Learn as much as you can about reverse mortgages before you talk to a counselor or lender. That can help inform the questions you ask, which could lead to a better deal.

Banks love reverse mortgages. They promote them for all kinds of needs. Don't use a reverse mortgage for home repairs or improvements. And don't use them to pay property taxes—unless absolutely necessary.

Instead, if you need help paying for home repairs or taxes, contact your local area agency on aging. These agencies are supposed to know about these programs. Ask about "loan or grant programs for home repairs or improvements." Or "property tax deferral" or "property tax postponement" programs, and then ask how to apply.

If you live in a higher-valued home, you may be able to borrow more with a proprietary reverse mortgage. But the more you borrow, the higher your costs.

The best way to see key differences between a HECM and a proprietary loan is to do a side-by-side comparison of costs and benefits. Many HECM counselors and lenders can give you this important information.

No matter what type of reverse mortgage you're considering, you must understand all the conditions that could make the loan due and payable. Ask your counselor to explain the "total annual loan cost" rates. They will give you the projected annual average cost of a reverse mortgage, including all the itemized costs.

Next Steps

Before deciding to get a reverse mortgage, calculate the costs and risks. Ask the following questions:

- Do I really need a reverse mortgage?
- Can I afford a reverse mortgage?

- Can I afford to start using up my home equity now?
- Do I have less costly options?
- Will I still be able to pay my costs of living if inflation rises?
- Will I be in my current home until I pass away?

If, after answering these questions, you still want to proceed, here's what to do:

1. Get information from a potential lender.

2. Get advice from a counselor (a free service).

3. Fill out an application, select a payment option, and receive estimated costs of the loan.

4. Receive an appraisal on your home. An appraiser determines the value and condition of your property. (You pay for the appraisal.)

5. Hire your own attorney and accountant to review everything.

6. If the loan goes through, the closing is scheduled and interest and closing costs are calculated. (You can finance closing costs as part of the loan.)

7. Access the money according to the option you selected. (Most people take it as a line of credit.)

8. You make no monthly mortgage payments during the life of the loan.

Reverse mortgages can be just the thing you are looking for. But they are generally more costly than other loans and come with risks. So before taking one, consider all other options.

CHAPTER 7

The MYGA:
A CD Alternative That Pays More

Earn 20-41% Higher Rates by Taking a New
Angle on This Popular Investment

By Grant Wasylik and Tom Dyson

A certificate of deposit (CD) is one of the most popular, easy-to-use, and trusted investments of all time.

A CD is a time deposit. You hand your money over to a bank. And the bank will pay you compound interest over a fixed term—typically, from six months to five years—until maturity.

These "high-yield" fixed-income investments pay more interest than other banking products—such as checking, savings, and money market accounts.

This chapter, we have another higher-yielding CD-like solution for your consideration.

If you use CDs, or are contemplating investing in them, you'll appreciate this vehicle.

CDs used to pay well. And they still pay well in relative terms. But in absolute terms, they pay *next to nothing*.

As of mid-2015, the average one-year CD that "laps" checking and savings accounts still yields only 0.2%. And the average five-year CD yields just 0.77% while tying up your money for five years.

Think about that: You lock up, say, $10,000 for five years, and it pays you just $390 over that time period. That's barely a monthly car payment for many people.

Even the best five-year CDs average only 2.25%.

Let me show you how weak the market is for safe-income seekers. Here are the highest-yielding five-year CD choices listed on Bankrate in mid-2015:

Top Yielding Five-Year CDs (Bankrate.com)

5 yr CD	
Institution	APY
synchrony BANK MEMBER FDIC ★★★★★	2.25% Wed May 27
Great Rates + Safety = Peace of Mind	
Barclays ★★★★☆	2.25% Wed May 27
Capital One 360 Bank ★★★★☆	2.20% Wed May 27
First Internet Bank of Indiana ★★★★☆	2.12% Wed May 27
EverBank ★★★★☆	2.04% Wed May 27

Even with these low rates, CDs are still popular with investors. In fact, they're the most popular short-term fixed-income investment for affluent U.S. households...

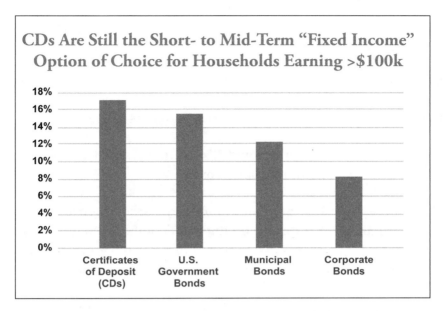

CDs Are Still the Short- to Mid-Term "Fixed Income" Option of Choice for Households Earning >$100k

In this chapter, we're going to show you how to do better than CDs. With the same level of safety, you can earn 20-41% higher yields.

We mentioned that the top five-year CD yields about 2.25%. Our alternative five-year investment yields 3.1%, which is 41% higher.

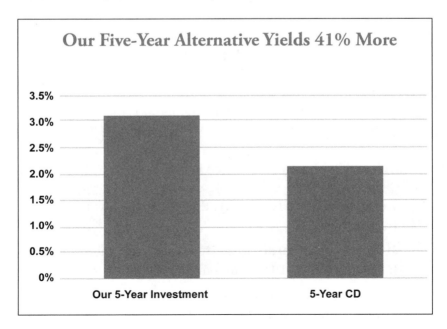

Our Five-Year Alternative Yields 41% More

The income you earn from a CD is taxable. This is where our alternative gets even better...

Our higher-yielding investment is 100% tax deferred. As long as you keep your money in this investment class, rolling it from one investment to the next, you'll pay no taxes on your income.

This finding is a creative strategy. It's so off the radar that most people don't even know this option exists.

The main reason: It's buried in a pool of 15 marketable products. The salesmen for this specific product don't bother with it because they hardly get paid on it (average commissions of 1% or less). And the commissions don't even come from its investors' pockets!

So, this unique arrangement has no out-of-pocket commissions... no fees... a short lock-up period... income tax deferral... and substantially higher rates than what CDs offer. Plus, it's one of the safest products in the financial universe.

We'll show you how to open up this type of investment shortly. But first, let's get into a little background about CDs themselves.

CD Refresher

When you open a CD, you agree not to withdraw the funds until the maturity date. If you break that agreement and access your money early, you'll pay a penalty.

CD returns vary based on these three factors:

- **Length of term** (generally, the longer the term, the higher the rate)...

- **Interest rate conditions** (today, interest rates are near historic lows—so CDs don't pay much)...

- **Frequency of interest payments** (the more often your interest compounds, the faster your money grows).

Back in the mid-1980s, you could earn double-digit returns on six-month, one-year, and five-year CDs. But by mid-2015, for non-jumbo deposits (less than $100,000), those national averages were 0.12%, 0.2%, and 0.77%, respectively.

These low rates have hurt the popularity of CDs. The number of people in households that owned CDs decreased from 25.2 million in spring 2008 to 14.4 million just six years later.

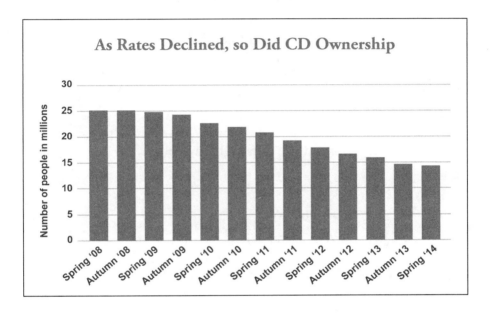

But CDs are still the most popular fixed-income investment for affluent households. Our earlier chart showed that 17.2% of U.S. households earning over $100,000 per year still own them. More households own CDs than U.S. government bonds, municipal bonds, and corporate bonds.

There are two main reasons...

First, CDs are safe. The FDIC (Federal Deposit Insurance Corp.) insures most CDs up to $250,000. So, you get the same protection as a checking or savings account.

Second, compared to regular bank accounts, CD rates are actually attractive. The national average for a checking account as of mid-2015 was 0.04%. And a savings account paid 0.06%.

If you don't need the money in a pinch, it makes sense to put it in a CD for a higher rate.

But, most investors don't realize there's another option to consider. It's just as safe as a CD. And it can pay an additional 20-41%.

Introducing the MYGA...

MYGA stands for "Multi Year Guaranteed Annuity." A MYGA is a fixed annuity. It applies a fixed interest rate to invested funds for multiple years in a row.

MYGAs are very similar to CDs in that they both:

- Have no market risk...
- Pay guaranteed interest...
- And protect your principal.

But MYGAs hold additional advantages over CDs:

- They pay higher fixed-interest rates...
- Your interest grows tax deferred...
- And, in some cases, you can take partial withdrawals of up to 10% annually (depending on the contract).

As we said earlier, most investors don't know about MYGAs because insurance agents don't earn much commission selling them. Agents prefer selling higher-margin products like indexed and variable annuities (commissions of up to 9% versus MYGAs' 1%). But that's a good thing for us... We like the simplicity and rock-bottom commissions of MYGAs.

We've already shown that they boast higher rates—we'll drill down with some examples later. Now, let's review another big edge they have on CDs: tax-deferred stature.

Tax-Deferred Compounding

When you earn interest from a CD (taxable account), you're taxed on that interest at the end of the year. Your gains are taxed as "interest income."

If you own a multiyear CD, this means you'll actually have to reach into your own pocket each year to pay the tax man.

MYGAs, on the other hand, push the tax puck down the ice...

In non-IRA accounts, MYGA interest grows and compounds tax deferred.

And thanks to the Internal Revenue Code's "Section 1035 Exchange" rule, you can transfer an existing annuity contract into a new one without it being a taxable event. This means you pay taxes only on the interest you earn when you take your money out. As a MYGA holder, it's your decision when to pay taxes.

MYGAs also work in IRA accounts because their yields are higher than CDs. However, you lose the tax benefit over CDs in an IRA where both options become equal.

Let's illustrate this "roll" feature to make sure you understand its benefits...

Let's say you own a three-year MYGA until maturity in a taxable account. You can then roll that money into another MYGA without paying any taxes. And you can continue to roll your money into new MYGAs indefinitely. You can also roll your MYGA maturity money into another annuity product if you choose (for example, a SPIA— Single Premium Immediate Annuity).

This tax-deferred status further widens the "yield lead" that MYGAs have on CDs. Let's revisit those five-year yields to see the significance of this.

Assuming a 28% interest income tax rate on CDs, our 3.1% MYGA yield is now 4.3% in pre-tax terms—almost double the 2.2% yield on the five-year CD.

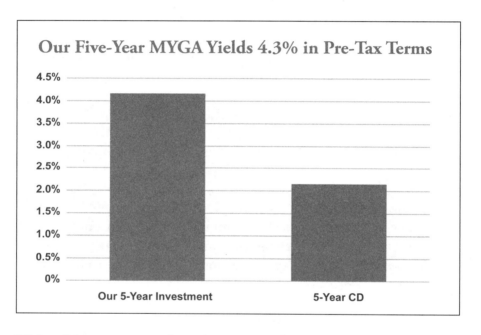

We're able to compound our investment faster thanks to our tax deferrals...

Let's say you put $10,000 into the top-yielding three-year CD. At 1.5%, you'll earn $457 in interest over that three-year period.

But at a 28% (ordinary income) tax rate, you'll owe $128 in taxes... which means you'll only "net out" $329 in total.

But, if you go with the MYGA instead, you'll earn 1.8% per year, which will total $550 in interest over those three years. And you'll be able to roll this entire amount into another three-year MYGA without any tax payment.

You'll have 67% more interest "in hand" ($550 versus $329) if you opt to roll your money into another MYGA versus putting it in a CD and removing it at the end of the three years.

So, MYGAs offer much higher rates than CDs. And their tax-deferred status increases the rate gap even more. But as *PBL* subscribers know, we always stress safe income. And it's easy to see that MYGAs are just as safe as CDs...

CD-like Safety...

An annuity is a contractual guarantee from an insurance company. The insurer, in the case of a MYGA, is guaranteeing an interest rate over a certain time. It's obligated to pay you that rate.

Just as we talked about in our SPIA chapter, insurance companies, safety-wise, stack up very well versus banks...

There have only been two notable failures in the last 25 years: Executive Life Insurance Co. and Standard Life of Indiana (no client lost a penny in either case because other carriers absorbed the guarantees). On the other hand, the FDIC lists 337 bank failures in just the last five years.

Speaking of FDIC insurance, annuities—including MYGAs—are backed by state guaranty funds per policy, per owner. State guaranty funds range from $100,000 to $500,000, depending on which state you reside in.

You shouldn't have to worry about state guaranty funds. As we said before, only two insurance companies have failed—without any client losses—in the last quarter century. Plus, we have two more safety features at work...

Comdex rankings are the best way to judge the financial strength of an insurance company. They're the average score an insurance company receives from all four ratings services: A.M. Best, Fitch,

Moody's, and Standard & Poor's. You can get these rankings and ratings—free, with no sign-up requirement—from annuity expert and *PBL* friend, Stan Haithcock ("Stan The Annuity Man").

Go to www.stantheannuityman.com/comdex-rankings/ and choose "DOWNLOAD your FREE Comdex Report" at the bottom of the page.

Plus, we're recommending MYGAs as short- to mid-term fixed-income strategies. Technically, you only need that insurance company to stay solvent for the duration of your MYGA(s). There's <u>less risk because of the short maturities</u> (unlike the typical annuity where you need that solvency for the rest of your life).

When searching MYGA quotes on Stan's website, you have two search options for ratings: (1) Check by credit rating in the drop-down box. (For example: selecting "A-" will show all MYGAs from carriers with "A-" and higher ratings.) Or (2) choose nothing for rating ("-"). This method will display quotes from "all carriers" regardless of rating—more reasonable with shorter-term contract lengths.

Now, let's walk through three investors' examples where MYGAs make sense for their portfolios (we're viewing quotes from "all rated" carriers).

Case Studies: Three MYGA Hypotheticals for Retirees and Near-Retirees

For these examples, we're using a free calculator provided, again, by Stan Haithcock. This calculator shows how much interest a MYGA will currently pay you.

You're welcome to use it, too. You can go to Stan's website and search for MYGAs by plugging in your own specifications and requirements. And there's no commitment or sign-up requirement (we don't know of another annuity website that offers a "free look" without a sign-up requirement). You can search by state, your age, premium, rating, length of contract, and more.

To access Stan's free MYGA feed, point your web browser to: www. stantheannuityman.com/annuity-strategies/the-annuity-man-steakhouse/fixed-rate-annuities-myga.

At the time of this writing, you can get a MYGA as far out as 15 years. Yet, with today's low-rate environment, we'd recommend sticking with shorter-term fixed annuities.

Please note: Currently, the shortest duration available is three years. However, this can change at any time depending on what insurance companies would like to offer. Sometimes, you may be able to get quotes on one-year and two-year MYGAs.

Now, let's get to our investor examples...

Example 1: Short-Term Cash

George Swift is 70 years old and retired. He's socked away $10,000 to take his extended family on a cruise three years from now. By then, all six grandkids will range from five to 10 years old—in his mind, the perfect time for this adventure.

George and his family can drive from his house to the port in under an hour. His savings will cover a weeklong trip and plenty of extras.

George has this money parked in a Charles Schwab government money market fund. He wants this money to be secure. But the paltry 0.01% interest rate disgusts him. Three years down the road, he'll have another $3 to spend on the cruise. George checked online three-year CD rates and found he can get 1.5%. That equates to $457 in interest payments.

It's a big improvement. But George can do even better.

He can make even more money with the same safety using a MYGA instead of a CD. Here are the top five quotes he'll see on Stan's website:

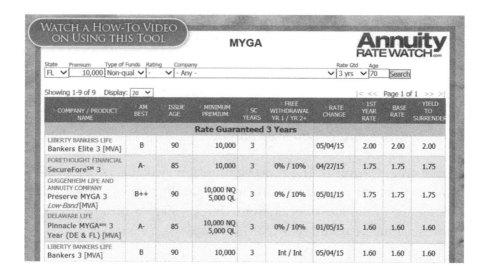

COMPANY / PRODUCT NAME	AM BEST	ISSUE AGE	MINIMUM PREMIUM	SC YEARS	FREE WITHDRAWAL YR 1 / YR 2+	RATE CHANGE	1ST YEAR RATE	BASE RATE	YIELD TO SURRENDER
Rate Guaranteed 3 Years									
LIBERTY BANKERS LIFE Bankers Elite 3 [MVA]	B	90	10,000	3		05/04/15	2.00	2.00	2.00
FORETHOUGHT FINANCIAL SecureFore℠ 3	A-	85	10,000	3	0% / 10%	04/27/15	1.75	1.75	1.75
GUGGENHEIM LIFE AND ANNUITY COMPANY Preserve MYGA 3 *Low-Band* [MVA]	B++	90	10,000 NQ 5,000 QL	3	0% / 10%	05/01/15	1.75	1.75	1.75
DELAWARE LIFE Pinnacle MYGA℠ 3 Year (DE & FL) [MVA]	A-	85	10,000 NQ 5,000 QL	3	0% / 10%	01/05/15	1.60	1.60	1.60
LIBERTY BANKERS LIFE Bankers 3 [MVA]	B	90	10,000	3	Int / Int	05/04/15	1.60	1.60	1.60

George can earn up to 2% annually. That means he'll have an additional $155 (above what his best CD would provide) to spoil his grandkids on the cruise.

Example 2: Intermediate-Term Cash

Fay Medial, 55, has $8,000 saved. She wants to pass it along to her daughter for her first year of tuition at college five years from now. It's sitting in a savings account at her local bank—earning 0.05% interest.

Fay can't afford to put this money at risk in the stock market—she wants it to be there for her daughter. But, she'd prefer to make more than $20 in interest over the next five years.

Her bank is offering 0.85% for a five-year CD (better than the national average). And Fay's considering it... This avenue would fetch her another $346 in interest. And her daughter could put that toward some used books for her classes...

Fay doesn't realize there's a better opportunity out there. If we plug her numbers into Stan's free fixed-annuity calculator, we get her MYGA earning power (top five quotes):

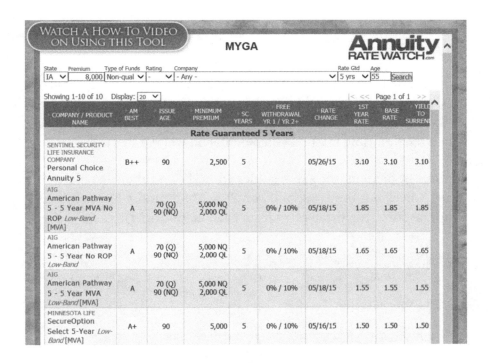

COMPANY / PRODUCT NAME	AM BEST	ISSUE AGE	MINIMUM PREMIUM	SC YEARS	FREE WITHDRAWAL YR 1 / YR 2+	RATE CHANGE	1ST YEAR RATE	BASE RATE	YIELD TO SURREND
Rate Guaranteed 5 Years									
SENTINEL SECURITY LIFE INSURANCE COMPANY Personal Choice Annuity 5	B++	90	2,500	5		05/26/15	3.10	3.10	3.10
AIG American Pathway 5 - 5 Year MVA No ROP *Low-Band* [MVA]	A	70 (Q) 90 (NQ)	5,000 NQ 2,000 QL	5	0% / 10%	05/18/15	1.85	1.85	1.85
AIG American Pathway 5 - 5 Year No ROP *Low-Band*	A	70 (Q) 90 (NQ)	5,000 NQ 2,000 QL	5	0% / 10%	05/18/15	1.65	1.65	1.65
AIG American Pathway 5 - 5 Year MVA *Low-Band* [MVA]	A	70 (Q) 90 (NQ)	5,000 NQ 2,000 QL	5	0% / 10%	05/18/15	1.55	1.55	1.55
MINNESOTA LIFE SecureOption Select 5-Year *Low-Band* [MVA]	A+	90	5,000	5	0% / 10%	05/16/15	1.50	1.50	1.50

Instead of a CD paying 0.85%, Fay could earn up to 3.1% using a MYGA. The $8,000 she's saved for her daughter's first year of college would turn into $9,319 five years from now. That's $1,300 more than a savings account would net. And almost $1,000 more than using a CD.

Example 3: Short- to Intermediate-Term Cash (Ladder Strategy)

Art Werner retired in 1998. He's now 78 years old and living comfortably in Arizona. He and his wife have a $1 million nest egg.

For a long time, Art has kept 10% of his savings (currently $100,000) in CDs. He likes visiting his local bank each month, chatting with the tellers, and checking out new deals for his money. But he's grown tired of the declining rates.

He just had a $30,000 CD come due. The best his bank could offer

---

him on a three-year CD was a measly 0.5%. Even five years out, he'd only get 0.9%.

Art has no idea when, or if, rates will rise, so he was thinking about a CD ladder. His plan would be to buy three-, four-, and five-year CDs ($10,000 apiece). Then in three years, he can reevaluate his options—when the first rung matures—depending on where rates are...

Art can implement the same ladder with MYGAs and earn higher rates. Check out the availability on Stan The Annuity Man's MYGA smorgasbord (top three rates from each ladder rung):

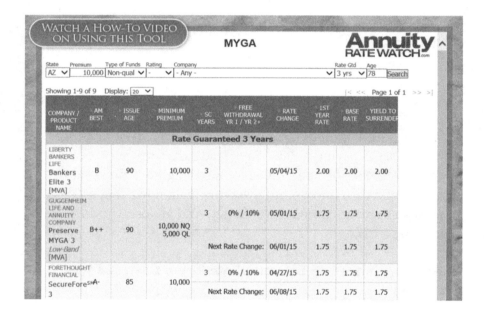

Showing 1-5 of 5   Display: 20 ▾ |< << Page 1

COMPANY / PRODUCT NAME	AM BEST	ISSUE AGE	MINIMUM PREMIUM	SC YEARS	FREE WITHDRAWAL YR 1 / YR 2+	RATE CHANGE	1ST YEAR RATE	BASE RATE	YIELD TO SURRENDER
Rate Guaranteed 4 Years									
GUGGENHEIM LIFE AND ANNUITY COMPANY Preserve MYGA 4 *Low-Band* [MVA]	B++	90	10,000 NQ 5,000 QL	4	0% / 10%	05/01/15	2.00	2.00	2.00
					Next Rate Change:	06/01/15	2.00	2.00	2.00
MIDLAND NATIONAL LIFE Guarantee Ultimate 4 *Low-Band* [MVA]	A+	90	10,000 NQ 2,000 QL	4	0% / Int	04/28/15	1.60	1.60	1.60
NORTH AMERICAN COMPANY Guarantee Choice 4 *Low-Band* [MVA]	A+	90	10,000 NQ 2,000 QL	4	0% / Int	04/28/15	1.50	1.50	1.50

Showing 1-20 of 37   Display: 20 ▾ |< << Page 1 of 2

COMPANY / PRODUCT NAME	AM BEST	ISSUE AGE	MINIMUM PREMIUM	SC YEARS	FREE WITHDRAWAL YR 1 / YR 2+	RATE CHANGE	1ST YEAR RATE	BASE RATE	YIELD TO SURRENDER
Rate Guaranteed 5 Years									
SENTINEL SECURITY LIFE INSURANCE COMPANY Personal Choice Annuity 5	B++	90	2,500	5		05/26/15	3.10	3.10	3.10
LIBERTY BANKERS LIFE Bankers Elite 5 [MVA]	B	90	10,000	5		05/04/15	3.00	3.00	3.00
LIBERTY BANKERS LIFE Bankers 5 Premier Plus [MVA]	B	90	10,000	5	Int / Int	05/04/15	3.60	2.60	2.80

By using a MYGA ladder (staggering his $30,000 evenly over three-, four-, and five-year MYGAs), Art can lock in rates ranging from 2% to 3.1% (remember, his CD options were paying 0.5% to 0.9%).

And after year three, he still has flexibility. Art can decide what to do with his short-term MYGA proceeds. He can take the cash—and either spend it or take it elsewhere. Or he can roll it into another MYGA or annuity product with no taxation.

Steps to Take If a MYGA Fits Your Investing Profile

If you're interested in earning a higher rate than a CD offers, check out a MYGA. It's simple...

Step 1: Go to Stan's website at www.stantheannuityman.com/annuity-strategies/the-annuity-man-steakhouse/fixed-rate-annuities-myga

Enter your search criteria... check the available rates... and decide if a MYGA makes sense for you.

Step 2: Compare the MYGA rates to your other comparable options: CDs, money market accounts/funds, Treasuries, etc. Remember, MYGAs compound tax deferred (assuming you keep the funds invested). In contrast, interest on CDs, money market accounts/funds, and Treasuries are taxed as interest income.

Step 3: If interested, call your trusted agent. Or call *PBL*'s preferred annuity expert, Stan The Annuity Man.

(If you go with your own annuity agent, make sure he or she can get you the same great rates quoted on Stan's site.)

You'll have to fill out some paperwork—just like you would with any annuity product. But, it's a quick turnaround (Stan says a realistic time frame—from start to finish—is a week).

STAN *The*
ANNUITY MAN™

| Annuity **Critic**
| Annuity **Consumer Advocate**
| Annuity **Expert**

800-509-6473 | **stan**@stantheannuityman.com

If you're in a similar situation as George, Fay, or Art, consider a MYGA. You can follow the same path we outlined for them. And you can earn up to 20-41% higher rates than CDs (even more when factoring in tax-equivalent yields).

Action to Take: Review your MYGA options via Stan's "free" live feed. Then, if interested, call your trusted agent or Stan at (800) 509-6473.

Note: If you plan to pull your money out of a MYGA and are under the age of 59-and-a-half, please consult your agent on the tax consequences. You may incur a penalty.

CHAPTER 8

Rental Real Estate 101

By Mark Morgan Ford

Almost everyone who invested in real estate between 2005 and 2008—and there were millions of Americans who did—lost their shirts. (Then again, investing is usually like this.)

The average investor always gets into a trend just when that trend is about to collapse. And then he's so traumatized by the experience that he can't bring himself to get back in when prices are right—even if he understands that investing is the smart thing to do.

Investing is scary. And the fact is that 80% of people reading this will not be able to get beyond their fears. But years from now, they will look back and realize they made a huge mistake.

I want to help you become wealthy, and real estate is one of the best ways to do so. And the good news is that real estate is not difficult to understand. It is very much a simple supply-and-demand sort of investment.

I have been able to make millions doing it and avoid the bubble without ever taking a course or getting a license or any of that stuff. With a little knowledge, you can do the same.

Do You Have What You Need to Succeed?

To be a successful rental real estate investor, you need three things: money, knowledge, and time. This is true of most investments, but the good news is that with rental real estate, you don't need a lot of any one of them.

You can get into rental real estate with as little as $10,000. The most important things you need to learn about it can be learned in less than 30 days. And the time it will take you to locate, purchase, finance, and rent your first property should be less than 40 hours.

The Money

I just said that you need only $10,000 to get into rental real estate. How, you may be wondering, did I come up with that number?

The typical down payment for a real estate investor to mortgage a single-family house is 20%. That's what a bank will require as a down payment for a rental property. An entry-level three-bedroom, two-bath rental in America costs about $80,000. Twenty percent of $80,000 is $16,000. But $16,000 is more than $10,000, you say. What's the trick?

The trick is that I am a strong believer in having partners in the rental real estate business. And having a 50% partner on a $16,000 down payment means that your share is only $8,000.

When you select a partner, you each kick in $8,000 for the down payment. Since you each have $10,000 cash total to use, you will each have $2,000 in cash left over for closing costs (minimal), repairs (also minimal, if you've done your homework), and getting it rented.

That's how I came up with the $10,000 number. But, in case you don't like the idea, let me make my case for having a partner. In terms of cash outlay, having 100% of one $80,000 home is the same as having 50% of two $80,000 homes. But I'd rather own

50% of two homes than 100% of one, because it lowers my risk and increases the chance of making above-market appreciation.

Of course, you have to know someone who (a) has $10,000 to invest and (b) is trustworthy. People who are trustworthy surround themselves with trustworthy people. If you are trustworthy, finding a partner won't be a problem.

Another option is to find a bank to give you a mortgage at 10%. Can you get a loan with a 10% down payment? It is possible, although banks are not as easy with money as they were during the bubble.

In any case, I don't recommend such loans. The traditional 20% requirement is there for a reason. It makes you think harder about the value of what you are buying and treat it more seriously. This is always a good thing in business.

If you don't want to partner up, you'll need a minimum of $20,000, or you'll have to find a rentable house for considerably less than $80,000.

The Knowledge

The most important knowledge you need to acquire in your journey to become a rental real estate magnate is about value. You'll need to learn the relative values of single-family homes in the market you will be buying.

The way to learn this is easy. Simply spend some time looking at and responding to real estate advertisements in the market you want to invest in. It's a simple and easy thing to do.

Read the listings. Get on a local realtor's email list to stay in the loop on properties that come to market. Talk to brokers. Go visit a dozen or so homes for sale. Before you know it, you'll have a good, instinctive feeling for how much any particular property in your area should be worth.

The other thing you have to learn is what you can expect to earn by leasing out the kind of houses you are shopping for. This, again, is as easy as pie. Look at the rental listings in your area. Talk to a broker who specializes in rentals. Browse websites such as Zillow, Trulia, and Craigslist to get a feel for what properties rent for in the areas in which you want to invest. And visit a dozen other properties for rent.

The Time

You can educate yourself on rental values at the same time you are learning about purchase values. A week or two of evenings or weekends should do the trick.

Once you have done that, it's time to look for a property to buy. Assuming you have selected the neighborhood, this process will take—as I said—less than 40 hours. You may not be able to cram those 40 hours into a single week. That's because your objective is to buy at the right price. And not every house that comes to market is priced right.

Success in real estate, in the short run, is dependent on buying right. (In the long run, this is much less important.)

There are times when becoming a rental real estate investor is easy. From 2009 to 2013, for example, this was the case. There were lots of inexpensive properties available—and plenty of inexpensive, easy-to-qualify-for financing.

As I write, the good deals are few and far between. They exist, but you have to go farther (perhaps to another state). Or you have to take on a bit more work (buying properties in working class neighborhoods that typically demand more work).

When conditions are like they are today, I'm still a buyer... I simply recognize that I won't be able to buy as much because there isn't as much on the market.

As the business cycle changes, plenty of properties will cycle back onto the market thanks to unemployment, foreclosures, and short sales. But there will also be plenty of guys out there with money who will be competing with you for the best deals. So for now, you may have to wait a few weeks or even a few months to find a property that is priced right.

That's okay. You never, ever want to run after any investment. There will be plenty of chances to cherry-pick individual properties over time, so don't feel pressured.

Once you have picked your property, it will take you a few weeks or a month to close on it. This process always takes a while—but the amount of time invested from you is minimal—filling out forms and signing contracts and such.

Soon enough, the day will come when you go to the closing and buy the house. And then, if you are properly prepared, you should be able to get it rented in a matter of days or weeks.

The Reward

The house you bought, fixed up, and rented for $80,000 total should bring you about $12,000 per year in rent. After the cost of financing (the mortgage), management fees (you can do this yourself if you want), and rental commissions (if you need to use a broker), your net profit should be about 7%, cash on cash. (That's my conservative estimate—most of my properties net more than that.)

[A cash-on-cash return is a common metric to measure a return on a rental property. It calculates the actual return on the cash you invest. In this case, you put down $20,000 (down payment and closing costs). If, after all of the expenses were paid, you cleared $1,400 per year, your cash-on-cash return would be 7% ($1,400 / $20,000).]

But that doesn't include appreciation. And here's where this business gets interesting. If your property appreciates at 3% per year, you are not making just 10% per year (the 7% plus 3%). That's because you haven't put down $80,000—you've put down only $20,000.

In fact, you would be making $3,800 per year on that $20,000 investment ($1,400 on net rent and $2,400 in appreciation). That is a total return on investment (ROI) of 19%!

[Return on investment, or ROI, is a performance measure used to evaluate the efficiency of an investment. To calculate ROI, the benefit (return) of an investment is divided by the cost of the investment. The result is expressed as a percentage or a ratio. So $3,800 divided by $20,000 = 0.19, or 19%.]

And it's a safe ROI, because your chances of actually losing money are nearly zero.

How to Buy "Right"

The most important rule of real estate investing is: Buy right.

You have probably heard that before. Or its equivalent: "You don't make money by selling real estate—you make money by buying it."

This rule, however simple it sounds, is often misunderstood. To many people, it means simply buying property when it seems cheap. But that is certainly not a good idea. You don't want any subjectivity in your buying decisions. After all, just because something *seems* right, doesn't mean that it *is* right.

The first property I invested in seemed very "cheap" when I bought it back in the late 1970s. It was a nice little one-bedroom condominium apartment in a refurbished building on Massachusetts Avenue in Washington, D.C. Our landlady convinced me to buy it by showing me how much prices had escalated in the recent past.

She told me that if I bought this unit "now," I'd stand to make a lot of money as it appreciated in the following few years. To make it even easier, she got me a "creative" loan from some bank that meant I had to put down nothing but a few thousand dollars in closing costs.

When my wife and I signed the mortgage and got the keys, we felt like we had made a great deal.

But Washington, D.C. real estate was bubbling up in the mid-1970s, and lots of people who didn't know a thing about real estate were jumping in. Including me.

To make a long, painful story short, it took me years to finally get rid of the apartment (and the deadbeat prostitute who was renting it from me). And it cost me about $30,000 to boot.

I made so many mistakes in that one transaction that I could probably base this entire series of lessons around it. But for today, I want to focus on just one part of that mistake: buying rental real estate without any idea of what a "good buy" really is.

When it comes to rental real estate, a good buy is getting the title to a property that can be fixed up and rented out at a profit right from the get-go.

From 2005-2008, millions of Americans were jumping into real estate. But they were doing just the opposite of buying right. They were buying homes at such high prices that it was impossible for them to make any cash profits from renting at all. The only chance they had for profits was if the property they bought kept appreciating in value. In other words, they were speculating that they would be able to sell their overpriced investments one day to someone even more foolish than they were.

So let's get to the question: What exactly does it mean to buy rental real estate "right"?

My answer is this: If you can buy a piece of property and have it fixed up and ready to rent for less than eight-times the yearly rent, you are "buying right."

Let me show you a specific example to make sure this is clear.

Let's say the house you rent goes for $1,500 per month. That would be $18,000 in rent each year ($1,500 multiplied by 12 months). As an investor in rental real estate, you should not pay more than eight-times this yearly rent amount to purchase this house if you want it for cash flow (i.e. you intend to rent it out to someone else). That means you should not pay more than $144,000 for it (8 multiplied by $18,000).

This is a ballpark rule of thumb, of course. But I've been investing profitably in real estate now for about 30 years, so I can say confidently that this rule of thumb is reliable.

If you can buy rental property at that ratio, you stand a good chance of making about 8-10% on your money if you buy it with cash, or about 20-25% if you use a mortgage. (The return is bigger because you're using less of your own money for the initial investment.)

Useful definition: This ratio I just told you about is called a gross rent multiplier (or GRM).

Eight-times yearly rent is the maximum you should pay for any rental property. If you live in an area that has high property taxes and home insurance, a GRM of 7 is a better bet. Your goal is always to pay the lowest GRM you can find for a rental property. Although they aren't as common as they were three years ago, there are still places where you can pick up property for GRMs of 6 or even 5.

The big point here is that when you invest in rental real estate, you should be investing for cash flow, not appreciation. Your object is to start making cash profits on your investment in the very first year. If you do that, you will likely see those profits increase year after year for as long as you hold the property.

Be aware: You can't always find rental properties for a GRM of 8 or less. There are places where either rents are too low or property prices are too high... or both. So these are places you should not invest in rental real estate.

There are also times when it is impossible or nearly impossible to buy rental real estate "right." You certainly couldn't have bought rental real estate for a GRM of 8 in Florida, California, Texas, and most other populous states between 2006 and 2008. The cost of property back then was too high, compared with the rents such properties could generate.

So the No. 1 rule to always follow is to buy rental property when you can get it at GRMs of 8 or less. If you do that, you should do very well as a rental real estate investor.

Be sure to check out areas with working-class people, students, and artists, and not so many professionals. It should be somewhere you feel safe, but it may be rough at the edges and still improving. You'll find far better yields in these areas. So scout out the better-yielding areas around you before you do anything else. All other things being equal, it's easier to manage properties close to where you live.

Let me give you a few specific examples of how I've used the GRM of 8 in my real estate investing. These come from investments that I have made with my brother, Justin, who is a very successful real estate developer and investor in Florida, Texas, and other states.

Around 2004, it became difficult to find properties in South Florida selling for GRMs of 8 or below. I managed to buy a few properties and even a few more in 2005, but by 2006, it was just impossible. At that time, I began advising my friends and colleagues that they should no longer be buying rental real estate.

After the bubble burst in 2008, prices went way down. Many single-family homes in my neck of the woods lost as much as 70% of their value from their peaks.

But I didn't jump in just because they were *relatively* cheap. I started buying again when I could get great GRMs. In 2009-2010, you could have bought properties with GRMs of 5! One of my clients, a doctor, was buying homes in Lake Worth, Fla., (about 30 minutes north of where I live) for GRMs of 4!

But not all real estate was too expensive during the early bubble years—from 2004-2006. Justin started researching other markets that had growing employment, growing population, a diversified and stable economy... yet still had low GRMs. He ended up buying properties in Knoxville, Tenn., in Jacksonville, Fla., and in Texas.

For example, in Austin, my brother bought a couple of four-plexes (buildings with four separate rentable units). They were "value plays," where he and his local Austin partner improved the performance and positioning of the properties.

Then, within two years, he sold the properties for six-figure gains. But the only reason he bought these properties out of state in the first place was because he was able to buy the properties at low GRMs of 5.5. That meant that, even if he didn't end up selling them for the prices he wanted, he could afford to hold on to them and collect good cash flow in the meantime.

So far, I've made the assumption that you are buying properties with cash. I did that to illustrate the main idea (buying right) and to keep it simple.

But if you want to become wealthy through rental real estate investing, you need to consider using mortgages. The reason for that is that a mortgage gives you leverage. And leverage will increase your returns.

For example, let's say you have $100,000 to invest. You have a choice. You can buy a ready-for-rental property for $100,000 and net $10,000 every year in cash. (That would be a 10% return on the cash you invested.)

Or you can buy five properties using an 80% mortgage (that means you would use a down payment of $20,000 for each one). Each of these five properties will give you only $5,000 return, but you will have five of them—for a total return of $25,000, or a 25% return on the $100,000 you invested!

Buying cheap does not mean buying property when it "seems" cheap—either because it is shooting up or because it is cheap *compared* with what it was before. Buying cheap means buying properties with GRMs of 8 or less.

If you do this, you'll stand a great chance that your property will flow cash as long as you manage it well. And when you buy at GRMs lower than the average in your area, your chances for capital gains are also greatly improved.

How to Estimate Rental Income

My rule of thumb for buying rental properties is to never pay more than eight-times gross yearly rent. Looking back at the 50-plus properties I've bought and sold over the years, I've never lost money when my purchase price was at a GRM of 8 or less.

If you stick with this ratio, you should have the same experience I've had: enjoying a positive cash return on each property you buy the first year and every year thereafter—even if you buy it with a mortgage.

Having this result depends, of course, on making an accurate assessment of how much rent the property you are buying will give you. If you overestimate the rental income, the formula will be useless.

That's why I am going to walk you through everything I know about how to accurately estimate rental income.

Don't worry: Estimating rental income is not difficult. There are basically three steps, each consisting of one or two procedures. Each of the actions you will be taking will be easy to understand and do. The challenge is to be thorough. If you take only one or two of these steps, your estimates will be less reliable than if you take all three steps. It's as simple as that.

To organize the data you will be collecting, you'll use a "rent survey." My brother Justin, who is a full-time real estate professional, created one. His rent survey is a table that displays the key factors in determining rental income values in a given area.

To determine accurate rents, there are three steps you need to take.

Step 1: Create a table like the one below.

As you can see, the table below identifies certain key characteristics that determine residential rental values. These include location, the type of structure, the number of bedrooms and bathrooms, and the square footage.

I prefer single-family homes with three bedrooms and two baths. These are obviously more expensive than homes with just two bedrooms, but the extra bedroom makes them more desirable and therefore easier to rent.

You're going to use this form to fill in the rent information you'll find.

Here is an example of the table Justin has created:

Rent Survey					
Address	Type	Sq. Feet	Monthly Rent	# BR/ Bath	Annual Rent per Square Foot
Etc., for a dozen properties in all					
Average rent per square foot:					

This is a template you'll be able to use over and over again.

Step 2: Start driving, calling, and browsing.

This next step is collecting data. Begin by driving around the area you're considering. Get a feeling for the neighborhood: the size of the homes, the income level of the residents, the proximity to schools and hospitals, the amount of traffic on the roads, etc.

You can't get a feeling for an area in a single drive-by. You will have to spend a half hour or so in the neighborhoods at least a half-dozen times. Be sure to visit the neighborhood in the morning, at midday, and at night. And spend some time walking around and speaking to the neighbors.

You can let them know you are thinking of buying a house in the area. Ask them frank questions about their experiences as residents. Take mental notes. After six such tours, you should have a very good idea if this is the kind of neighborhood you and—better yet—a tenant would want.

Also, while you are driving around, take down any phone numbers of advertised rental properties you come across.

When you call the agent or owner, ask for the key data on each property. You're looking for the size (in square feet) of the house, the number of bedrooms and bathrooms, the availability and kind of heating and air-conditioning, the availability of amenities such as pools, hot tubs, etc.

You can also ask them about monthly rents in that neighborhood. Not every agent will know these numbers. And some, if they suspect you are a rental real estate investor, will exaggerate the rents, but you should ask nonetheless, because most of the time, brokers have a fair idea and will tell you the truth.

After you've gotten a feeling for the neighborhood by the half-dozen visits and the necessary data from local brokers, you should double-check what you've learned by doing some online research.

There are several websites that can be very helpful in finding rental values in your market. Here are a few:

- Rent.com
- Apartments.com
- Rentometer.com
- Zillow.com
- Trulia.com
- Craigslist.org.

You should also locate and interview at least one real estate agent who specializes in renting properties in your target area. He is an expert in estimating rental revenues. He will have a good feeling for how much rent you can expect to get from every sort of property in that area.

When interviewing him, you can admit that you are an investor, or you can pose as a renter. The former approach allows for a fuller, more detailed conversation. But there is always a chance that he won't be interested in speaking to you since he won't see you as a source of future business.

If you do pose as a renter, he will be able to give you current listings from the multiple listing service (MLS) that agents and brokers have access to. This will give you the actual asking rents in that area. Of course, what property owners are asking for and what they are getting might be two different numbers. This is another reason I personally prefer to be honest with the agent: I can ask about actual rents, not asking prices.

Another very important question you should ask is how long it normally takes to get a renter. As you can imagine, this is a very important factor in figuring out your first year's cash flow.

Also, ask how long renters typically rent for in that area. In some neighborhoods, the term might be two or even three years. In other neighborhoods, it might be only six months. This is important, because it will cost you money every time you have to re-rent your property.

You might think that contacting such an expert is the only thing you need to do. But I don't feel comfortable trusting any single source of information, especially when it is critical to my success. I prefer to contact rental agents after I've done the other work I've listed above. By that time, I already know a good deal about the area and I can ask better questions and better determine whether he is giving me reliable advice.

In addition to speaking with rental real estate agents, you can get on their email lists. Several real estate agents have websites where prospective buyers, sellers, and renters can sign up for daily email alerts free of charge.

The best agents tie their websites to the MLS itself. You can customize the daily email alert by price range, bedrooms, bathrooms, and area. These daily emails are pure gold. You'll get information on rental properties that come to market each day for your rent survey table.

As you take these steps, enter all of the relevant data into a journal. That data should include "hard" information that will go into your rent survey table and "soft" data (such as proximity to schools and hospitals, the sort of employment residents have, the amount of traffic in the area, etc.) that will be useful later when it comes to finding good tenants.

And keep all of this data in a safe place.

Step 3: Fill out your table.

Once you've collected at least a dozen rental quotes from making

HUD and "Section 8"

If, for any reason, you are having a hard time gathering information, you can go to the website for the Department of Housing and Urban Development (HUD). Then check out its rental rates for "Section 8" tenants in your area.

Section 8 is a rent-subsidy program. Under this program, HUD pays for all or some of the rent of low-income people. It bases the pay scale on the income the person makes and the size, type, and location of the property.

As far as the property is concerned, HUD has fair market rent (FMR) guidelines for different areas. For instance, the HUD FMR for a 2/1 apartment in Smithtown, N.Y. might be $700.

In the one Section 8 deal I've done, I found that the HUD guideline was 10% higher than the actual market value. My brother Justin confirms that this has been his experience as well. This is a good thing. It means the rent that HUD guarantees may be higher than the rent you could get elsewhere.

If the local Section 8 agency is good at selecting good tenants and ensuring they don't trash your property (this has been the case for me), then you are doubly blessed. You will be getting a higher rent, and you will have a government agency doing some property management for you.

For HUD's database of fair market rents, visit www.hud.gov.

calls and browsing websites, you can fill out the table you created in Step 1. This will make it easy to analyze and compare the data on an apples-to-apples basis.

Here is the same table Justin created above, with some fictional data:

Rent Survey

Address	Type	Sq. Feet	Monthly Rent	# BR/Bath	Annual Rent per Square Foot
10 Atlantic Ave., 1A	Apt.	750	$700	2/1	$11.20
755 Lee Ave., Unit 3	Apt.	875	$750	2/1	$10.29
51 Hollywood Ct.	Apt.	850	$775	2/2	$10.94
5 Glenwood Ct., 3D	Apt.	925	$875	3/1	$11.35
120 Enfield Rd., 6B	Apt.	1,025	$925	3/2	$10.83
1201 5th St.	House	1,100	$950	2/2	$10.36
1450 5th St.	House	1,500	$1,200	3/2	$9.60
22 Ave. L	House	1,250	$1,000	2/2	$9.60
22 4th Ave.	House	1,850	$1,350	3/3	$8.76
Etc., for a dozen properties in all					
Average rent per square foot:					$10.25

Making Sense of the Rents

As I said in the beginning, the purpose of the table is to be able to accurately estimate the rental income you will be getting for the kind of property you intend to buy.

The hard data you put on the table accounts for 80-90% of the rental income you will get. The "soft" data you will record in the journal accounts for the other 10-20%. Let me explain...

Traffic, proximity to schools and hospitals, the class of resident, the condition of the house, and the availability of amenities are all examples of soft data I've already mentioned.

Another factor is curb appeal. Houses that look good at a glance are usually easier to rent.

These soft data do matter. But as I said, they are only 10-20% of the equation. The hard data (location, number of bedrooms, number of baths, etc.) will always be the most important factors.

There is a reason that soft data doesn't matter as much. It is because the typical renter of this sort of property is cash-strapped. He won't be able to pay extra for these extra benefits.

So that's one important "inside" tip for you. If you can buy properties in great condition with extras at or below "average" prices, then do so. But don't pay much extra for these. You won't get the return from them.

Another factor you should consider is the physical condition of the property. Both inside and out. As a general rule, older houses tend to require more maintenance. But many newer houses may be in poor condition and in need of repair. Keep these factors in mind.

You will notice that my brother takes note of the size of the property in terms of square footage. The size of the house is not as important as the number of bedrooms and baths in terms of rental income. Later on, if and when you decide to sell the house, it can become important. So it's a good idea to include that in your comparison table.

Look at the table above. As you can see, my brother divides the monthly rent by square footage. Then he multiplies it by 12. He does this to come up with the yearly rent per square foot.

For example, look at the last property in the list—22 4th Ave. It is an 1,850 square-foot home. It rents for $1,350 per month. So... divide $1,350 by 1,850 square feet. By doing this, you get $0.73 per square foot. But that number is per month.

So then, multiply $0.73 by 12 months. Now you get $8.76 per square foot of house space annually. Or said another way, based on the $1,350 monthly rent, a tenant will pay $8.76 for each square foot of space each year.

Now you can use this number to easily compare different sized houses. (Square footage is important when it comes to buying commercial properties such as office buildings or warehouses.)

What Residential Renters Look For

Let's look at everything we've just discussed from a different point of view. What does a renter look for?

The location is usually the residential renter's first consideration. He knows that the quality of the neighborhood is going to have the greatest impact on the quality of his family's experience there.

The next most important factor is the number of bedrooms he needs. Obviously, a couple with three children will much prefer to rent a house with three bedrooms than two.

All other factors being equal, a 1,250-square-foot, two-bedroom house will get a higher rent than a 1,000-square-foot, two-bedroom house. But it won't be 25% higher rent just because the square footage is 25% higher. It might be only 5% or 10% more.

Similarly, a three-bedroom house won't get 50% more rent than an otherwise identical two-bedroom house. Even though there are 50% more bedrooms, the rental value may be only 20-30% more.

Fill in details for at least a dozen properties on your table. Then calculate the yearly rent per square foot for each one as we showed you above. You'll quickly develop a sense for what any given property type could rent for.

Sometimes There's the "Rental Value"... and Then There's the Real Rental Value

If the property you're looking to buy currently has tenants, your task is easier. There's an established rental value on the property. It's at least the amount the tenants are currently paying.

If the tenants are on a lease, better still. Chances are you won't have to find a tenant right away. Plus, existing leases tend to make banks happy. They also improve your chances of getting a loan to purchase the property.

As I alluded to above, be cautious of the validity of advertised rental income. This will be important when and if you decide to purchase commercial rental property such as apartment buildings.

Some owners and brokers state the income at maximum pricing and 100% occupancy for all units. They are giving you a best-possible scenario of the building fully rented, rather than the actual rents.

Ask for the owner's actual income statement on the property. And if you go to contract, ask for the owner's tax returns for the property, as well.

When shopping for apartment buildings, it is helpful to have a good sense for local rental values. Sometimes you can use this knowledge to buy a property at a very good price.

My brother and I were involved in the purchase of a half-vacant, 10-unit apartment near the beach. At the time, tenants occupied only half of the units. The other five were being offered at $800 apiece.

We bought the building and completely restored it for $475,000 and then were able to gross $102,000 in rents the very first year. We had a great, renovated property, within a block of the beach for less than five-times yearly rent!

But to secure deals such as this, you *must* understand the local rental market.

Go Figure

Now you have collected the data on several rental properties. You've determined the rental economics of the neighborhood you're looking in. Now you can calculate, with some precision, just how much you should pay for any piece of property in that neighborhood.

Remember that you should never pay more than eight times the gross yearly rent you can expect from the property. And when I say "pay," I mean to include both the purchase price of the property and any money you need to spend on getting it up to speed.

Let's say, for example, your calculations indicate that the house you are looking at will give you $1,000 per month (or $12,000 per year) in rent. As an investor you should not put more than $96,000 into it. That includes the cost and any renovations.

Of course, if you can get if for less than $96,000, so much the better.

Now It's Your Turn

Identify a 10-block stretch in an area where you'd like to buy rental properties. Go through the steps I've listed above to gather rent details for the area.

Next, use some of the websites and agencies listed above to find out which properties are available for sale in that area.

Once you're certain you understand how much those properties can rent for, calculate each one's GRM:

Purchase Price + Closing Costs & Renovations Needed Divided by Annual Rent

If the GRM is higher than 8, keep looking. If the GRM is 8 or lower, you've likely found a decent candidate for a rental property.

PART 3:

Safe, Cash-Generating Options

CHAPTER 9

The Banker's Code: How to Make Money 98% of the Time in the Secondary Stock Market

By Tom Dyson

While I was working in London at the trading desks of Citigroup and Salomon Brothers, the other traders and I used a secret strategy I called "the Banker's Code."

It was powerful.

So powerful, in fact, that we made money on almost every trade. Day in, day out. Up market, down market. While other investors frantically chased trends, gambled on the latest "hot" stock, and tried to discover the next big thing, we quietly and safely followed the Banker's Code.

And it made us money almost every day, on nearly every trade we entered.

Unfortunately, most investors don't do it this way.

The Dalbar financial research firm recently released a report that showed investors "guessed right" in the market only 42% of the time last year.

I don't want you to guess right only 42% of the time. In fact, I don't want you to guess at all. That's why I'm sharing the Banker's Code with you.

Now, I have been involved in income investments for a long time. And over my career, I have studied every different type of income investment that exists—from the stock market to bonds, to insurance, to real estate...

I've studied them all, and I can categorically say—without any hesitation or doubt—that the Banker's Code secret we're going to show you in this chapter is the single-best way I know to earn income from the stock market.

I am not exaggerating.

I have a **98%** win rate using this strategy. I have every reason to believe that you will enjoy this tremendous success as well.

The bottom line is, if you're going to be in the market, you have to know this strategy. It's a huge advantage. It _will_ make a difference in your income.

It's one thing for me to tell you this. But let me _show_ you I'm speaking the truth.

I've been using the Banker's Code strategy with selected individuals since January 2012. Not long ago I paused to evaluate our track record—at the time of this writing we've made money on 120 of our 123 trades.

I'd love to take credit for this success, but I can't. It wasn't my intelligence that resulted in this phenomenal win rate—it was merely following the simple strategy of the Banker's Code.

I'll say it again: This strategy is powerful. But it's also vital. Now, more than ever, it's a crucial skill every investor should have in their toolbox. Why?

Because the cards are stacked against you.

To begin, it's just not easy to earn income anymore. And I put the blame squarely on the Federal Reserve.

In 2008, the Federal Reserve set interest rates at nearly zero. For people such as you and me, this was possibly the most financially destructive move the government could have made.

You see, with rates this low, the Federal Reserve is preventing little guys like us from earning a fair, safe return on our money.

It used to be that you could earn 4% in a savings account or government bond. No longer. Today, these accounts pay just a hair above 0%. Where do you earn safe income? How do retirees, who rely on fixed income, generate cash?

For most people, there's simply no good answer.

That's why I am furious about the Fed's actions. I believe it is nothing less than evil.

But this is the reality: Interest rates are practically zero right now. And they're going to stay low for years to come. Perhaps decades.

Facing this unpleasant reality, many people have given in. They either park their savings in cash (earning nothing) or buy junk bonds or high-yielding stocks in an effort to earn what was once "the norm" in savings accounts. The problem with this is that it significantly increases risk.

I hate risk.

The paradox of the Banker's Code is that, despite its good returns, it's safe. Safer than high-yielding stocks. Safer than junk bonds. And far safer than flash-in-the-pan growth stocks.

And not only is it safe, but it also works in any kind of market—bull market, bear market, sideways market...

It doesn't matter. The Banker's Code churns our money, regardless.

The old ways of earning safe income may not work anymore, but that's all right. In this chapter, I'll show you a better way. Actually, today I'll show you the best way.

The Banker's Code Will Make You Money... Period

The Banker's Code strategy stuffs your pockets with cash. But rather than me just telling you this, let me show you what people who are using this strategy are saying:

> *"I am thrilled with the results and averaging more than $2,000 per month. In six months, **I have made $13,890**."—Paulina*

> *"I have done every trade you have recommended so far and have **made money on every one of them**. I am very happy with your service."—Lionel*

> *"I made about $4,000. This has been transforming for me at many levels. [I] know I can **CONFIDENTLY make money** for the rest of my life."—Rick*

Real people are making real money with the Banker's Code.

But is it for everyone?

Absolutely. Whether you're 29 or 89, you will make money with this strategy. And you don't have to be a financial whiz to make it work, either.

Even my father is making good money with the Banker's Code. In fact, it saved his retirement.

See, Dad lost nearly all of his retirement savings in the stock market crash in 2008. Two of his largest holdings were in Lehman Brothers and Citigroup.

The money he had in Lehman literally disappeared. Its value went to zero as the stock became worthless. And Citigroup? Its price went from $410 per share in August 2000 to less than $15 by February 2009. The crash practically destroyed my father's retirement income overnight.

What was he to do? What income would he live on? I decided to teach him the Banker's Code strategy, although he had zero prior understanding of it.

Flash-forward to last week—my dad was ecstatic to tell me that the strategy had just made him more than $2,000 in cash... in one day.

I will use this strategy for the rest of my life. So will anyone else who is willing to learn it. And it will make us money for as long as we want.

How You'll Make Money—The Big Picture

Let's start with a high-level overview, sort of a big picture of how this strategy works. I'll use an analogy we all can understand—buying a house.

Imagine a beautiful mansion located right on the beach. It's listed at $1 million, except you don't want to pay $1 million. You want to pay only $750,000.

You know that $750,000 is an extraordinary price for this mansion. And you have the cash in your bank account to pay for it.

Let's assume you approach the owner and say, "I'd like to buy your home for $750,000."

The owner says, "Thank you, but my asking price is $1 million. However, I'll keep your offer in mind... and if I change my mind, I'll let you know."

Then the owner does something that surprises you. He hands you a check for $5,000. All you have to do is promise to buy his house for

$750,000 anytime in the next month if the he decides to sell it for that price.

Why would he do this?

Because it's a good deal for both of you. The homeowner gets a month to search for a buyer willing to pay more. But he has the assurance of you paying $750,000 if no other offers materialize.

If the homeowner doesn't sell you the house, you get $5,000... free and clear. But if he does sell you the house, you get exactly what you wanted in the first place.

Actually, it's better than what you wanted. You'll pay $750,000 and keep the $5,000 he gave you as part of the agreement. That means you'll buy this new, beautiful home for only $745,000.

What I've just described is the essence of the Banker's Code strategy.

Earning Income by Making Low-Ball Offers

The Banker's Code revolves around the following principal:

> Making low-ball offers on assets you want to own anyway, then receiving income for making those offers.

It's simple, powerful, and profitable. And whether or not you ever actually acquire those assets doesn't matter. Why? Because your primary goal is to generate cash from making low-ball offers. And that will happen regardless of whether or not you're able to buy the valuable asset.

Let's apply the Banker's Code strategy to the stock market, which is where it works best. In our example above, what we wanted was premium, beachfront real estate.

What is the equivalent of that in the stock market?

Quite simply, the equivalent is the best blue-chip companies in the world. Companies that make products that will never go out of fashion... that have the strongest brand names... that produce billions of dollars in cash every year.

These companies pay out hefty dividends. They buy back mountains of their own stock. They have zero, or very little, debt. They boast the most conservative management teams. And they do business all over the world.

These are companies such as McDonald's, Johnson & Johnson, or Microsoft... the very best companies. The names you know. The products you use every day. They're the beachfront companies of the stock market.

Normally, these companies aren't cheap. They never get really cheap, because everyone knows they're the best companies. Just like beachfront property, they usually don't come at a discount.

Because of this, what you're going to learn to do is make low-ball offers for these excellent companies. You'll submit offers with asking prices below the current market prices these stocks are at. And in exchange, the current stockowners will pay you cash.

A Low-Ball Offer on the Best-Known Company in the World

Let's walk through the process of making a low-ball offer. Seeing the concept illustrated with an actual stock will help you understand how it all works.

We're going to make a hypothetical low-ball offer on **Coca-Cola (NYSE: KO)**.

Why Coke? Because it's one of the best stocks in existence.

Both globally and in the U.S., Coke dominates the liquid-refreshment beverage industry. It has a 42% market share in the U.S. While it's best known for its sodas, Coca-Cola has 500 other beverage brands that sell in more than 200 countries worldwide.

It boasts the single most recognized brand in the entire world. People all around the globe know and love Coca-Cola products. If that's not enough for you, Warren Buffett, arguably the world's greatest investor, has made billions investing in Coke. He now owns 400 million shares, valued at $16.07 billion.

Year in, year out, Coke is one of the world's most elite stocks. This is "beachfront property" at its finest.

At the time of this writing, Coca-Cola stock trades for about $41 per share. But we don't want to pay $41. Even though it's worth that price, we want to offer to buy it at $36 per share. But with one catch… we're willing to keep this low-ball offer on the table for only six weeks. After six weeks, we'll take our offer off the table.

We now have our game plan. A $36 low-ball offer, which will expire six weeks from the day we make it. Now, best of all, we're going to get paid to make this offer.

Our low-ball offer is valuable to the current owner of the Coca-Cola stock. You see, our low-ball offer gives the current owner some flexibility. It's a "Plan B," so to speak.

Under the circumstances we both agree to, he'll be able to sell us his stock. But he doesn't have to, either. It's his choice—and that's valuable. He pays us for this value.

In this case, the owner of those Coca-Cola shares pays us $70 cash. The amount of cash we receive will change on a trade-by-trade basis. In this case, it was $70. The next trade could be $105. The next, $55.

Six weeks from our low-ball offer, if we don't own Coca-Cola stock, our offer expires. What happens to that $70? Do we have to return it? Nope. It's ours. We never have to pay it back under any circumstances.

You might be wondering: "Well, what happens if someone does take us up on our offer and sells us their shakes of Coca-Cola?"

We'll get to that in a bit, but for now, we just want you to understand the main strategy of the Banker's Code: We make low-ball offers on the world's safest, most profitable, best-run companies, and we're paid cash to do it.

It's really that simple.

Three Real Low-Ball Offers That Have Stuffed Cash in Our Pockets

Let's move from our hypothetical Coca-Cola trade and look at some actual trades I've recommended over the last 6 months:

Walgreens (NYSE: WAG) is the largest drugstore chain in the U.S. Chances are, you are familiar with it. It operates 8,221 locations nationwide... and serves more than six million customers each day.

On August 12, 2014, we made a low-ball offer on Walgreens. In exchange, the Walgreens' shareowner paid us $126 to keep our offer on the table for five weeks.

At the end of the five weeks, we didn't get to buy Walgreens, so our low-ball offer expired worthless, but we kept the $126, anyway. Our return? 2.1% in just five weeks. That might not seem like a lot, but that's an annualized return on our investment of 20.2%.

Apple (NASDAQ: AAPL) is the largest publicly traded company in the world by market cap. As you likely know, the tech titan designs and creates consumer electronics such as the iPad, iPhone, and Mac notebooks.

On September 30, 2014, we made a low-ball offer on Apple. In exchange, the owner of Apple stock paid us $17 to keep our offer on the table for a little over seven weeks.

But after only 28 days, we were able to close our low-ball offer and didn't buy Apple. But we kept the $17, anyway. This time we earned 1.6% in about four weeks. That's the equivalent of earning 21.4% on our cash each year.

Intel (NASDAQ: INTC) is the most dominant semiconductor chipmaker on the planet. It controls nearly 80% of the market worldwide.

On October 21, 2014, we made a low-ball offer on Intel. In exchange, the owner of Intel stock paid us $39 to keep our offer on the table for a little over four weeks.

But at the end of just two weeks, we captured most of our profit and closed our low-ball offer. We didn't buy Intel, but we kept the $39. We earned 1.1% on the 14-day trade... an annualized return on our investment of 28.7%.

These are real trades we've done. The annualized returns were 20.2%, 21.4%, and 28.7%. Let's put that into context.

Warren Buffett has been successful enough to earn 19.7% annualized compound returns for his shareholders over the past 48 years.

Individual trades using this simple strategy earned us returns that raced past those numbers. Will every low-ball offer have high returns like this? No. But they don't need to. We just make steady streams of cash from routine low-ball offers.

I hope you're beginning to see just how powerful the Banker's Code truly is.

Learning the Language of Options

As you now know, stock owners are willing to pay us for our low-ball offers. Why? Because our offers give them flexibility. Under certain circumstances, they could sell us their stock or not. It's their choice. Our offer gives them options.

And that, literally, is the name of the game. We're trading options.

We've used the term "low-ball offer" so far. But you need to know the specific term your broker will recognize. See, in the financial world, people don't call them "low-ball offers." They go by a different name: put options.

Here's a trick—you might think of it like this: You're giving a stock owner the right to "put" his stock on you under certain circumstances.

Financial professionals call the Banker's Code a "put option selling strategy."

You might have heard some scary stories about options. And that's for good reason. Some people, with no experience at all, barrel into options trading with "get rich overnight" fantasies. When that happens, it often ends badly.

That's because the reality is that a whopping 80% of options traders lose their money. And most options strategies are very risky.

But rest assured, we don't fall into that 80%. And what we're doing is the safest strategy of them all.

Why? This statistic largely derives from options investors who **buy** options, hoping that stock prices will go to the moon and they'll make gobs of money.

That rarely happens. Those investors are gambling. Pure and simple.

That's not the Banker's Code strategy. We don't gamble. We don't speculate. We aren't trying to hit a home run. We just quietly and consistently earn chunks of cash on each trade by **selling** options. The returns snowball over time.

Remember the track record of trades we put together as of the date of this writing: 98% winning trades. 120 out of 123 have made us money. You cannot argue with the numbers.

Back to the official language of options...

As I just told you, the Banker's Code strategy sells put options. In our Coca-Cola example, we were selling Coca-Cola share owners a put. This gave them the right, but not the obligation, to "put" their stock on us under certain circumstances. In exchange, we earned cash that's ours to keep forever.

In our opinion, the easiest, safest way to make money with options is by selling put options.

What Is the Risk Here?

If you're like me, I'm sure you're thinking... What is the risk? How can I lose money?

Let's look back to our Coca-Cola example.

In our hypothetical situation, Coca-Cola stock was trading at $41. We made our low-ball offer for $36 for a six-week period. In our example, we didn't end up buying the Coca-Cola stock owner's shares. Our offer expired worthless, so we pocketed the money we made for the offer.

But sometimes, the price of a stock we're making an offer on will fall just below our offer price. In these situations, the owner will ask us to buy his stock per our agreement. Depending on the price you choose as your low-ball offer, the likelihood of this happening could be very small. Nevertheless, it does happen sometimes.

If someone accepts your low-ball offer and you end up buying a stock, the only way you would lose money is if you agreed to buy Coca-Cola (in our example) at $36, but the current market price is now, say, $32.

In this case, you would be paying $4 more per share than the current market value of the stock. Your "loss" would happen if you immediately sold your Coca-Cola stock on the open market. You would lose that $4-per-share difference between the current stock price and the price at which you bought Coca-Cola.

But let's remember a few things:

- First, you don't have to sell. You would own a world-class, elite stock. I can all but guarantee you that, in time, a stock such as Coca-Cola will increase in value and make you even more money.

- Second, the top-quality companies you should make low-ball offers on typically won't experience tremendous price drops that would leave the stock trading significantly lower than your low-ball offer.

- Third, you've already partially offset any potential losses by making money selling your low-ball offer.

- Fourth, when you own elite stocks like Coca-Cola, they pay you dividends, so you're still generating income as you hold the stock.

In addition to all this, there's one more thing you can do if you end up owning your low-ball offer stock. And it will earn you even more income.

What is it? It's the opposite of the low-ball offer... it's the "high-ball listing."

A high-ball listing is the mirror image of the low-ball offer, except it's the process in reverse.

Instead of offering to buy someone else's stock, you're now offering to sell someone your own stock. But just as in a low-ball offer, your high-ball listing will be for a specific price, and your offer will last only a specific length of time. And most importantly, you'll earn cash making this offer.

We'll get into high-ball listings in another chapter, but the important thing to know is it's another smart secret with the Bankers Code available to you if your low-ball offer is accepted.

Making Lots of Money, Bit by Bit

You might be saying to yourself, "Wait a second—making $75 on a trade doesn't seem like a lot of money."

You're right.

$75 all by itself isn't a great deal of money. But we do this every week, in up markets, down markets, and sideways markets. This money adds up, and even better, it adds up safely.

Look at some of these returns from people who have used the Bankers Code strategy:

- Over the course of three months, Y.F. collected $5,000, then $7,000, then another $5,000
- J.H. made $6,500 in one month
- T.A. collected $13,355 in two months
- And Brian M. even made $83,000 in seven months.

Don't let "$75" fool you. Real money is made using the Banker's Code strategy. Remember the real returns we made on our own trades:

20.2% with Walgreens, 21.4% with Apple, and 28.7% with Intel.

Let's illustrate the kind of money that's possible with these returns.

Let's assume you start with $25,000 for use in the Banker's Code strategy. And let's be very conservative and assume that we earn just half of the smallest of the percentage returns above. That would be the 10% (half the return from the Walgreens trade).

If you reinvest your earnings back into the strategy, compounded at 10% year after year, how much money do you think that $25,000 would grow to at the end of 15 years?

$104,431.

After 25 years, that turns $25,000 into $270,868. And after 35 years into $702,561.

The Banker's Code strategy makes money, bit by bit, slowly but surely. And if you keep investing your earnings back into the program, over time, it blossoms into a fortune.

Keep in mind, we do this safely. We're not taking huge risks here.

In baseball terminology, the Banker's Code tries to hit only "singles". We want just to get on base. Because we know, over time, consistent singles lead to lots of runs scored. See, we're not like the average investor who swings for home runs every time.

"Why invest in a boring, old, 'safe' stock when this red-hot biotech is soaring? It has three new products that will revolutionize the industry! I've heard it may quadruple my money in the next eight months!"

Too many naïve investors chase after this illusion, constantly searching out the latest "get rich quick" stock pick. It rarely ends well. And all the while, we're in the background, making money... bit by bit... dollar by dollar... turning it into a fortune.

Our strategy is safe. Our strategy is conservative. But best of all, our strategy works.

I keep pointing back to our track record, because it's the best way I know to prove to you what the Banker's Code can do: As of this writing, we made money on 120 out of 123 trades.

In fact, Eric J. wrote to us and said:

> *I absolutely love the Banker's Code. I've made close to $1,000 in just a few months. And now that I fully comprehend the concept, I will be making much more in the near future.*

And then Joan G. also told us:

> *I'm so happy I had the insight to purchase and learn the Banker's Code. I am 77 years old and had never made money in the stock market until now.*
>
> *So this note is to say thank you for helping the people who need it the most. It's been one year since I joined the Banker's Code. To date I have made $4,556.30 with your guidance.*

And Steven H. writes:

> *My son Josh and I have been following your advice in the Banker's Code for over a year. My goal was to generate enough income to replace my wife's current income from her job. She wants to retire and go on more vacation cruises. So far, I have been able to more than triple her current income.*
>
> *This exceeds my expectations and is far beyond what I am getting in my checking account. Thank you for showing me a way to create a stream of income that is over 90% successful. I wish I had known this income-producing strategy 20 years ago. Keep up the good work. It has been fun and very profitable.*

I suggest you think of the Banker's Code as a steady, reliable second income. That kind of return is incredibly attractive in any market—but even more so today, as government bonds and savings accounts are paying close to nothing.

I hope you'll give it a chance to see just how powerful it is.

CHAPTER 10

The "3-Minute" Money Primer

How to Earn Safe Income With Options

By Tom Dyson and *The Palm Beach Letter* Research Team

In this chapter, we're giving you one of the most powerful wealth-building tools you'll ever use.

With it, some investors will be able to generate hundreds... thousands... even hundreds of thousands of dollars.

How? Selling put options—what we call "low-ball offers"—on the highest quality companies in the world. We'll be going into more detail on the "Banker's Code" from our prior chapter.

It's so simple that after you learn how to do it, you'll be able to make trades in just three minutes. That's why we call this the "3-minute" money primer. In this chapter, we will tell you everything you need to know to research, analyze, and pick your own trades.

In essence, you have in your hands everything you'll need to collect a generous stream of income for the rest of your life.

We call our proprietary screening method the COIN system.

We'll give you a list of 30 elite stocks that you can use for potential trades. Then, we'll show you three simple steps you can use to

---

narrow down this list. Finally, we'll show you how to select the top trade based on the key metrics of income and safety.

When you are finished with this chapter, you'll be ready to begin creating your own "3-minute" moves. You'll have the tools needed to grow your bank account month after month... year after year.

Let's get started...

Every Trade Begins with the Right Company

A great low-ball offer begins with a great Company.

That's the "C" in COIN. We're particular about the type of companies we make low-ball offers on. We pick only the best.

We focus on blue-chip companies that are safe, profitable, and shareholder friendly. We do this for a very specific reason. When we sell a put option on a company, we are agreeing to buy shares if they fall to a certain price.

That's why we only make low-ball offers on companies we'd be happy to own anyway.

Because of this, the first step in our process is the fundamental analysis of a company. We evaluate a company as if we were going to buy the stock and hold it long term.

[Fundamental analysis is a method of evaluating a stock. With fundamental analysis, you examine and analyze a stock's economic and financial condition. You're trying to determine the real worth of the company given all its assets, liabilities, and projections of future earnings.]

Here are the criteria you should look for when analyzing the fundamentals of a company...

1. **Is the company safe?** To determine a company's safety we look at different indicators. How long has it been in business? Is it the dominant company in its industry? What is its market capitalization? (This tells us how big a company is.)

   Also, does it sell or make something that has a lot of demand that won't disappear? Or does its product face obsolescence? A current example of this is Blockbuster Video. Blockbuster failed to recognize that the trend in entertainment media rentals was moving toward online downloads and rentals via mail. Blockbuster ultimately filed bankruptcy.

   Another way to measure safety, and one our favorites, is to look at the company's cash position. Does it have more cash than debt? If it has a lot of debt, is the interest rate low and easily covered by the company's cash flow?

2. **Is the company profitable?** Even better, if it is profitable, are those profits growing consistently? To measure a company's profitability, we analyze the company's income statements. We look for growing revenues and positive net income. We also look at a company's cash flow. Many times, earnings can be manipulated by various accounting tricks.

   Cash flow, however, never lies. We make sure the company is generating positive cash flow. Again, it's even better when a company is generating growing positive cash flow.

3. **Is the company shareholder friendly?** Most of the companies we select pay dividends. Dividends are important because they show that the business is committed to rewarding its shareholders. And if one of our low-ball offers is accepted, we want to make sure we make as much income as we can from our new shares. Receiving a dividend gives us another income stream.

   We also measure shareholder friendliness by looking at a company's stock buybacks. A stock buyback is simply when a company retires shares from the open market by buying them back. When a company does this, it reduces the overall share count. This makes each remaining share more valuable.

Think of it as a pizza. Would you rather have a pizza that's cut into eight different slices or six slices? Well, if you're like me, you'd rather have the pizza with six slices, because each slice will be bigger and, therefore, more valuable.

Another great thing about share buybacks is that they're a nontaxable event (as opposed to a dividend payment). When a company retires shares and makes the remaining shares more valuable, you won't get a tax bill for the increase in value.

Countless authors have written entire books and research papers dedicated to fundamental analysis. It is a critical, but time-consuming process. The good news is, we've done a lot of the work for you.

We've vetted a list of 30 elite stocks that are safe, profitable, and shareholder friendly. Many of these we've already featured in our weekly trading service. Others are new names.

Whenever you want to generate your own ideas for low-ball offers, you can refer to this list.

Let's see what companies made the list...

The "Elite 30"

We've evaluated the list of 30 stocks and can confidently recommend them to you as fundamentally strong companies worthy of considering for a trade.

Does this mean a stock is "less worthy" if it doesn't make the list? Not necessarily. There are plenty of great companies out there. Ones we could safely make low-ball offers on. But we wanted to narrow down this list to a smaller number of companies.

Later in this report, we'll show you how to create a custom portfolio that tracks all 30 of these companies.

Here are the "Elite 30":

Note: We haven't ranked these companies in order of potential profitability. We've organized them alphabetically for your convenience.

1. American Express Co. (AXP)
2. Apple Inc. (AAPL)
3. AT&T (T)
4. Baker Hughes Inc. (BHI)
5. BP Plc. (BP)
6. Cisco Systems Inc. (CSCO)
7. Coca-Cola Co. (KO)
8. Colgate-Palmolive Co. (CL)
9. ConocoPhillips (COP)
10. CVS Caremark (CVS)
11. Disney (DIS)
12. EMC Corp. (EMC)
13. Express Scripts Holding Company (ESRX)
14. Google Inc. (GOOG)
15. Intel Corp. (INTC)
16. Johnson & Johnson (JNJ)
17. Kellogg Co. (K)
18. Lorillard (LO)
19. McDonald's Corp. (MCD)
20. Microsoft Corp. (MSFT)
21. PepsiCo Inc. (PEP)
22. Pfizer Inc. (PFE)

23. Procter & Gamble Co. (PG)

24. Sysco Corp. (SYY)

25. Teva Pharmaceuticals Industries (TEVA)

26. United Parcel Service, Inc. (UPS)

27. Walgreen Co. (WAG)

28. Wal-Mart Stores (WMT)

29. WellPoint Inc. (WLP)

30. Wells Fargo & Co. (WFC)

How to Narrow Down the "Elite 30"

You're probably wondering, "If all 30 of these companies are great, how do I decide which one to make a low-ball offer on?"

While we feel that all of the stocks in the "Elite 30" are fundamentally sound companies, that doesn't mean each one always offers a great low-ball-offer opportunity.

That's because a good low-ball offer requires a cheap price.

Sometimes these companies are too expensive to make low-ball offers on. Other times, the share prices have risen too high too quickly, so the risk-reward balance is out of whack. In other words, we'd have to set aside too much of our capital for too little return.

Therefore, we've created three specific guidelines you can follow at any given time to help you decide which company to trade. These guidelines will help you narrow this list of 30 stocks down to a handful.

Guideline No. 1: The P/E Ratio Should Be Cheaper than the Market's P/E Ratio

"P/E" stands for "price-to-earnings." A P/E ratio tells you how many years of earnings it would take to earn back the total value of your investment. Investors use this metric to determine how cheap or expensive a stock is. You can calculate it by dividing the stock price by a company's earnings per share.

Our low-ball offer strategy gives us the potential to own great companies at a discount... We like getting a good deal.

The principle behind our "cheaper P/E ratio" is the same. Why pay full price for something if we can get it at a discount? We measure the P/E ratio of the market by using the **S&P 500 (NYSE: SPY)**.

As we write, the P/E ratio of the S&P 500 is 15. This means if we invested our money into SPY, it would take 15 years of earnings to earn back our entire investment.

Remember, we want to make low-ball offers on companies that are trading cheaper than the S&P 500. That means we would be interested only in companies from our "Elite 30" list that have a P/E ratio lower than 15. (Remember, these numbers are accurate at the time I'm writing this. Be certain to check current numbers when you're researching your own trades.)

Guideline No. 2: The Stock Cannot Be Trading at the High of its 52-Week Range

We prefer to sell options on companies that are "Off" their highs. (The "O" in COIN.)

This rule also ties into our principle of never paying "full price" for our investments. If a stock is trading near its 52-week high, there is danger it could suffer a sell-off. Even if there's nothing really wrong.

Perhaps current shareholders will take profits? Maybe momentum sellers will short shares at what they feel is the top?

[Investors "short" shares when they are betting against a stock. In other words, they believe that the stock price is going to fall in value.

They borrow money to sell at current prices and plan to buy the stock to cover this sale in the future when prices have fallen.]

Here's a rule of thumb you can use: Don't make a low-ball offer on a company if it is trading within 10% of the top of its 52-week range.

Let's look at an example using the hypothetical stock of Acme Corp...

Over the last 52 weeks, Acme shares have traded in a range of $46-50 per share. This means the 52-week range is $4 ($50 - $46 = $4). Ten percent of $4 is $0.40. Therefore, in general, we wouldn't open a trade if Acme Corp. is trading above $49.60 ($50 - $0.40).

Guideline No. 3: Headlines Create Trades

The financial media and Wall Street have a way of frustrating many investors. But not us.

We love it when one of our 30 stocks are "IN the news." (The "IN" in COIN.)

You see, the media and Wall Street can be great allies to put option sellers. They create sensational headlines and stories, which can lead to broad sell-offs. These, in turn, often create wonderful trading opportunities.

We've found that many times, Wall Street overreacts to bad news. When we dig deeper, we often find that the company affected is still fundamentally solid, profitable, and rewarding shareholders. It just stumbled a bit.

But Wall Street acts as though the company is doomed. A broad sell-off ensues. That's when we step in and make a low-ball offer. We do this when we feel that Wall Street is overreacting and mispricing a great company.

Some of our recent trades in our trading service, *Palm Beach Current Income,* are great examples of this:

We made a safe 9.5% annualized return when Wall Street overreacted to one of Microsoft's earnings releases.

We generated an 18.6% annualized return when Wall Street threw a tantrum based on one of Cisco's earnings releases.

And we earned a 12.5% annualized return from BP as they rebounded from relentless negative press stemming from the *Deepwater Horizon* oil spill.

These are just a few examples of how we've used Wall Street overreactions or media headlines to generate safe, immediate income.

> **Here's an important point to remember:** Make sure to do your homework and study the "bad news." Sometimes it will warrant staying away from the company for a while. A good example of this would be something such as:
>
> "Apple announces decision to begin manufacturing VHS players."
>
> Obviously, manufacturing obsolete products such as VHS players would make little sense. This should cause you to dig a little deeper and make sure Apple is still on the right track.

We're constantly keeping our eyes and ears open for sensational headlines or news stories that might tip us off to a potential trading opportunity. You should as well.

How to Track the "Elite 30"

Alright, so we have our list of 30 "Elite" stocks. Now we need a simple, effective way to monitor this list for trading opportunities.

You could build an Excel spreadsheet from scratch and update the information by hand almost daily. But this is a time-consuming and inefficient process.

Fortunately, you can use Yahoo Finance's "Portfolios" feature to track these companies for you. Let's walk through the steps necessary to create your custom portfolio.

1. Go to www.finance.yahoo.com.

2. Click on "My Portfolios" > "Sign in to access your Portfolios."

3. If you already have a Yahoo ID and password, enter it now. If not, click on "Create New Account."

4. On the next screen, name your portfolio. We're using the name of our trading service, "The *Palm Beach Current Income* Elite 30."

5. After you name your portfolio, enter the ticker symbol for each of the "Elite 30" listed in this report. When you're done, all 30 stocks should be in your new portfolio.

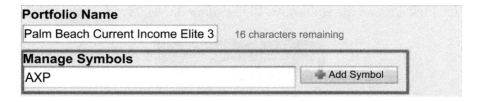

6. Under the "Default View" tab, select "Basic."

7. Scroll down a bit and click the check box for "Sort positions alphabetically by symbol."

8. Click "Save."

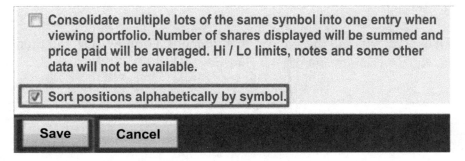

9. Once you advance to the next screen, click on "Add Custom View."

This is where you will instruct Yahoo to provide the specific information you need based on our three guidelines. Make sure you select the options shown in the screenshot below:

10. Pick a name for your view. We've named ours "Trade Analyzer."

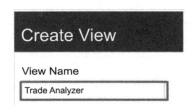

11. Next, add eight fields to your analyzer. They are:

a. Symbol

b. Price

c. Volume

d. 52-Wk Range

e. P/E

f. Ex-Div Date

g. Yield

h. Mkt Cap

I'll explain what all these mean in a moment. For now, just add them in. Here's a screenshot of how your page should look:

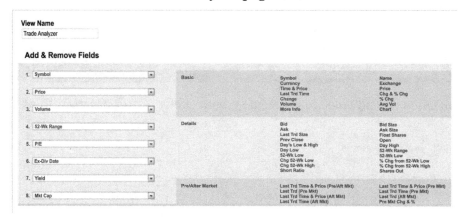

---

12. Click "Save" at the bottom of the page.

Congratulations, your new portfolio is set up. Now's let's look at the important data your portfolio shows you.

Here's a screenshot from our portfolio:

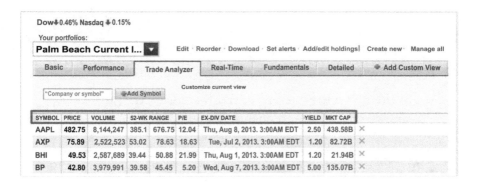

For the sake of space, this screen shot shows only four of our "Elite 30" stocks, instead of all 30. The important thing at this point is to understand each of your eight new fields:

1. **Symbol**—This tells us what company we're looking at. For example, "AAPL" is Apple Inc.

2. **Price**—This is the stock's current market price.

3. **Volume**—This is a simple way to make sure there are plenty of shares trading. Since we focus on large, safe blue-chip stocks, volume should always be high. But if you ever notice abnormally low volume (for example, less than 100,000 shares), that's a warning sign. At that point, you'd want to dig deeper to figure out what's going on.

4. **P/E**—This tells you the current price-to-earnings ratio. We explained this ratio under Guideline No.1: The P/E Ratio needs to Be Cheaper Than the Market. You're going to compare this number to the S&P 500's P/E ratio. Let's walk through how to do this.

---

a. Pull up a separate Yahoo Finance page by going to finance.yahoo.com.

b. Enter "SPY" into the "Symbol Look Up" box in the upper left-hand corner of the screen and click on "Look Up."

c. Write down the current P/E ratio of the S&P 500. We've marked it on the screenshot below:

At the time we write this, SPY's P/E ratio is 15. Remember, using Guideline No. 1, you are going to target trades with a P/E ratio less than SPY's. This means that from our list of the "Elite 30," we are going to look at stocks with a P/E ratio of 14.9 and lower.

Doing a scan of the first few positions in our portfolio, you can see there are two stocks trading with a P/E ratio less than 15:

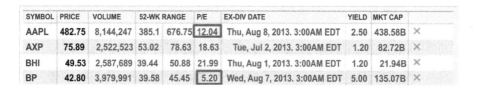

Both Apple and BP have a P/E ratio under 15. This means they would pass Guideline No 1.

5. **52-week Range**—This tells you the stock's range over the last 52 weeks. This addresses **Guideline No. 2: The Stock Cannot Be Trading at the High of its 52-Week Range**. Remember, we don't want to make a low-ball offer on a company if it is trading within 10% of its 52-week range high.

    Earlier, we showed an example of this guideline using a hypothetical company, Acme Corp. Let's walk though Guideline No.2 using a real example from our "Elite 30" portfolio.

    Over the last 52 weeks (at the time of this writing), BP has traded as low as $39.58 per share and as high as $45.45 per share. This means the 52-week range is $5.87 ($45.45 - $39.58). Ten percent of $5.87 is $0.59. Therefore, you wouldn't want to open a trade if BP is trading above $44.86 ($45.45 - $0.59).

    BP's current price is $42.80. Since this is less than $44.86, BP would meet Guideline No.2.

6. **Ex-Div Date**—You need to own a stock before this date in order to receive a company's dividend. We pay attention to this date because it tells us whether we will earn a dividend if the market accepts one of our low-ball offers. The timing of an ex-dividend date might affect what expiration date we choose.

    It's also important to see if a company has an ex-dividend that falls just before your low-ball offer will expire. This is because—theoretically—on the ex-dividend date, a company's stock price will fall by the amount of the dividend payment. Depending on how big the dividend is, that may affect whether or not the market accepts your low-ball offer. We'll talk more about ex-dividends in the next section.

7. **Yield**—This is the dividend payment shown as a percentage. You calculate it by dividing the dividend payment by the share price.

   For example, if Acme Corp. is trading for $100 per share and pays a $5 per share annual dividend, its annual dividend yield is 5%.

8. **Market Cap**—A company's market cap is the total value of all outstanding shares. You calculate it by multiplying the total number of shares outstanding by the current price per share.

   The reason we track this is that we only make low-ball offers on large, safe blue-chip companies. These companies have multibillion-dollar market caps. Apple Inc., for example, has a market cap of $438 billion at the time of this writing.

   If any stock you're analyzing has a market cap that drops below $1 billion, that would be cause for concern. You'd want to investigate why and possibly remove it from your list of potential trades.

What about **Guideline No. 3: Headlines Create Trades?**

We'll show you a great way to keep up with news and headlines for your portfolio. Go to your "Portfolio" page on Yahoo Finance. Scroll about halfway down the page, and you'll notice a heading that says "Recent News."

Recent News

Saturday September 28, 2013

AAPL   Can Apple's iOS 7 Make You Sick? at Wall St. Cheat Sheet 9:04pm EDT

AAPL   An Interview with Steve Cheney: On Apple, Tim Cook and The Future of Mobile at Forbes 8:50pm EDT

AAPL   Microsoft's Smartphone Ambitions Are Too Lofty at Motley Fool 8:02pm EDT

AAPL   Why Apple Didn't Fix Its Biggest Problem at Seeking Alpha 06:45pm EDT

In this section, you'll see updates, headlines, and stories that relate to the stocks in your portfolio. We recommend checking this section often for trading ideas.

Narrowing Down the "Elite 30"

Alright, let's recap where we are in our process. We've established three guidelines to help us identify potential trades. We created a custom portfolio to track our "Elite 30" stocks. Now, we need to narrow down this list of 30 stocks into a potential trade.

After running our "Elite 30" portfolio through our three guidelines, we've trimmed down our list. Of the stocks that made the cut, we've decided to further evaluate three of them: BP **(NYSE: BP)**, ConocoPhillips **(NYSE: COP)**, and Cisco **(NASDAQ: CSCO)**. At the time we write this, these three stocks are trading with a current P/E ratio less than 15. This means they pass Guideline No. 1.

> **Note:** Please remember that we are using the numbers available to us as of the date we write this report. As you are reviewing this and other sections (and come back to them from time to time), the individual numbers may have changed. Don't worry, though. The important thing is to understand and apply the principle behind each guideline.

As we write, all three stocks are trading below 10% of their 52-week range. So we're all clear on Guideline No. 2.

As far as media headlines go (Guideline No. 3), at the time of this writing, there's no horrible news on BP or ConocoPhillips. But Cisco's stock price is still down from several weeks ago when it suggested its earnings would slow in the coming quarter (Wall Street threw a temper tantrum, and Cisco's stock suffered a large sell-off). That means we'll want to pay extra attention to Cisco.

Should the lack of bad headlines on BP and ConocoPhillips stop us from considering them as trades? Absolutely not. Our "headline" guideline is just that—a guideline. It can be a great tool that helps us find quality, low-ball offers. But that doesn't mean there <u>must</u> be a sensational headline to trade around every time.

Now that we've narrowed our list of 30 stocks down to three, we need to decide which one makes the best overall trade. To do this, we use another set of analytics. These analytics will help us decide which company (BP, COP, or CSCO) makes the best hypothetical trade today.

The Six Safety and Income Metrics

1. **Annualized Return**—This is the return we generate per trade. We annualize each return so that we can compare potential low-ball offers on an "apples to apples" basis.

   For instance, is Trade A (a $22 low-ball offer paying $0.50 per share over 31 days) better than Trade B (a $22 low-ball offer paying $0.70 per share over 61 days)? You might answer "Trade B, because it's paying more money per share."

   But when you factor in the length of the trades, Trade A is actually a more profitable low-ball offer. To help us see this more clearly, we "annualize" all our returns. This means we find out what return our trade would generate if we were able to earn it for an entire year.

You can always use the formula below to calculate your annualized return for any given trade:

$$\text{(Income Received / Capital Set Aside for Low-Ball Offer)} / \text{(Number of Days in Trade)} \times 365 \text{ days} \times 100$$

Here's a brief description of each part of our equation. We'll also walk through a hypothetical example to make sure you understand it:

- **Income Received**—This is the cash we receive for making our low-ball offers.

- **Capital Set Aside for Low-Ball Offers**—This number represents our total potential purchase obligation in dollar terms.

- **Number of Days in Trade**—The day you enter a trade is "day zero." The third Friday of the month, when your option expires, will be the last day.

With our trades at *Palm Beach Current Income*, we target annualized returns of 12-25%.

Now, when the markets are volatile, we'll get returns at the higher end of this range. But there will be periods of calm when volatility is low and annualized returns are smaller.

Let's calculate the annualized return for a hypothetical trade with Acme Corp. For this example, let's assume we sell the November 2013 $20 put for $0.50. Finally, we'll use October 1, 2013 as the day we open our trade.

Here's what that means...

Income Received—This would be $50 ($0.50 of income per share multiplied by the 100 shares that come in a single contract).

Capital Set Aside for Low-Ball Offer—This would be $2,000 ($20 strike price multiplied by the 100 shares that come in a single contract).

Number of Days in Trade—This would be 45 (the expiration date of 11/15/13 minus the open date of 10/01/13).

Therefore, the annualized return equation would look like this:

$$($50 / $2,000) / (45 \text{ days in the trade}) \times 365 \text{ days} \times 100 =$$
$$20.3\% \text{ annualized return}$$

It also walks you through the pros and cons of closing a trade early... and the corresponding impact on your annualized return.

2. **Cushion**—A trade's cushion is just the difference between a stock's current market price and the price we pick for our low-ball offer (known as the "strike price"). You could think of this cushion as a moat around a castle. A small, stream-sized moat won't protect the castle much. But a wide, river-sized moat will.

In the same way, large cushions give our low-ball offers more protection. You see, even though we make low-ball offers only on safe, profitable companies we'd be happy to own, the lower the prices we can own them at, the better.

Having a bigger cushion means that if someone accepts your low-ball offer, they've accepted it at a large discount to its current market price. That means you get a better deal.

Here's the formula for how to find your percentage cushion (we use percentages so we can compare cushions on low-ball offers of different sizes):

$$[(\text{Current stock price} - \text{Low-ball offer strike price}) /$$
$$(\text{Current stock price})] \times 100$$

The amount of cushion you decide to include in a trade is up to you. It depends on your own risk tolerance given the volatility of the stock and overall market conditions.

Keep in mind if you have a smaller cushion, your annualized return will be higher. If you want a bigger cushion, your annualized return will be lower.

As we write this report, under current market conditions, we typically target cushions of 4-10%. Again, in a market with much lower volatility you might need to use smaller cushions to get the returns you want.

Because of the personal nature of this, it's difficult to provide a "one size fits all" suggestion for how much cushion to target.

3. **Length of Time in the Trade**—We prefer to sell options with an expiration date one to three months out. There are two main reasons for this: options pricing and safety. I'll talk about options pricing first.

The further out in time you go, the higher the premiums are. This makes it appear as though you could make more money selling options with distant expiration dates.

However, most times, selling options with closer expiration dates means you'll collect more income per unit of time (remember, calculating "annualized yields" will help you see this).

You see, options lose value with every day that passes. Think about it like this: Each day you get closer to the option's expiration, that's one less day in which something crazy or unexpected could happen to the underlying stock.

You'll sometimes hear financial analysts call this "time decay." As options sellers, we like time decay. That's actually value we're receiving. But the thing is, options don't lose the same amount of value every day at the same rate. We've found that the greatest amount of time decay comes when an option is around 4-6 weeks from expiration.

The second reason why we typically choose trades of this length is for safety. Let's say the broad market suffers a pullback. If we're locked in a trade for six months, we're not able to adapt to the new market conditions easily. We have money tied up for a long time. If we had to buy back our low-ball offer to protect us from large losses, it would be expensive because of the long trade length.

But if the low-ball offer expired only four weeks out, we have more flexibility. It won't cost us as much to buy back our low-ball offer if necessary. We can adapt more easily.

4. **Open Interest**—This simply measures how many outstanding contracts there are for a particular option. We evaluate this to make sure the options we are selling are liquid enough to buy and sell easily.

   [Liquidity refers to the degree to which an asset or security can be bought or sold in the market without affecting the asset's price. Liquidity is characterized by a high level of trading activity. Assets that can be easily bought or sold are known as liquid assets.]

   Let's look at an example. Look at the screenshot of Cisco's November put options to the right:

Put Options					Expire at close Saturday, November 16, 2013		
Strike	Symbol	Last	Chg	Bid	Ask	Vol	Open Int
17.00	CSCO131116P00017000	0.02	0.00	0.02	0.03	5	1,940
18.00	CSCO131116P00018000	0.03	0.00	0.03	0.05	2	702
19.00	CSCO131116P00019000	0.08	↑0.03	0.06	0.08	33	265
20.00	CSCO131116P00020000	0.14	↑0.06	0.13	0.14	73	759
21.00	CSCO131116P00021000	0.26	↑0.08	0.25	0.26	956	3,504
22.00	CSCO131116P00022000	0.47	↑0.14	0.46	0.48	6,987	5,326
23.00	CSCO131116P00023000	0.84	↑0.21	0.83	0.84	4,124	11,368
24.00	CSCO131116P00024000	1.37	↑1.25	1.37	1.39	2,144	22, 899
25.00	CSCO131116P00025000	2.10	↑0.37	2.09	2.11	763	7,942
26.00	CSCO131116P00026000	2.95	↑0.40	2.93	2.96	120	6,756
27.00	CSCO131116P00027000	2.84	0.00	3.85	3.90	8	3,914
28.00	CSCO131116P00028000	4.85	↑1.09	4.80	4.90	3	4,529
29.00	CSCO131116P00029000	5.48	0.00	5.80	5.95	10	15
30.00	CSCO131116P00030000	5.82	0.00	6.60	6.95	13	142
32.00	CSCO131116P00032000	7.70	0.00	7.25	9.20	61	103

We've boxed in the "Open Interest" column. As you can see, some options have more liquidity (open interest) than others. As we write, Cisco is trading for $23.33 per share. Options with a strike price that's a bit above and below $23.33 have plenty of liquidity.

You'll notice, however, that options with strike prices far away from Cisco's current price don't have as much liquidity. The CSCO November 2013 $19 put option, for example, has only 265 open contracts. Depending on how many contracts you wanted to sell, this might give you pause.

The CSCO November 2013 $22 put option, however, has 5,326 open contracts. Much more liquidity than the $19 put option.

There's no hard and fast rule we use for how much or how little "open interest" we look for in any particular option. It's always a judgment call. But in general, the greater the number, the easier for you to trade

5. **Timing of Earnings Reports**—Earnings reports are financial reports companies file with the SEC. They are a

type of corporate "report card." Companies will disclose figures for revenues, costs, free cash flow, and other various data.

The important thing to remember about earnings reports is that they can create a lot of short-term volatility in stock prices. Wall Street watches these reports very closely. If traders perceive weakness in a company's earnings report, it can result in brutal short-term sell-offs in the stock.

On the other hand, if the earnings report is positive, shares can race higher.

Because of this uncertainty, we try not to make any low-ball offers that expire within the two weeks after an earnings report is due for release.

We also don't want to open a trade within the two weeks before an earnings release.

Typically, two weeks is enough time for the market to digest the news and correct a mild overreaction.

During earnings season (the time when the majority of companies report their earnings), you might be in a situation in which no matter what company you're looking at, your low-ball offer expires somewhere in that two-week window.

In this case, use your best judgment. Do you believe in the company's underlying fundamentals? Has the company been growing profits and cash flows relentlessly quarter after quarter? If so, you might still feel comfortable making a low-ball offer.

That said, we generally try to avoid bumping into earnings.

Now that we know what earnings reports are, how do we know when they're released?

Go back to Yahoo Finance and enter your desired stock symbol into the "Symbol Lookup" search bar. Hit "Enter." We've used ConocoPhillips' symbol, "COP."

This will bring you to the stock's main screen. On the screenshot below, we've boxed in where the earnings release date is displayed. It is in the same spot for any stock you research on Yahoo Finance:

Write down this date. As you're analyzing a potential low-ball offer, try to pick an expiration date that is greater than either two weeks before or two weeks after that date.

6. **Timing of Ex-Dividend**—The ex-dividend date is the date before which you need to own a stock in order to receive a company's dividend. We pay attention to this date because if the dividend is large, it might affect what expiration date you choose for your low-ball offer.

For example, let's say you're evaluating a low-ball offer on Company A. You're wondering if you should pick an expiration date in October or November. (We're assuming the annualized yields of the two trades are the same, so there's no clear advantage.)

You could look to see when Company A's ex-dividend date is. Let's say it's in early November, before the November expiration date.

In this case, you could choose to sell the low-ball offer expiring in October instead of November. That's because if the market accepts your October offer, you'd own the stock before the ex-dividend date. That means you'd be eligible for the next dividend and you'd earn more income.

But if you made the low-ball offer expiring in November, you would miss any chance at owning the stock before the ex-dividend date.

It won't work every time, but it's worth checking to see if you can organize your trade around receiving a dividend. We talked about this before, calling it our "Triple-Income Play."

How to Pick a Winner

Alright, we're almost at the finish line. We've narrowed down our list of 30 stocks to three choices using our three guidelines. The three stocks we are analyzing are BP, ConocoPhillips, and Cisco.

We've covered the six safety and income metrics.

Now, we need to compare our three stocks using these six metrics. We chose a put option for all three companies that expires November 15, 2013, for our comparison.

Here's how they compare...

Company and Option Symbol	BP- BP131116P00041000	COP- COP131116P00067500	CSCO- CSCO131116P00022000
Current Share Price:	$42.80	$70.31	23.33
Low-ball Offer Strike Price	$41.00	$67.50	$22.00
Put Premium:	$0.62	$1.00	$0.47
Annualized Yield:	12.27%	12.02%	17.33%
Cushion %:	4.2%	4%	5.7%
Time in Trade (Days):	45	45	45
Open Interest:	1,209	2,452	5,326
Next Earnings Report:	N/A	10/21/13	11/13/13
Ex-Dividend Date:	8/7/13	7/18/13	7/1/13

Let's see how each stock stacks up:

1. **Annualized Return**—All three stocks pass our target of 12-25% annualized returns. BP, COP, and CSCO generate returns of 12.3%, 12%, and 17.3%, respectively. CSCO, however, clearly has the highest annual return.

2. **Cushion**—CSCO wins this category, with a cushion of 5.7%.

3. **Time in Trade**—This is a tie across the board, as all three put options expire on Friday, November 15, 2013.

4. **Open Interest**—CSCO wins this category as well, with an open interest of 5,326 contracts. COP comes in second with 2,452. BP comes in last with 1,209 contracts outstanding.

5. **Next Earnings Report**—BP has not published its next earnings date. When this happens, you can look back at when the company released earnings for the same quarter the previous year. That's often a good proxy. Last year, BP reported on October 30th. We'll use that as a guide. COP is set to announce earnings on October 21, 2013. CSCO will be announcing earnings on November 13, 2013.

Remember, in general, we try to avoid low-ball offers that expire within two weeks of an earnings release. That would mean that BP and COP would both meet this guideline.

Unfortunately, CSCO's earnings will come two days before the November expiration. That means we'd rule out CSCO.

6. **Ex-Dividend Date**—BP and COP are left. They both offer large dividends, so the timing of their ex-dividend dates might affect which one we pick for our low-ball offer.

    However, when we inspect the timing, we find that both companies' ex-dividend dates will fall before the November expiration. That means, in this case, the ex-dividend date isn't a factor.

Who's the winner?

Well, CSCO won the "annualized returns," "cushion," and "open interest" categories. However, we had to disqualify it based on its earnings date.

Between BP and COP, BP provided a higher "annualized return" and a larger "cushion." It has less "open interest" than COP, but there's still plenty of liquidity for a low-ball offer.

After analyzing all this information, we'd choose BP as our winner.

(**Note:** Please remember this is only an example on how to create your own low-ball offer. This is not an official trade recommendation.)

As you build your own low-ball offers, you'll often run into situations such as this, in which a few trades look great and you have to decide which one(s) to pick. As time goes on, you'll be able to use your judgment to pick the best low-ball offers that fit with your goals and trading style.

So congratulations! You've learned the COIN system.

We've now armed you with the knowledge necessary to begin creating your own low-ball offers.

CHAPTER 11

How to Make Your Own High-Ball Listings

How to Earn Safe Income With Options

By Tom Dyson and *The Palm Beach Letter* Research Team

You've done everything right...

You found a safe, profitable, shareholder-friendly company trading at a great value. You used the skills you learned from reading our last chapter, the "3-Minute Money Primer," to make a low-ball offer.

You earned instant cash for your offer... and waited until option expiration day.

When that day comes, the stock price is trading below your low-ball offer strike price... so the market accepts your low-ball offer.

What now?

That's the question we answer in this chapter.

By the time we're through, you'll know exactly what to do when the market accepts any of your low-ball offers.

This strategy, what we call "putting your shares up for sale with a high-ball listing," will put even more cash in your pockets beyond what you earned with your low-ball offer.

So, let's get to it...

Why High-Ball Listings Are Nothing to Fear

So, let's imagine this hypothetical...

It's at the end of the trading day on options-expiration day. Some weeks back, you had sold a low-ball offer and put cash in your pocket by doing so. Today, that offer is expiring.

You go to your broker's website to see the status of your trade. When you look at the stock price, you realize it's below your strike price. That means you're about to buy a stock at a higher price than its current market value. In other words, you're about to be sitting on an unrealized capital loss.

If that happens, the first thing to do is... relax.

For newer options traders, the tendency at this point is to worry... especially if the stock you're about to buy has experienced a sharp drop.

But whether it's a sharp decline or a just small drop, the same advice applies: Relax.

Under our system, we only make low-ball offers on companies that pass our strict fundamental criteria. These companies are safe, profitable, and shareholder friendly. Due to their strength and dominance, they tend to bounce back over time.

The overwhelming majority of these companies will eventually recover any losses. To see this concept in action, take a look at this 20-year chart of the S&P 500.

S&P 500 20-year Chart

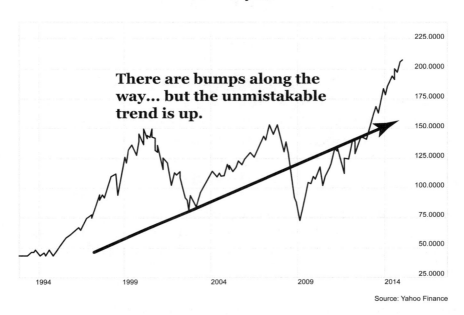

There are bumps along the way... but the unmistakable trend is up.

The S&P 500 is an index that tracks the 500 largest companies in the U.S. It's a good barometer for us because the index contains the types of companies we focus on.

As you can see, there are times when the market sells off. But over time, things recover and stocks resume their upward march.

So back to our original question... If we're only making low-ball offers on great companies... what do we do when the market accepts one of these offers?

Making Even More Cash From High-ball Listings

A high-ball listing is our term for a covered call option. By selling a covered call, we earn cash by selling someone the right to buy our shares if they are trading at or above our chosen strike price on option-expiration day.

(Though, again, an option buyer can technically exercise their right

---

to buy our stock at any time... but it's very uncommon to exercise a call option if the share price is trading below the strike price.)

Let's look at a hypothetical example...

Say the market accepts our low-ball offer to buy Acme Co. for $10 per share (the put strike price). Once we own the shares, we immediately agree to sell them (by selling a covered call) to someone else for $11 per share (the call strike price) by expiration day on, say, Friday, January 16th. The other trader in this example pays us $1 per share ($100 per contract) for this right.

Once January 16th rolls around, we check Acme's share price. If it's trading at $11 or above, the trader who bought our covered call option takes ownership of the shares. At this point, how do the numbers look?

Well, we'll keep the $1 per share ($100 per contract) we earned for selling the covered call. We'll also earn $1 per share ($100 per contract) in capital gains (the difference between the $11 sale price and the $10 low-ball offer strike price).

And don't forget—we've still banked the premium we originally received for making the low-ball offer in the first place. As a final bonus, we'll keep any dividends we earn during the time we hold Acme Corp.

What happens if Acme is trading below $11 on January 16th (expiration day)? The covered call (high-ball listing) will expire worthless... and we'll hold onto our Acme shares.

And guess what... we'll do the whole process over again.

We can immediately put our shares up for sale again with another high-ball listing. We'll repeat this process over and over... earning cash each time... until someone eventually buys our shares from us.

How to Pick the Right High-Ball Listing

Now that we know what a high-ball listing is, how do we pick the right one?

We've found the "sweet spot" that works well for us. But as always, as you develop a feel for this strategy, you can adjust things to fit your trading style.

Step 1: Only place a high-ball listing at or above the strike price of your original low-ball offer.

By following this rule, you'll avoid locking in a loss. Let's use our Acme example from earlier...

Let's say instead of selling someone the right to buy our Acme shares for $10, we sold the $9 covered call strike price instead. (The assumption here is that Acme's shares fell into the $8-range over the life of our low-ball offer.)

This could be tempting because the option premiums will be higher for the $9 vs. the $10 strike price. (The lower the covered call strike price is relative to the current stock price, the higher the premium.)

But remember, the market accepted our low-ball offer at $10 per share. So if we sell our shares at $9, we're locking in a $1 per share capital loss. Not good.

That's why we pick covered call strike prices <u>at or above</u> our original low-ball offer strike price. Hence the name "high-ball listing."

Now, there will be times you need to have patience to follow this step. Every so often, a stock will suffer a steep sell-off. At this point, the covered call premiums at the strike price you need might not be high enough to support a good trade.

Our earlier advice applies—relax!

Wait for your stock to drift back up. This might happen quickly, or it may take some time. But as the market price approaches your original low-ball offer strike price, the covered call premiums will increase. At this point, you can sell a covered call. If your shares aren't called away, repeat the same process.

Wash. Rinse. Repeat.

Now, one quick word on the downside of having to wait while a stock price drifts higher...

If you have to sit on your shares for a while before selling a new high-ball listing, it means you're not putting your money to work for you. In other words, you have a chunk of capital tied up in a stock, not actively invested in an options trade. This will lower the overall full-cycle return of your trade.

While you shouldn't like lower returns, you should recognize that lower returns are still better than locking in a loss by making a high-ball listing for a price lower than your purchase price.

Plus, since you should only be making low-ball offers on companies you'd be happy to own, you should feel comfortable holding shares. And remember, while you hold shares, you're entitled to any dividends.

> **Editor's Note:** In Step 1, we mention to only pick a covered call strike price at or above your original put option strike price. But what happens when a trade moves against you? If the current market price is way below the strike price you were assigned at...
>
> There is an advanced trading method called "rolling an option." You can roll an option "up" (as in a higher strike price) and/or roll an option "forward" (as in a later expiration date).
>
> In this case, you sell a covered call below your original low-ball

offer strike price in order to get a larger option premium. Then, if the stock rises toward this strike price, you roll the call forward and up. To do this "buy to close" the option you sold, then "sell to open" a new covered call with a higher strike price and a later expiration date.

While this is a valid strategy, it is an advanced strategy and outside the scope of this chapter.

Step 2: Choosing the right strike price.

Take a moment to think back to the last chapter. In it, we spent a lot of time talking about the trade-off between cushion and return when evaluating trades. Remember, cushion is the difference between the stock price and the strike price. The tradeoff comes down to a decision—more income and less cushion, or less income and more cushion?

With a high-ball listing, there's a similar type of trade-off...

Here, the question is: Book more cash now from a lower covered call strike price (which makes it more likely your shares will be called away)... or book less up-front cash, but gamble on a higher strike price. This means you'll earn greater capital gains if the stock surges in price (though a higher strike price reduces the odds your shares will be called away).

Let's illustrate with an example.

If we own Acme shares at $10 per share, the $11 covered call will have a higher premium than the $15 call. This is because there's a greater chance that Acme will rise to $11 than to $15 by expiration.

Now, if our shares are called away at $11, we'll keep the covered call premium, say $0.50 per share for this example, plus the $1 capital gain ($11 strike price - $10). That's $1.50 in total income. But if Acme rises past $11, we won't get any of those capital gains.

On the other hand, what if we sold the $15 covered call? The up-front premium would be much lower, say $.015 per share. But, if Acme surged to $15 and beyond by expiration, we'd bank $5 in capital gains ($15 - $10). That's $5.15 in total income.

Of course, there's no guarantee that Acme will rise to $15 per share (or $11 per share for that matter) by expiration.

As with any trading decision, there's no "right" answer or golden rule here. It's part art, and part science. As you develop your own trading style, you'll find the right mix of desired capital gains versus up-front covered call premiums.

Step 3: Once you pick the right strike price, choose your expiration date.

Given market conditions at the time we're writing this report, we like to sell options that expire in one to two months. We've found this to be the "sweet spot" of risk vs. reward. It hands us the right mix of premium and time decay (more on this in a moment). And it allows us to cycle our money many times throughout the year. However, it doesn't lock us into a long trade, which could leave us vulnerable to major market moves—up or down.

In general, the further out in time you go, the higher the option premiums will be—in absolute value (for instance, $1.50 vs. $1). But, you get less money per unit of time (for instance, $0.25 per week vs. $0.20 per week). Options are decaying assets. This means, over time, their value whittles away.

Think about why. If I hold an option that expires next week, there are 5 days between now and then in which the market can bounce around. It can affect my trade. But if I hold an option that expires tomorrow, there's far less time for something unexpected to happen that affects my trade. So as time decreases, so does the value of an option.

And as sellers of options, this "time decay," or time value, works in our favor. And based on the intricacies of option pricing, the most decay happens when an option is 4-6 weeks from expiring... hence our target time frame of one to two months.

Let me show you what I mean...

For this example, let's use a real company. Let's say the market accepted a low-ball offer on **AT&T (NYSE: T)** at $35 per share. So we now own AT&T shares, based on a $35 purchase price. As I type, shares trade for $34.80.

Following step one, we need to sell a covered call with a strike price of $35 or higher. To keep things simple, we're going to choose $35 as our strike price. (We're not targeting large capital gains for this trade.) Now, we need to pick an expiration date.

Let's walk through the steps we'd take...

(Remember, these figures and screenshots are accurate as of the time of this writing. The exact figures will be different when you read this chapter. But the process will be the same.)

First, go to www.finance.yahoo.com. Your screen will resemble the screenshot below.

I've put a box around the "Quote Lookup" search bar. Since we're evaluating AT&T, type in its ticker symbol ("T") here. Then hit "Go."

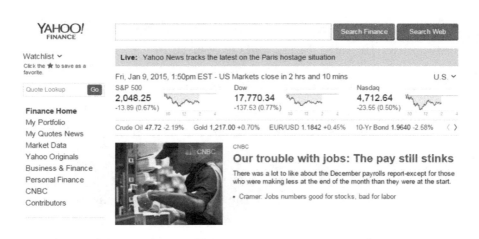

When you do, here's what you'll see:

Here, I've drawn a box around the "Options" link. This is where you'll find all of AT&T's available put and call option expiration dates and prices.

Click on "Options."

For our example, we're going to look at three different expiration dates: July 17th, August 21st, and October 16th.

The first option below expires July 17th. Here's how it looks:

35.00	T150717C00035000	0.52

You're looking at the $35 strike price (identified by the "35.00" on the left-hand side of the screen), the option symbol in the middle (which is a combination of the expiration date and the strike price), followed by the cost of the option (which, in this example is $0.52).

The next call option expires Friday, August 21st, and has a higher premium ($0.74):

35.00	T150821C00035000	0.74

And this last one expires Friday, October 16th, and offers the highest nominal price of all ($0.95):

35.00	T15016C00035000	0.95

As you can see, the October 16th expiration date has the highest "nominal" premium (meaning, "face value"). But that doesn't necessarily mean it's the best choice from a "return" perspective. For that, we need to run some numbers through our Trade Evaluator (which we'll do in a moment).

Step 3(a): Check for any upcoming ex-dividend dates.

There's one additional step when we are picking an expiration date for a covered call trade. We check for any upcoming ex-dividend dates.

Why? Well, as long as we own shares at least one day before a company's ex-dividend date, we're entitled to the dividend payment. Don't let the term "ex-dividend" trip you up. All it means is that you need to own shares before this date.

Think about why this date matters... Remember, this strategy is all about generating income. We sell options (puts and calls) but we also collect dividends when possible. After all, the more income the better.

Here's where a bit of strategy comes in. When picking an expiration date for your covered call, you can choose one that expires just after a company's ex-dividend date. This would enable you to earn the covered call premium... bank the next dividend payment... and free up your money for a new trade if your shares are called away at expiration.

We call this a Triple Income Play. The first income stream is the original low-ball offer. The second income stream comes from selling the covered call. And the third is the dividend payment.

We'll tell you more about this at the end of the chapter.

At this point, there are a couple of other considerations we'd like to cover before moving on...

First, some call buyers will exercise their call options early based on the ex-dividend date. This usually happens when the stock is trading at or above the covered call strike price... and when the dividend payout is relatively large.

There's no hard-and-fast rule here. It's up to the option buyer if and when he wants to exercise early. But just be aware that it's more likely to happen when the trade is already profitable for the call buyer, and he can bank the upcoming dividend.

This isn't a bad thing for you. If you sell a call at the right strike price, you'll bank your profit on the trade earlier than expected. Your money will free up, and you can move onto the next trade.

Also, at market open on the ex-dividend date, the stock price drops by the amount of the next dividend payment. For example, let's say Acme Co. closed at $20 per share the day before its ex-dividend date. The next dividend payment is $0.20 per share. Acme would open at $19.80 ($20 - $0.20) the day of.

In general, the share price tends to drift back up after the ex-dividend date, but be aware of this pricing action. It might affect whether or not your shares are called away if your expiration date falls right after the ex-dividend date.

Alright, now that we know how ex-dividend dates can affect your expiration choice, let's walk through some real-world scenarios.

Step 4: Run the numbers through your Trade Evaluator.

Once you've identified your possible expiration dates, it's time to evaluate their annualized returns (if you need a refresher on how to calculate an annualized return, please see the previous chapter).

After we crunch the numbers, we see that if we sell the AT&T July 2015 $35 call option, we'd generate a full-cycle annualized return (minus commissions) of 12.5%. (We assume a flat commission of $12.95.)

Let's compare this result to the returns of the calls with other expiration dates.

After doing the math, we get the following results:

Expiration Date	Full-Cycle Annualized Return (minus commissions)
July 17th	12.5%
August 21st	11%
October 16th	11.5%

This table clearly shows what we mentioned earlier... Although the call options that expire further out in time have higher premium amounts, the annualized returns are lower (since your money is tied up longer).

So, which covered call option do you choose?

We'd choose the July 17th expiration. To us, it offers the best trade. If someone takes us up on our high-ball listing, our $3,500 in trading capital will free up for another lucrative low-ball offer.

But again, as you develop a feel for this strategy, choose the option that best fits your trading style.

Further Considerations

Do earnings dates matter for high-ball listings?

When we sell puts, we use a "two-week rule." With this rule, we avoid making a new low-ball offer if a company is set to announce earnings within the next two weeks. We do this because earnings can be volatile events. And we don't want a trade to get blown out of the water right out of the gate if shares plummet after earnings.

With our high-ball listings, we still pay attention to earnings, of course. You always should. But, since we already own shares, they're not a material part of our decision-making process.

That said, there are a few ways you could look at an upcoming earnings release...

Let's say the market just accepted your low-ball on Acme Co. The company will release earnings a month and a half from now. For the quarter, the company's been selling a hit new product hand over fist. Customers just can't seem to get enough.

You think that the earnings release might show a big uptick in sales from this new hit product. These positive results could cause a surge in the share price.

So, you decide you want to sell a covered call today in order to bank some income, but have it expire before the next earnings release. This way, if your shares aren't called away, you'll own shares "uncovered" on the earnings announcement date. The benefit of doing this is that if the earnings are, in fact, blockbuster, and the stock does surge higher, you can ride these capital gains.

Then, you can decide to either cash out of the trade entirely, or sell another covered call at a higher strike price.

Of course, earnings are very unpredictable. There's a chance that the "hit" product wasn't such a hit after all. There's also a chance Wall

Street could find something unrelated that it doesn't like… and send shares lower.

But, this example illustrates the mindset you could use as you evaluate expiration dates in light of upcoming earnings announcements.

Do volume and open interest matter for high-ball listings?

When we sell puts, we pay attention to volume and open interest. As a quick refresher, volume measures how many options contracts trade in a day. Open interest is the total number of open contracts for a specific option. In general, if an option has higher levels of volume and open interest, that means it will be easier to trade in and out of the position.

When evaluating a new high-ball listing, checking the volume and open interest doesn't hurt. But even if your desired option has low volume and open interest, that doesn't necessarily mean you should avoid it.

The key is making sure there is an active bid-ask spread. As long as there is, then the option market makers (the people who facilitate the buying and selling of options) will work to fill your order.

For example, let's say you're looking at the August 2015 $11 call option for Acme Co. The daily volume is five contracts and the open interest is 80 contracts.

This bid price on the option is $0.45 per share. That's the limit buyers are willing to spend to buy the option. The ask price is $0.55 per share. This is the lowest price sellers are willing to accept to sell the option. This is an example of an active bid-ask spread.

An inactive bid-ask spread is when there isn't a bid or ask price. This typically only happens with small, illiquid stocks. For example, check out this option chain on micro-cap **USA Technologies Inc. (NASDAQ: USAT)**:

Calls	Bid	Ask	Last	Change	Vol	Op Int	Strike	Puts	Bid	Ask	Last	Change	Vol	Op Int
2.5 Call	--	--	--	0.00	0	0	2.50	2.5 Put	--	--	--	0.00	0	0
5.0 Call	--	--	--	0.00	0	0	5.00	5.0 Put	--	--	--	0.00	0	0
7.5 Call	--	--	--	0.00	0	0	7.50	7.5 Put	--	--	--	0.00	0	0

USAT Jul 17 2015 51 Days to Expiration Collapse

No bid price. No ask price. No last price, volume, or open interest. In short, don't waste your time trying to trade options in a company with an options chain like this.

As an aside, as smart options traders, when we sell options, we're trying to receive the highest possible price. So in our example above (with the active bid-ask spread), we could try to sell this call option for $0.55 per share. Or, we could try to split the bid-ask spread for $0.50 per share. Finally, if we wanted to get filled right away, we could sell at the bid price of $0.45 per share.

Should valuation metrics such as the P/E ratio affect my covered call decision?

Valuation plays a big role in the decision-making process behind making a low-ball offer.

Ideally, we target companies that are trading at a discount to the market by one or more metrics (such as the P/E ratio).

But once we're at the high-ball listing stage, you're already past this point. The market's accepted your low-ball offer (that you thoroughly researched, of course), and you now own shares.

Your focus at this point is turning your shares into more cash by selling a covered call.

The Key to Great Long-Term Returns Is Great Risk Management

Following the four-step process above is an excellent way to turn your stock holdings into extra cash flow if the market accepts one of your low-ball offers.

But there's always a chance, however remote, that something completely unexpected happens to one of our trades. That's why we base our strategy on three core tenets:

1) Only make low-ball offers on elite, dominant companies we'd be happy to own if someone accepts our low-ball offer.

2) Don't put more than 20% of your options capital into any single trade. That way, if a trade turns against you, it only affects, at most, one-fifth of your options trading portfolio.

3) Use our 25% stop loss rule to prevent small losses from becoming big losses.

We base this stop loss on our cost basis (strike price minus all income received). Let's use our Acme example from earlier to illustrate this rule.

With our low-ball offer, we agreed to buy Acme at $10 per share. Let's say we earned $0.50 per share ($50 per contract) for our offer. At this point in the trade, our cost basis is $9.50 per share ($10 - $0.50). So for the low-ball offer period of our trade, our 25% stop loss is $7.12 per share ($9.50 multiplied by 75%).

Now, in this chapter, we're assuming the market accepted our low-ball offer. We put our shares up for sale with a high-ball listing (covered call). We agreed to sell them for $11 per share in exchange for a payment of $1 per share.

So what's our cost basis now? Remember, our cost basis is the low-ball offer strike price (what we paid for our shares) minus total income received. Here's how the calculation looks:

$10 (original low-ball offer strike price) - $0.50 (low-ball offer premium received) - $1 (high-ball listing premium received) = $8.50

This means our updated 25% stop loss is $6.37 per share ($8.50 cost basis multiplied by 75%).

If no one took us up on our high-ball listing to sell Acme for $11 per share, we'd sell another covered call... bank more cash... and reduce our cost basis by the amount of the new premium received.

You can follow this same process for any of your positions.

Now, what happens if Acme closed at or below $6.37 per share? We'd close and exit our position immediately... no questions asked.

To do so, we'd "buy to close" our covered call (high-ball listing), and sell our Acme shares at current market prices.

Remember, we use stop losses to prevent a small, manageable loss from becoming a catastrophe. That's why we use a pre-determined 25% stop loss at the outset of every trade... it prevents our emotions from getting in the way if a trade turns against us.

And one final note... The market is dynamic and ever changing. In our weekly trading service, we reserve the right to change the stop loss levels as conditions merit. If we do so, however, we'll send out an alert right away.

The same rule applies to your personal trading. If a different stop loss level fits your trading style better—or even just one particular trade—feel free to adjust as needed.

Bonus Lesson

Let's end this chapter with a bonus trading trick...

What would you rather have... one cash payment... or two... or three? This isn't a trick question. The obvious answer is three cash payments.

Let's go through a trading technique to time some of your low-ball offers to position yourself for three income streams in one. We call this technique a Triple-Income Play.

As you'd expect, a Triple-Income Play is comprised of three parts: the initial low-ball offer (the put option), the high-ball listing (the covered call), and a dividend payment.

A good Triple-Income Play gets all three of these components to sync up.

In order to do that, you need to time your low-ball offer to expire right before a company's ex-dividend date (the date by which you must own shares to receive the dividend). So, clearly, one of the most important pieces of information is a company's next ex-dividend date.

For our "how-to" example, we're going to use **AT&T (NYSE: T)** again.

(Keep in mind, the dates and figures for this example are accurate as of the time of this writing. They will not be the same by the time you read this. But, use this example to learn how to set up a Triple-Income Play... not to do this specific trade on AT&T. Also, the optimal expiration date to earn the dividend payment might not always coincide with the best return and safety for a specific trade.)

Okay, first go to free, online resource Morningstar.com. Once there, type AT&T's ticker symbol (T) into the "Quote" search bar. When you do, your page should look such as this (I've drawn a box around the "Performance" tab):

Click on the "Performance" tab. When you do, here's what you'll see:

Click on the "Dividends & Splits" option. That takes you to this screen:

The top portion of the page will show you any upcoming dividend payments. The goal is to time your low-ball offer to expire right before the next ex-dividend payment.

As you can see, AT&T's next ex-dividend hasn't been announced yet. If it had been, the date would be listed here. We'd then use this date to time our low-ball offer.

But since it's not, you're probably wondering, "What if Morningstar doesn't show the next dividend payment yet? Or, what if I just missed the last ex-dividend date?"

Well, we'll need to figure out when the next ex-dividend date will be.

How?

In general, the elite companies we make low-ball offers on pay dividends on or around the same dates each year.

You can see this clockwork-like action on display on the second half of the screen. Take a look:

Five Year Dividend History T

Annual Dividends

	12/2010	12/2011	12/2012	12/2013	12/2014
Dividend Amount	1.68	1.72	1.76	1.80	1.84
Year-end Yield %	5.72	5.69	5.22	5.12	5.48

*Dividend Amount is calculated using the ex-dividend date

Dividend History

Ex-Dividend Date	Declaration Date	Record Date	Payable Date	Dividend Type	Amount
▼ 2015					
04/08/2015	03/27/2015	04/10/2015	05/01/2015	Cash Dividends	$0.47
01/07/2015	12/18/2014	01/09/2015	02/02/2015	Cash Dividends	$0.47
▼ 2014					
10/08/2014	09/26/2014	10/10/2014	11/03/2014	Cash Dividends	$0.46
07/08/2014	06/27/2014	07/10/2014	08/01/2014	Cash Dividends	$0.46
04/08/2014	03/28/2014	04/10/2014	05/01/2014	Cash Dividends	$0.46
01/08/2014	12/13/2013	01/10/2014	02/03/2014	Cash Dividends	$0.46
► 2013					

Based on the date of this writing (June 17th), we can conclude that AT&T's next ex-dividend date will be on or around July 8th.

So for this trade, you'll need to make a low-ball offer that expires right before this date. This way, if the market accepts your low-ball offer, you'll own shares before the ex-dividend date.

For this step, pull up AT&T's option chains on Yahoo Finance or your brokerage account. When you do, choose an expiration date right before the next ex-dividend date. In this case, the ideal expiration date is Friday, July 2nd.

If the market accepts your low-ball offer on July 2nd, you'll own shares before AT&T's next ex-dividend date. And you'll be in line for a $0.47 per share dividend payment.

As you can see, using our Triple-Income Play strategy, you can position yourself to earn three income streams from one low-ball offer. This can have a significant impact on the expiration date you choose for your high-ball listing... and it can boost your returns if done correctly.

Tying It All Together

Let's take a moment to bring this strategy full circle. Here's how to think about the order of any Triple-Income Play:

Step 1: Make a low-ball offer that will expire before (but close to) a company's next ex-dividend date. The put premium from your low-ball offer is your first income stream.

Step 2: If the market accepts your low-ball offer, put your shares up for sale with a high-ball listing (covered call). This will put a second cash payment in your pocket.

Step 3: Since you timed your trade right, you'll hold shares for the company's next dividend payment. This is your third income stream.

One... two... three income streams. As you can see, this strategy does take some planning. And we wouldn't recommend it for a stock with a spotty history of dividend payments... timing the trades would be too difficult.

And as always, just because you *can* make a Triple-Income Play doesn't mean you *should*. Every company must pass a strict review of the fundamentals. It must be safe... profitable... and shareholder friendly.

Never get lazy. Always review a company's fundamentals before putting your hard-earned cash on the line.

And there you have it... another valuable strategy for your "trading for income" toolbox.

PART 4:

Safe Stock Market Income

CHAPTER 12

"Special" Dividends for Hidden Yield

Our 19 Favorite Companies That Pay Extra Dividends Regularly

By Grant Wasylik and Tom Dyson

Investors who need income have a problem... our government is robbing them.

Thanks to the Federal Reserve's zero-interest-rate policy, living off of fixed-income investments doesn't seem likely... or even possible... anymore.

Bank accounts used to pay more than 5% interest. Today, they pay less than 1%... and in many cases, they pay nothing. You used to be able to get nearly 10% from bonds and bond funds, even the safe ones. Today, there's nothing of quality paying much more than about 5%.

You used to be able to find high yields in the stock market, as well. When I first started looking at high-yield stock investments 10 years ago, the safe investments paid 10%, and the risky ones paid 20%. Today, even the riskiest high-yield stocks pay less than 10%.

What is an income investor supposed to do?

We've found the answer in something called a "special dividend."

You see, for nearly a decade now, a select group of America's top-shelf companies have been paying unscheduled special dividends to shareholders.

As you know, dividend stocks typically pay out four times per year. But this special group of companies I uncovered pays shareholders five times each year—sometimes more. Most investors have no idea these opportunities exist. That's because the financial media don't report them. It takes a lot of work to uncover them. By our count, of the 5,000 companies on the American stock exchange, only a relatively small portion of them distribute this "special dividend." And they don't advertise these secret payments—somebody has to go looking for them.

In this chapter, I'm going to tell you everything you need to know about this secret section of the market. I'll also tell you four of the best companies to buy to build your wealth using this special dividend strategy. And I'll give you our own "watch list"—which contains 15 more special dividend payers.

These companies provide the best, safest way to generate big income in today's "zero-income" environment.

The "Special" Dividend That's Providing Huge Returns

Let's begin by making sure you understand the difference between "regular" and "special" dividends...

Most investors are familiar with regular dividends. They're what companies pay regularly to investors, typically on a quarterly basis. The popular financial websites list regular dividends.

Below is a screenshot from Yahoo Finance for Coca-Cola. I've boxed the reported dividend and dividend yield.

The Coca-Cola Company (KO) - NYSE ★ Follow

38.28 ↑ 0.31(0.82%) 11:44AM EDT - Nasdaq Real Time Price

Prev Close:	37.97	Day's Range:	37.88 - 38.28
Open:	37.95	52wk Range:	36.83 - 43.43
Bid:	38.14 x 6100	Volume:	4,772,490
Ask:	38.15 x 1800	Avg Vol (3m):	16,236,300
1y Target Est:	43.83	Market Cap:	168.66B
Beta:	0.34	P/E (ttm):	20.08
Next Earnings Date:	15-Apr-14 📅	EPS (ttm):	1.90
		Div & Yield:	1.22 (3.20%)

What many people don't know is certain companies distribute a second type of dividend to shareholders called a "special dividend."

What's the difference between "regular" dividends and "special" dividends?

Special dividends are "one-off" dividends. In other words, they are non-recurring.

Companies pay special dividends when they want to return extra cash to shareholders, but they don't want to cause a spike in their regular dividend payments.

Why would a company not want to increase its regular dividend? Well, imagine we have a company—it has a year of windfall profits and raises its dividend to share these profits with investors. But what happens the following year if the company doesn't make as much money?

It might be unable to maintain that increased dividend payment. That would mean it may have to cut its dividend.

That's a problem. You see, most investors hate it when a company cuts its dividend. A smaller dividend means less money to shareholders. So many investors will sell a stock when the company cuts its dividend. That pushes down the share price.

You can see how a company wouldn't want this to happen. Therefore, increasing the regular dividend isn't always a smart idea.

What's the solution, then? How does a company with extra cash return this cash to shareholders without locking itself into a permanent dividend increase?

A special dividend.

As I mentioned above, a special dividend is non-recurring. It simply means a company returns some amount of profits to shareholders in a one-time payment. No one expects it to continue on a regular basis.

Shareholders love special dividends. That's because in addition to the regular dividends they receive every quarter, they get another distribution of cash from the company in the form of this special dividend. It means more money in their pocket.

Best of all, these special dividends are often much larger than regular dividends.

Most times, the special dividend will be over two or three times more than a single quarterly dividend.

But there's a problem...

Leading financial sites such as Yahoo Finance, Bloomberg, CNBC, MarketWatch, Google Finance, and *The Wall Street Journal* don't report special dividends the same way they report regular dividends. In fact, the financial media don't report them at all on the main pages of their sites.

I'll show you...

The following company—let's call it Company A—is a great insurance business. It's paid investors dividends for 150 straight quarters. Its regular dividend is $0.68. At a stock price (as I write this) of about $44.50, that's a dividend yield of 1.50%. Here's how it looks on Yahoo Finance:

RLI Corp. (RLI) - NYSE ★ Follow

44.50 ⬆ 0.31(0.70%) 4:00PM EDT

Prev Close:	44.19	Day's Range:	44.29 - 44.96
Open:	44.56	52wk Range:	34.56 - 52.57
Bid:	41.99 x 100	Volume:	140,531
Ask:	50.00 x 400	Avg Vol (3m):	161,759
1y Target Est:	38.00	Market Cap:	1.91B
Beta:	0.75	P/E (ttm):	15.34
Next Earnings Date:	Apr 14 - Apr 18 (Est.)	EPS (ttm):	2.90
		Div & Yield:	0.68 (1.50%)

Now, a dividend yield of 1.50% is nothing to get too excited about. But that 1.50% yield isn't totally accurate...

That's because Company A pays "special dividends."

You see, the company paid a $5 special dividend in 2012 and 2011 (its quarterly dividend during those years was never greater than $0.16). It even paid a mammoth $7 special dividend in 2010.

This past December, Company A announced a special dividend of $3 for 2013. That bumped its annual yield up to about 4.5%.

But you would never have seen this by checking Yahoo Finance or any other similar financial data website. That's why so many investors miss these opportunities.

So how do you find these special dividends? Well, it's not easy.

Reading through annual reports is one option. But that's time consuming. Another method is scrolling through a stock's dividend payment history. That's a long, drawn-out process, as well.

Which company do you start with? And who has the time to do that anyway?

Fortunately for you, we do. Finding these companies isn't easy, but we're happy to uncover these hidden payments. We actually enjoy doing the hard work to track down these companies.

Four of Our Favorite Special Dividend Companies

Now, we'll give you the names of four of our favorite companies that regularly declare special dividends. These companies are providing investors with a great "stealth" income in today's low-interest-rate market. We hand picked them out of the hundreds of companies that have declared special dividends in the past. We chose them because they're a good value (at the time of this writing), have a history of declaring special dividends, have the potential to grow, and thus, are likely to declare more special dividends in the future.

If you're looking for special dividend candidates to buy, start your analysis with these four. (Be sure to evaluate each company based on current data at the time you're considering a purchase.) And afterward, we'll share 15 more special dividend payers that you should also keep on your "watch list."

Special Dividend Company #1: Buckle

Buckle (NYSE: BKE) sells casual clothing, shoes, and accessories to middle- and upper-income young adults—or, as Buckle calls them, "fashion-conscious young men and women." We'll translate that for you... "trendy teenagers and young adults."

Buckle now has more than 450 stores in 43 states. Even with that, it's still expanding.

The expansion is leading to strong earnings growth. For instance, 10 years ago, Buckle's revenues were about $400 million. Last year, that number came in at $1.1 billion. That's about 200% growth.

But the reason we really like Buckle is that it's paid a special dividend every "holiday season" since 2008. I write "holiday season" because the company tends to announce its special dividend around one of two holidays. Some years it's closer to Halloween. Other years, it happens just before or after Christmas and New Year's.

Regardless of when Buckle announces it, this isn't a small special dividend we're talking about. Take a look for yourself—this table shows Buckle's holiday dividend payments since 2008:

Month-Year	Special Cash Dividend
Jan. 2015	$2.77
Jan. 2014	$1.20
Dec. 2012	$4.50
Oct. 2011	$2.25
Dec. 2010	$2.50
Oct. 2009	$1.80
Oct. 2008	$2.00

And remember, this is in addition to Buckle's quarterly dividends. Here's what Buckle has actually yielded from 2010 through 2014. Notice how much larger its actual combined (total) yield is than its stated yield from its quarterly dividends alone (which is the number you'll see on a site such as Yahoo Finance).

Year	Regular Dividends	Special Dividends	Total Dividends	Stated Yield	Combined Yield
2014*	$0.88	$2.77	$2.77	1.7%	7.1%
2013*	$0.80	$1.20	$1.0000	1.5%	3.8%

2012	$1.00	$4.50	$1.0000	1.8%	9.9%
2011	$0.80	$2.25	$1.0161	2.0%	7.6%
2010	$0.80	$2.50	$3.30	2.1%	8.7%

(Also please note that we're grouping Buckle's January 2014 and January 2015 special dividends with the previous calendar year for consistency, since they were paid during that year's "holiday season.")

Special Dividend Company #2: Cohen & Steers

Cohen & Steers (NYSE: CNS) has been managing funds for individual investors and U.S. and foreign institutions since 1986. The company has offices in the U.S., Europe, and Asia-Pacific.

Cohen & Steers manages investments in global real estate securities, commodities, global listed infrastructure, MLPs (master limited partnerships), preferred securities, and large-cap value stocks. It has $50 billion in assets under management. For context, in 2012, Cohen & Steers made *Institutional Investor*'s list of America's Top 300 Money Managers. It ranked No.105 in total assets under management.

Cohen & Steers is the first investment company to specialize in listed real estate. Currently, the company boasts the industry's largest global investment team dedicated to real estate securities. Professional investors consider this company to be the world's authority on real estate.

But enough background on the company. Remember, what we're most excited about is Cohen & Steers' dividends—including special dividends.

CNS has issued special dividends in 2010, 2011, 2012, 2013, and 2014. And like Buckle, our annual combined yields are much higher for CNS than its stated yields:

Year	Regular Dividends	Special Dividends	Total Dividends	Stated Yield	Combined Yield
2014	$0.88	$1.00	$1.88	2.1%	4.5%
2013	$0.80	$1.00	$1.80	2.0%	4.5%
2012	$0.76	$1.50	$2.26	2.4%	7.1%
2011	$0.45	$1.00	$1.45	2.1%	6.8%
2010	$0.40	$2.00	$2.40	1.5%	9.0%

Special Dividend Company #3: Capitol Federal Financial Inc.

Capitol Federal Financial (NASDAQ: CFFN), or "CapFed," has been in business since Grover Cleveland was president—but it still doesn't garner much investor attention.

It's based in Topeka, Kansas—closer to Main Street than to Wall Street. Which is fine for management, since it makes its money doing community banking rather than investment banking.

This Midwestern community bank started in 1893. It operates 47 branches in Kansas and Missouri. It is the premier residential lender in Kansas with over $9 billion in assets.

CapFed has been a family run business for the last 70-plus years. Henry Bubb—hired as an office boy in 1926—became president in 1941... his son-in-law, Jack Dicus, became president in 1969. And grandson John Dicus took over as president in 1996. John is the current CEO and chairman of the board.

Since it went public in 1999, CapFed hasn't missed a quarterly dividend payment. A streak of 62 dividend payouts in a row.

It's also paid special dividends to shareholders every year since 2008. And lately, it's even paid out these special dividends multiple times per year. Since 2011, the company has paid two separate special dividends each year.

Here's what CapFed's combined actual yield looks like. Since 2010, it's averaged a combined yield of 7.5%.

Year	Regular Dividends	Special Dividends	Total Dividends	Stated Yield	Combined Yield
2014	$0.30	$0.51	$0.81	2.4%	6.5%
2013	$0.30	$0.43	$0.73	2.5%	6.1%
2012	$0.30	$0.70	$1.00	2.6%	8.7%
2011	$0.30	$0.70	$1.00	2.6%	8.7%
2010	$2.00	$0.30	$2.30	6.7%	7.7%

Special Dividend Company #4: HollyFrontier

This company plays in the U.S. oil fields. In the early 1900s, the U.S. was the top oil producer in the world. This status has since moved to the Middle East. However, the U.S. is in the midst of another energy boom that will benefit this company.

The name of this company is **HollyFrontier Corp. (NYSE: HFC)**. Based in Texas, it's one of the largest independent petroleum refineries in the U.S. It operates five large refineries.

HollyFrontier produces gasoline, diesel, jet fuel, and other petroleum products. It is a result of a 2011 merger between Holly Corp. and Frontier Oil Corp. Before the merger, each company operated for 60-plus years.

HollyFrontier also usually pays multiple special dividends each year. Thanks to these hidden payouts, HFC has averaged a 7.5% yield from 2011 to 2014:

Year	Regular Dividends	Special Dividends	Total Dividends	Stated Yield	Combined Yield
2014	$1.26	$2.00	$3.26	3.4%	8.8%
2013	$1.20	$2.00	$3.20	2.4%	6.4%
2012	$0.55	$2.50	$2.75	1.3%	7.2%
2011	$0.17	$0.75	$0.92	1.4%	7.6%

Fifteen More Special Dividend Payers To Watch

We constantly monitor our own watch list of our favorite special-dividend-paying companies. If a company continues to perform well and its stock becomes an attractive buy, we'll promote it from our watch list and formally recommend it to our readers.

We just shared the four best companies on our watch list. Here are 15 more that we're keeping an eye on. We're including each company's stated yield and comparing that with its combined yield (which includes special dividends).

We're also listing the number of special dividends each company paid from 2010 through 2014 in the right-most column.

Special-Dividend-Paying Company Watch List

Company	Symbol	Industry	Stated Yield	Combined Yield*	No. of Specials Divs Paid 2010-2014
Apollo Global Mgmt	APO	Asset Management	5.9%	9.7%	13
Bassett Furniture	BSET	Home Furnishings	1.1%	5.0%	4
Booz Allen Hamilton	BAH	Consulting	1.8%	15.3%	5
CME Group	CME	Financial Exchanges	2.0%	4.2%	4
Diamond Hill Inv Group	DHIL	Asset Management	0.0%	8.4%	5
Gluskin Sheff	GS.TO	Asset Management	3.3%	8.5%	7

Haverty Furniture	HVT	Home Furnishings	1.5%	3.1%	4
L Brands	LB	Specialty Retailer	1.8%	7.9%	6
National Presto	NPK	Conglomerate	1.4%	8.4%	5
PACCAR	PCAR	Truck Manufacturer	1.4%	2.8%	5
RLI	RLI	Insurance	1.5%	9.1%	5
TransDigm Group	TDG	Aircraft Components	0.0%	7.2%	3
Universal Insurance	UVE	Insurance	1.7%	6.4%	5
Vale SA ADR	VALE	Metals & Mining	4.9%	5.8%	11
Wynn Resorts	WYNN	Resorts & Casinos	4.8%	6.1%	5

CHAPTER 13

An Ultra-Safe 6-8% Income Source

A Star Portfolio Manager That Delivers With Almost No Risk Involved

By Grant Wasylik and Tom Dyson

"It sounds like a gimmick. I wouldn't put a penny of our firm's money into this."

At that point, everyone started laughing...

I (Grant) had just presented what I thought was a slam-dunk opportunity to the other six members of our investment committee. And my former boss was not impressed...

It was 2012. Our firm had $1 billion in assets under management.

I was our firm's lead research analyst and head trader, and I was responsible for coming up with new investment ideas. Every month, I had to stand up before the investment committee and make investment presentations. It was a vital part of my job.

Just prior to this recommendation, I had been in the library combing through academic journals. That's when I noticed a college professor's essay on this new investment offering. I had never heard of it. Or the guy running it.

After reading this dissertation, I realized there was something genius about the strategy this guy was running. A way to beat the markets.

I started researching who this guy was. I found he had an impressive pedigree. He was a tireless worker... two famous value investors schooled him... and he had carved out this secluded spot in the markets—unknown to everyone else—all for himself.

Although this fund was tiny, I could see he was generating solid returns with no risk. So I decided to present it in that month's investment committee meeting.

But my boss—the firm's president—did not think my best idea was worthy of *any* of our investment dollars.

I could tell right away he wasn't pleased with my presentation. He had a big scowl on his face. Plus, he was making jokes about it. It was worse than I thought...

He didn't even speak to me for a couple days...

Why was he so mad?

Well... he'd never heard of the guy directing the strategy... it was hard to understand... too new to be credible.... and its assets were so small that a minimum allocation (about $25 million) from our firm would make us majority owners.

I was embarrassed by how my boss handled it. But it was more than that—I was irked.

You see, I knew the idea was superb.

I did more research. I understood the strategy better. And I was sure this thing was an undiscovered treasure.

Undaunted, I told the investment committee about it again six months later. It had gained more traction—which meant it had more investment dollars. And it could now absorb our company's minimum investment level.

Once again, the investment committee said "no." But it wasn't a quick dismissal this time. I could tell my colleagues were more interested.

In fact, one committee member pulled me aside after our meeting. He wanted the symbol—so he could buy it in his taxable account and his wife's IRA!

Yet they still didn't want to invest the firm's money in it. They considered it too risky. And my boss's quips continued... "Are we sure this guy even has an office?" he snickered as I finished my presentation.

Now, you might think I'm crazy. But I refused to let the idea go...

I was stubborn. I kept researching... tracking... digging... and number crunching. I even contacted the company. And I was able to speak with the founders themselves.

They were very engaging. And smart. So I booked a trip to visit their office in New York. I met the head guy and had an in-depth conversation with him.

He gave me more details about the secret "nice return, no risk" strategy he was running so successfully.

I figured this idea deserved one more chance. Even if I were to lose my job over it. No one in my company's history had ever recommended the same investment opportunity a second time, let alone a third. But after letting the dust settle for several months, I recommended it again to the investment committee.

Well, the third time was a charm.

Thanks to my extra "boots-on-the-ground" work, the investment committee approved it.

We bought it for some of our best clients. The investment was providing 4% annualized returns with almost no volatility. It was almost like a super-charged bank account.

I was glad that I refused to throw in the towel on this diamond in the rough. In its first three years, it generated positive returns in 34 of 36 months. (The two down months were off 0.2% and 0.1%—hardly anything to fret about.)

Our clients were happy—which meant my boss was finally happy as well. I even bought it for my mother's retirement account...

Now, this investment is no longer available. It soon grew to $750 million in assets and shut its doors to new investors.

But that's okay, because today I *can* recommend something from the same people that's even better...

You see, I regularly attend Morningstar's Annual Investment Conference. It's one of America's top investment gatherings. I rub shoulders with financial gurus for three full days. And it was there in the exhibit hall that I ran into many old acquaintances...

Including some of the people who sparked the three-round boxing match with my old investment committee.

In our conversation, I learned that this investment manager had just launched a similar investment offering. And this one is still available to new investors today.

It's safe. It's paying <u>even higher income than my old favorite</u>. And it has the same experienced captain at the helm. In other words, it's a fantastic way to address the "safe income" challenge so many people face today.

I liked what I was discovering about this investment... but first, I needed to better understand the strategy. If I'm going to recommend that you allocate your hard-earned money to an investment, I feel a personal responsibility to do everything I can to eliminate uncertainties or surprises about that investment.

I learned that it was similar to the former strategy, but had some differences. I brushed up on the firm—and its investment approach—by talking to company management several times over the course of the next few months. I culminated my research with a two-hour call with company VIPs (more details on that conversation later).

Everything I learned made me increasingly eager to recommend it.

When you buy it, you'll get a star portfolio manager that nobody has ever heard of. He'll bring you 6-8% returns per year. And he'll do it safely, with very little risk involved.

Now let's get into the details...

This "Odd" Strategy's Secret Sauce

There is no other fund in the world that makes money this way.

It's so unique that Morningstar doesn't even know how to classify the fund. The leading financial data provider throws it into the "multisector" bond category. That's a catchall category for odd fixed-income strategies.

And this particular "odd" fixed-income strategy involves high-yield bonds, asset-backed securities, distressed securities, preferreds, bank loans, and other income-producing securities.

But the strategy itself is not that complicated. It's actually very simple:

Generate high income. And do it safely.

The fund manager targets 6-8% annual returns. He told me personally that he feels "very comfortable" about hitting the 6% number over the next three years.

But he also made it clear to me that he will not reach for returns.

He said:

> *When the market sells down, we protect capital and we're very defensive. When the market jacks up, we lag. I think that's pretty consistent. We take great pride in managing the risk profile of the fund.*

He avoids capital losses at all costs. This means that some years we may have to "settle" for a safe 6% return. He refuses to reach for that extra 2%.

It's a pure, absolute return vehicle. That means, by design, the strategy will earn mid-to-high single-digit returns every year—no matter what the markets do. It consistently hits singles. And it doesn't rely on homeruns for returns.

The man who hits these safe, high-yielding singles month after month is David Sherman.

I've been a fan of David's for years. Let me tell you why...

Who Is David Sherman?

David graduated from Washington University in 1987 with a business degree. There, he also became a registered stockbroker *while attending college.*

Taking classes and studying for the Series 7 exam is plenty to keep the typical college student busy. But not David. He worked for Leucadia National's insurance company during the school year.

(Leucadia is known as a "baby Berkshire Hathaway." It's a value shop famous for investing in undervalued and distressed companies.)

Then, when summers rolled around, David interned as a junk bond analyst in Los Angeles. He cut his high-yield teeth working for

Michael Milken—the "Junk Bond King."

After college, David continued to work for Leucadia. Management made him responsible, as treasurer, for the company's $4 billion insurance operation. He investigated whatever investments Leucadia put on his plate. Anything from Russian equities... to bankrupt and distressed entities.

In 1996, David left to start his own company: Cohanzick Management. His first investor was his previous employer. Leucadia gave David $100 million of high-yield money to manage.

But they only wanted "money good" bonds. That meant if David dropped dead... or Cohanzick went out of business... Leucadia could hold these bonds to maturity without worry.

In other words, these bonds were perfectly good loans that would pay all interest and return principal upon maturity.

David's hedge fund returned Leucadia and its other investors about 10% per year. And he did this with much less risk than typical high-yield strategies employ.

Remember, he's a singles hitter. More on this later.

In 2010, David joined forces with the RiverPark Funds.

Before this partnership, investors had to pony up at least $1 million—the required minimum to get into his hedge funds.

But when David started the **RiverPark Short-Term High Yield Fund (RPHIX)**, his skilled high-yield bat became available to individual investors.

In this fund, he employs an "ultra-short duration strategy." It is so safe that investors can use it as a cash-like substitute. And it returns 4% per year with barely any volatility.

And investors can elect to receive their 4% in cash if they'd like.

The only thing better than a smooth 4% per year is a smooth 6% per year. Which is what David delivers with his second fund.

In 2013, David launched the **RiverPark Strategic Income Fund (RSIVX)**. RiverPark's clients had been asking for a strategy like this for a couple of years.

RSIVX gives David the opportunity to use his skills in some other areas of the market. This fund is similar to the first one. Except it has the potential for higher returns.

That's because it allows David to fish in obscure, yet profitable, investment ponds that he knows quite well...

Where David Fishes for Safe Yield

When I spoke to him, he explained the five "odd" investment ponds in which he fishes.

1) Money Good is the cornerstone of David's strategy. As I mentioned earlier, these bonds provide above-market yields with limited credit risk. Remember, no matter what happens to our fund manager, these bonds are going to pay out.

2) Short-Term High Yield is high-yield debt that matures in three years or less. Its short-term nature makes it safer than regular high-yielding bonds.

3) Above the Fray are securities of issuers that are experiencing industry or credit stress. They will benefit from being "higher on the totem pole" in the capital structure. Longer-term restructuring is possible—and if that happens, bondholders such as David are paid first.

4) Off the Beaten Path means not widely followed, or less liquid securities. Either of which offer better yields than alternatives. David knows these well because he's been searching them out for 25 years.

5) Opportunistic Plays are asset-backed, distressed, and equity-like securities. They are perceived as being risky—but they're not. They have enough assets to cover their debt payments.

Now let's talk about some specific examples of the kind of bonds David buys...

He bought investment-grade-rated URS bonds. URS is an infrastructure company. David's firm invested in three-month investment-grade bonds with a yield of 1.5% to 2%. At the time of his purchase, URS had just announced that it would soon be acquired by rival firm AECOM.

When the transaction settled, holders had the option of selling the bonds back to the company at a premium. And URS sold the bonds back to AECOM, as expected, just three months later.

That may sound modest, but that's an investment that annualizes to 6-8%—which is exactly David's target.

He also bought bonds in Stratus Technologies—yielding between 10% and 12%. Stratus is a computer server manufacturer that David's team has been following for years. It's a well-managed business with strong, growing revenues.

Stratus was soon sold to Siris Capital Group. The new parent company bought David's bonds back from him for full value. And it paid him all the interest it owed him.

So he was able to bank 5-6% returns in just six months... and get all of his principal back afterward.

As we write, Cohanzick holds American Piping 12.875% senior-secured notes. They're due in two years.

American Piping distributes specialty metal products. It has a huge inventory and offers fast delivery of mission-critical parts that are otherwise unavailable on short notice.

Since Cohanzick bought American Piping's notes, the yield has tightened from 13.4% to 7.3%. Remember, bond yields and prices have an inverse correlation. A potential refinancing would yield close to 8%. But David and team anticipate a yield above 8% based on a later takeout.

"Money good" is an important, recurring theme with David. It's a broad term that defines the fund's investment strategy.

It means the manager is *very, very sure* that he's going to get 100% of his principal and interest back, no matter what happens...

I want to show you how the Cohanzick team breaks down their search for "money good" investments.

How David's Team Finds Bonds That ALWAYS Pay Back

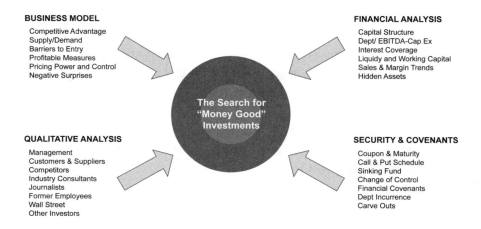

BUSINESS MODEL

Competitive Advantage
Supply/Demand
Barriers to Entry
Profitable Measures
Pricing Power and Control
Negative Surprises

FINANCIAL ANALYSIS

Capital Structure
Dept/ EBITDA-Cap Ex
Interest Coverage
Liquidy and Working Capital
Sales & Margin Trends
Hidden Assets

The Search for "Money Good" Investments

QUALITATIVE ANALYSIS

Management
Customers & Suppliers
Competitors
Industry Consultants
Journalists
Former Employees
Wall Street
Other Investors

SECURITY & COVENANTS

Coupon & Maturity
Call & Put Schedule
Sinking Fund
Change of Control
Financial Covenants
Dept Incurrence
Carve Outs

This might look like a lot to digest. But here's the key takeaway: David's research team turns over every stone before committing capital to any new bond investment. They take due diligence to the extreme.

But they've been doing this for 15-plus years. This latest fund is just the next evolution of bond strategies David's been orchestrating. He's an expert on finding obscure, safe bonds with attractive yields.

And remember, David is adamant that he won't stretch for yield. He puts "money good" before return.

That's great, because he's protecting our capital first.

Safety Comes First

David emphasizes a "don't get greedy" approach. A mentality far from what most other hedge fund managers practice. This is his controlling theme. He does not deviate from it.

Let's walk through some of the safety features of this fund...

First, the fund has low volatility. It's a smooth ride. David's investors have never had a month with him where they've lost more than 0.4%. That's excellent.

Think about the most reliable dividend-paying stocks that you own. Even the steadiest are likely to drop a few percent in a month if the market tanks. David's fund, on the other hand, has never dropped as much as half a percent from month start to month end.

This all looks great. But I needed to verify—so I called up David and asked him point-blank: I'm assuming you own this fund for your mother...

> *I feel very comfortable with my mother owning the fund. I think the concept of "money good" goes right to the concept of being happy to buy it for the widows and orphans.*

And if it's not money good, then that's a different profile. We do have currently one investment that's less than two percent of the portfolio, but we think is extremely attractive at the current price. I mean, we're very comfortable because current market price is dramatically less than what the business is worth.

So the answer is yes to that.

Mom has a safe investment. So do the widows and orphans.

And they also have four competitive advantages over other investors, as well...

Not Only Safe—Four More Great Features

First, the fund has a short duration. If you're nervous about rising rates, you have nothing to worry about here.

David thinks there's a good shot that rates aren't going to rise as quickly as people think. But he's not investing that way. He would rather invest defensively.

This fund is not vulnerable to rising rates the way most bond funds are. Rising rates would actually help this portfolio. Let me explain...

The fund's average duration is under two and a half years. And the short-term, high-yield bucket provides a constant flow of maturing bonds. This means that David can apply the brakes and "cash in" if he sees rates starting to rise.

He can then sit back and wait to buy bonds at better (higher) rates.

Second, Cohanzick and RiverPark believe in their products. They eat their own cooking. Cohanzick management, at the individual and business level, has over $10 million in both of their funds.

And RiverPark's CEO and founding partner, Morty Schaja, has about $1.5 million in the RiverPark Strategic Income Fund. When management owns a big stake in their product, their interests are aligned with those of their shareholders.

Third, David has a stranglehold on this specific market. He has no competitors. This strategy makes up a tiny slice of the fixed-income market. And no one else is using this strategy.

Why?

Bigger mutual fund families can't operate in this space. The PIMCOs, Vanguards, and T. Rowe Prices can't function here. Their assets are simply too big for this little corner of the market.

This benefits David's investors because he can take advantage of situations that larger players cannot.

There's a large barrier to entry as well. David is the first call in the short-term yield market. When dealers, brokers, and big institutions want to get rid of a bond, they call Cohanzick first. People know it's a major buyer of short-term, high-yield paper.

Take Goldman Sachs, for instance. Cohanzick went from being unknown to Goldman... to now being one of its favorite high-yield accounts. Goldman calls David regularly to see if he's interested in deals.

No one else has these kinds of connections. If someone off the street tried to enter this small slice of the fixed-income market, they'd be at a severe disadvantage. David's connections are invaluable. And so is his expertise.

Fourth, management genuinely cares about its shareholders. They closed the original short-term, high-yield fund at $750 million in assets. They just didn't believe they could execute their bond strategy as effectively if they took in much more money than this.

Now that's a small asset base in the mutual fund industry. But, not according to RiverPark...

In fact, if assets in the new fund grow to the point where it's hard to run the strategy effectively, Cohanzick will close this one as well.

Shareholders never have to worry about watered-down returns.

RiverPark isn't interested in becoming a giant fund. It just wants to run its niche strategy effectively.

And this high-yield strategy is even safer than another favorite tactic of mine—collecting dividends. Here's why...

Complimentary Safe Yield Thanks to a "Day of Reckoning"

To build a truly diversified portfolio, you should buy assets that are not going to trade in tandem with each other.

This means if you're looking for yield, and you own many of our dividend stocks, then you should look to add issues that have a completely different "strategy."

That is, buy something that has a different time duration than a stock. Such as a fund of "money good" bonds.

David explained why his fund is a complementary holding to our other dividend payers...

> Let's compare our strategy to a dividend strategy, which you've written a lot about.
>
> In a dividend strategy, you have much longer durations.
>
> You have the duration of a stock, and the duration of the stock is longer in perpetuity.
>
> There is no day of reckoning. There's no maturity. My portfolio has a day of reckoning. And a maturity.

Each of David's portfolio holdings have that "day of reckoning" to reduce his downside. For example, if interest rates rise, the maturity date gets him out of each position.

This is the exact opposite of a stock investor who does not use stops. He or she has the potential to lose everything in a market crash.

It's why David's largest monthly drawdown is only -0.4% so far.

We'll Make 6-8% Returns with Minimal Risk...
But You Need to Buy Now

This fund has a monthly distribution policy. If you need income, you can choose to have monthly distributions paid in cash. This cash can help meet your immediate income needs.

But if you don't need income right now, you can choose to reinvest all dividends and capital gains—letting the power of compounding work for you.

My phone call with David actually turned into a two-hour conversation. I closed it by asking him what type of investor should buy his fund...

> *This is an ideal investment for somebody who wants a component of their portfolio to be fixed income—such as where they are interested in protecting capital and getting income.*
>
> *We make monthly distributions for those who need monthly distributions. And we let those reinvest if they want to continue to build and reinvest.*
>
> *It's an income product. If you think that owning a portfolio of money good bonds that's going to yield you a net return in a target range of 6% to 8% is an attractive yield... this is a great investment for you.*

I agree that it's great. But remember, David closed his last fund when it hit $750 million in assets. He might have to close this one soon...

Which means you need to buy it right now.

Action to Take: Buy RiverPark Strategic Income Fund (RSIVX) at NAV (net asset value). We're not using a stop loss. Do not invest more than 10% of your portfolio in RSIVX.

Additional Notes: Since this is a mutual fund, you will place a buy order in dollars. This is a no-load and no-transaction-fee fund.

If you choose to buy RSIVX through RiverPark, the minimum is $1,000. Minimums at online brokerage firms vary (RSIVX is available through all major custodians: Schwab, TD Ameritrade, Scottrade, Fidelity, Vanguard, etc.). Mutual funds are bought and sold at NAV at the close of each business day. So you may not see the transaction until the following morning.

You can opt to reinvest all dividends and capital gains. Or if you want the "cash" income, you can select "no" or "none" for reinvestment.

If you have the option, buy RSIVX in your retirement account. Not only does it pay steady income, it can pay short- and long-term capital gains. RiverPark is estimating a short-term capital gain of $0.01—only about one-tenth of a percent—at the end of this year.

* If you're able to invest $100,000 in this strategy, you should opt for the institutional shares (RSIIX). This share class is 0.25% cheaper.

CHAPTER 14

A New, Backdoor Way to Play Dividends

*Why the "Jelly Roll" Is Safer Than <u>Any</u> Dividend-Paying Stock...
and Should Average 8-11% Returns per Year*

By Grant Wasylik and Tom Dyson

Take a look at the chart below...

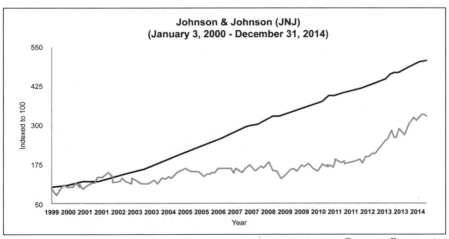

Source: Compustat

It shows two different ways to play **Johnson & Johnson (NYSE: JNJ)**. Which line would you rather own?

Of course, you'd pick the darker line. It increased by 406% in 15 years and never went down. The light line rose 225%—about half as much—and chopped up and down quite a bit.

Now, check out this chart. Each line is a way to invest in **IBM (NYSE: IBM)**. Which one would you buy?

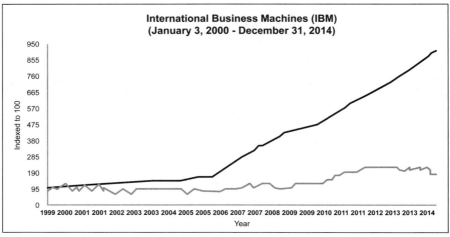

International Business Machines (IBM)
(January 3, 2000 - December 31, 2014)

Source: Compustat

Once again, it's an easy call. You'd take the investment that rose 804% without ever declining... versus the one that whipsawed sideways for 15 years, returning only 82%.

The light lines in these charts—the ones that go up and down and don't rise nearly as much—are the **total returns of each stock** (price appreciation + dividends). As you can see, even the two blue chips we chose were anything but a "one-way" ride over this period.

But the dark lines—the ones that *always* went up and far outpaced the light lines (total returns)—represent the **dividends each stock paid**.

So, while the "total return" lines are susceptible to the whims of the market (which sends prices up and down)...

The "dividend-only" lines are far more stable. That's because they reflect management's commitment to maintaining a steady, growing dividend—rather than the uncertainty of the stock market.

Until now, it's been almost impossible for the average investor to isolate this dividend growth and invest in it without putting capital at risk of the market's whims...

To get those rising dividends, we had to buy the stock and hold it... through ups and downs... just to collect the dividends and "hope" that a rally would follow each pullback.

It doesn't matter whether it's Johnson & Johnson, IBM, or any other blue-chip company. Every stock price can go down as well as up—even if the business is continually growing earnings and paying higher dividends. As a result, investing in good fundamentals has never guaranteed good returns.

Until now...

In this chapter, we have a new investment that actually lets you invest in the "dividend-only" line. <u>Without having to worry about stock prices that yo-yo around these steady payouts</u>.

It's a brand-new, backdoor strategy that barely anyone knows about. Until December 18, 2014, it wasn't even available to everyday investors. (It looks to us that the SEC thought it was *too* good to be true... and took a little extra time to approve it.)

Now, some professional investors have used a similar method to "isolate" dividends before. But it was only reserved for large institutions with billions of assets under management.

By following our instructions today, you'll finally be able to isolate dividends as well. And you'll have a chance to average 8-11% returns without any stock market risk whatsoever.

Now, let's discuss how this new strategy came about.

He Quit His Job to "Isolate" Dividends

Eric Ervin was happy with his job at Morgan Stanley...

And he was successful by any measure.

After 14 years, he and his partner had accumulated $300 million in assets under management. His office was in the top 2% of all Morgan Stanley advisors. And he had 125 clients who were counting on him to guard their nest egg. (Many clients—such as Eric—had built up a business themselves, and were now living off the proceeds.)

But one thing frustrated him on an almost daily basis...

The waiting.

You see, he could buy good businesses, and eventually the stock price would rise to meet the company's fundamentals. If his clients could wait long enough.

But some weren't patient enough. And many were retired or approaching retirement. They couldn't stomach all the intraday market fluctuations.

Nor could they afford to take a big loss. Even if a stock was likely to bounce back "someday," a 33% loss meant they'd need a 50% gain just to get back to even.

Eric understood his clients' concerns. He also hated the daily fluctuations. He and his partner had built a 40% allocation to alternative investments (typically, not stocks, bonds, or cash) because of it. They didn't want their clients' portfolios rolling up and down with the stock market.

Inside his alternatives allocation, there was one particular alternative strategy that Eric was very fond of. A few of his hedge fund manager friends had showed him this technique...

It was a way to invest in "pure dividend growth"... and *only* dividend growth.

In short, Eric had found a rare way to isolate and capture just the growth of stock dividends... This approach focused on the long-term financial health of companies without any exposure to their stock prices. It's exactly what we showed you in the charts above.

He told his clients about it. And a few of them really latched on to the idea. One of Eric's wealthiest clients—Charlie Silver—was so impressed with this unique strategy that he had bigger plans for it.

One day in the fall of 2011, Charlie marched into Eric's office with a radical idea. Eric's life was about to change...

Charlie asked him to quit his job at Morgan Stanley.

He wanted Eric to bring this elite strategy to the average Joe. He knew regular investors, who never had access to this strategy or even knew about it, could benefit greatly. Charlie was so confident that he even offered to help fund the new business.

Eric took Charlie up on his offer. In less than two weeks, he resigned from Morgan Stanley.

It took Eric two and a half years to assemble his team... conduct the research... build the analytics... and establish the trading platform.

Then there was the regulatory red tape that Eric had to navigate. You see, this was a brand-new concept that the Securities and Exchange Commission had never seen before. So it was even more stringent than usual in reviewing and approving Eric's product.

But after 30 months of 65-hour-plus workweeks, Eric finally got the go-ahead from the regulators. On December 18, 2014, Reality Shares—Eric's ETF business—launched the world's first publicly traded vehicle centered on "pure dividend growth": **Reality Shares DIVS ETF (NYSE: DIVY)**.

How I Discovered DIVY

I (Grant) found this unusual ETF when I met Eric at the world's largest ETF conference, "Inside ETFs " in Hollywood, Florida—and learned of his groundbreaking strategy.

DIVY is totally unique. No one can duplicate it. That's because Reality Shares has written the book on isolating dividend growth. It has protected its strategy with index licenses and methodology copyrights.

That means you're getting a "safe" investment idea that's the only one of its kind... And very few people know about it...

It's a complex strategy. But that's where Eric comes in. He's implementing the strategy so that we can invest in it simply by buying his ETF.

Let me explain how it works...

The Most Creative Dividend Strategy in the World

If you wanted to capture the dividend—and only the dividend—of a single stock, you might be tempted to try the following...

Buy the stock sometime before its next "ex-dividend date"—the date by which you need to own a stock in order to receive its dividend. Then sell the stock on the ex-dividend date, or shortly after, having pocketed the dividend payment. Investors call this a "dividend capture" strategy.

It sounds easy enough. And every now and then, it might work. But most of the time, it doesn't. That's because, in principle, on a stock's ex-dividend date, the stock price should drop by the amount of the dividend the company is paying out. So even though you'll be receiving the dividend (since you own the stock by the ex-dividend date), the value of those shares you own will drop by the same amount.

It's a bit like holding a wad of cash in your right hand, then switching it over to your left hand. You still have the same amount of cash—it's just in a different location.

Plus, since you own that stock, you're exposed to the market for however long it's in your portfolio. This can be dangerous...

Maybe some market event pushes the stock price down. For example: an employment report, a data breach, an oil shock, or a Vladimir Putin comment.

Point is, you're exposed to the resulting price fluctuations while you hold the stock, trying to capture the dividend. And one negative piece of news could wipe out your dividend payment in an instant.

Eric has a better—safer—way to capture dividends. He hedges against price movement so that he's left with only pure dividend growth. Here's how...

Instead of buying the stocks themselves, he buys and sells a combination of options on the major market indexes. By doing this, he has figured out a way to have the options cancel out any price moves. And he's left with only "long" dividend growth.

Now, if you aren't familiar with options, you might find this a bit confusing. That's okay. You don't need to know all the details.

He buys a "call option" on an index at a certain expiration date and price. And he sells a "put option" on the same index at the same expiration date, and the same price. Here, Eric is "long" the index.

Next, to complete the option pair, he also buys and sells another matching option. The strike price remains the same. But for this combination, he sells a call and buys a put (the reverse of the first paired trade)... and extends the expiration date by one year. With this step, Eric is "short" the index.

Eric makes these trades at the same time. Here's an image to show what it looks like:

How DIVY Captures Expected Dividends

TRADE 1:

BUY ONE YEAR CALL & SELL ONE YEAR PUT → **LONG THE INDEX** (One Year)

We buy a call and sell a put with the same strike price and expiration, this is equivalent to a long position.

TRADE 2:

SELL TWO YEAR CALL & BUY TWO YEAR PUT → **SHORT THE INDEX** (Two Year)

We buy a call and buy a put with the same strike price and expiration, this is equivalent to a short position.

LONG THE INDEX (One Year) - **SHORT THE INDEX** (Two Year) = **EXPECTED DIVIDEND** (Market Neutral)

Again, if this is confusing to you, don't worry—here's all you need to know...

The net result is that Eric's two pairs of options cancel out any potential price movement in the underlying index. Whether the index goes up or down, the four options result in a net wash.

But even though these options cancel each other out, they give Eric one year of a "synthetic long" position in the underlying index. This means that Eric gets to participate in the dividend growth of this index during this time frame. Without any price risk!

[The main risk Eric faces is dividend cuts. If dividends go down rather than up, this strategy will lose money. But we'll explain later why this is unlikely to happen for any extended period of time.]

In option trader lingo, Eric's strategy is known as a "jelly roll." The "roll" is the option combination built around dividends. It's rolled forward from one expiration to the next (typically annually). And the "jelly" is the yummy dividends captured in the middle of the option expirations.

It's as close to a free lunch as you can get on Wall Street.

Notice we said Eric uses an index instead of a stock. His investor-friendly strategy—DIVY—works best with index options. There's much more liquidity in index options than individual stock options. And you capture the potential dividend growth of around 600 stocks for diversification instead of just one stock.

As I write this, DIVY's options have a 90% weight in the S&P 500 index and 10% in the Nasdaq 100 index. The goal is to increase the Nasdaq 100 weighting over time—30% is the target.

How Is This Strategy So Profitable?

After returning from the ETF conference, I talked to Eric and his team several times. I needed clarification on something...

How is it possible for this near-risk-free trade to be so profitable? And why hadn't options prices adjusted to eat away these returns?

His response surprised me. First, options prices don't fully factor in dividend increases.

Second, the pricing of the dividend component in this option strategy tends to be "undervalued." In other words, there's a "dividend discount" available in the options market.

For example, in early April 2015, the options market was pricing in a $0.47 June dividend for Apple. That was 0% dividend growth.

But Wall Street analysts (according to *Bloomberg*) were forecasting a $0.50 dividend for AAPL that June—a 6% increase. And some other forecasters were projecting an 8-10% dividend increase.

Apple actually announced an 11% dividend increase on April 28, 2015. Once again, the options market had priced in a "dividend discount" that was too steep.

And this discount should continue for at least the next three years. Dividends on the S&P 500 and Nasdaq 100 are selling at considerable discounts to analyst estimates...

S&P 500 Dividends Through 2017
Are Priced at a 21-30% Discount

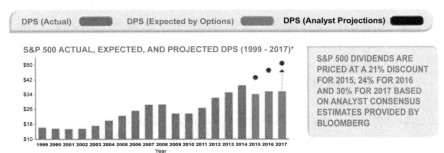

Source: Bloomberg

Nasdaq 100 Dividends Through 2017
Are Priced at a 30-39% Discount

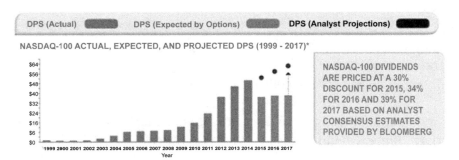

Source: Bloomberg

Eric is buying at these steep discounts. He's able to do this because of supply and demand in the options market. There are more sellers of dividends than buyers when it comes to derivatives.

Traders, market makers, and structure product engineers are more concerned about short-term market moves than little dividends. So they "sell off" the dividend risk.

The simple takeaway is: this benefits Eric. He's on the other side of this dividend trade. Plus, he's using the options market to get rid of price risk either way. He's chowing down on the jelly dividends only.

That's how DIVY works. Now, let me tell you about its "forced" special payout feature...

A Special Rule Mandates a Special Dividend...

If overall dividends rise in the S&P 500 and Nasdaq 100, then all of DIVY's price appreciation will be paid out as a special dividend each year (when its options expire).

From 2000-2014, the DIVS index (DIVY aims to match this index) back test returned 13.2% annually—more than triple the S&P 500's return over that same time. And with 12% less volatility...

A "DIVS Back Test" Tripled the S&P 500... and Was Steadier

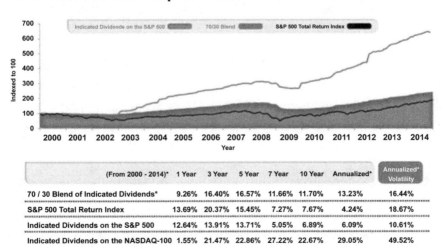

(From 2000 - 2014)*	1 Year	3 Year	5 Year	7 Year	10 Year	Annualized*	Annualized* Volatility
70 / 30 Blend of Indicated Dividends*	9.26%	16.40%	16.57%	11.66%	11.70%	13.23%	16.44%
S&P 500 Total Return Index	13.69%	20.37%	15.45%	7.27%	7.67%	4.24%	18.67%
Indicated Dividends on the S&P 500	12.64%	13.91%	13.71%	5.05%	6.89%	6.09%	10.61%
Indicated Dividends on the NASDAQ-100	1.55%	21.47%	22.86%	27.22%	22.67%	29.05%	49.52%

*70/30 Blend represents 70% S&P Dividend Growth and 30% NASDAQ-100 Dividend Growth
*Jan 3, 2000 - Dec 31, 2014

Source: Bloomberg, Compustat

On average, you would have received close to a 13.2% payout at the end of each year in the form of a special dividend (technically, a special distribution).

And while DIVY's special dividends won't be taxed at normal dividend rates (because they're not actual dividends), they are tax advantaged compared to taxable bonds and short-term gains...

Because DIVY's underlying investments are broad-based stock index options, it classifies as a "Section 1256 Contract" investment by the Internal Revenue Code. Your accountant will be happy to know that DIVY's year-end distributions qualify for 60% long-term and 40% short-term capital gains rates.

Safer Than Buying General Electric, UPS, or Walt Disney...

When overall dividends grow, DIVY goes up. And if overall dividends decline, DIVY goes down.

But because dividends, in aggregate, go up almost every year, it's almost a guaranteed outcome. According to Howard Silverblatt (senior index analyst for S&P Dow Jones Indices), there have been 169 increases and only five decreases so far this year (97% of dividend actions were increases).

The S&P 500 index (90% of DIVY's dividend growth allocation) has generated positive dividend growth in 40 of the last 43 years. Hypothetically, this means DIVY's strategy would have made money 93% of the time. For comparison, the S&P 500 lost money in nine of those 43 years (positive returns 79% of the time).

S&P 500 dividend growth didn't go down anywhere near as much as the market during negative calendar years.

For example, let's look at a few of the worst years for the stock market over the last 15 years. We'll compare three "so called" safe-haven stocks, the S&P 500 index, and the S&P 500's dividend growth.

Annual Return	2000	2001	2008
General Electric	-6.0%	-15.1%	-53.0%
United Parcel Service	-33.3%	-6.1%	-19.5%
Walt Disney	-0.4%	-25.8%	-28.6%
S&P 500 Index	-9.1%	-11.9%	-37.0%
S&P 500 Dividend Growth	**-2.9%**	**-1.8%**	**0.3%**

<u>Note, the third-worst year ever for the S&P 500 was 2008. Yet, the S&P 500's dividend growth still managed to grind out a positive return.</u>

Buying DIVY, which tracks the dividend growth of the best companies in the world, is safer than owning any of the stocks themselves.

Reality Shares has the index back tests to prove it. The following study uses a 70%/30% split (DIVY's targeted allocation) between the dividend growth of the S&P 500 and Nasdaq 100. It shows results from three different times of major stock market losses.

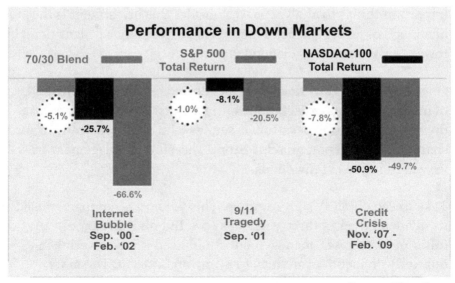

Source: Bloomberg

As you can see, three separate market implosions... Yet, the DIVS index (which DIVY mimics) held up...

- The Nasdaq 100 dropped 67% in the Internet bubble collapse... the DIVS index was down just 5%.

- The 9/11 tragedy sent the S&P 500 down 8% and the Nasdaq 100 down 21%... the DIVS index was flat.

- And the credit crisis chopped 50% off both major market indexes... the DIVS index lost less than 8%.

Most investors would have loved that performance in those difficult times.

We can't predict when the next big market downturn will come. But we know we'll get one. Holding the defensive DIVY will help calm your nerves the next time the market gets turbulent.

Future Dividend Growth Looks Bright

DIVY's returns rely upon dividend increases. So one of the most important things to analyze as we consider this investment is the likelihood of future dividend increases. Fortunately, all signs point toward years of strong dividend growth.

Once companies start raising dividends and establishing a history of increases, it sets expectations for investors. If a company cuts its dividend after this expectation is set, it's a huge disappointment for shareholders and potential investors. Therefore, management tries very hard not to cut dividends.

Take Ensco plc (ESV), for example. The oil and gas company raised its dividend the last three years in a row. But on February 25, 2015 (after market close), management announced it was lowering its quarterly dividend from $0.75 to $0.15, an 80% cut. The news caused a sell-off. ESV dropped 8.1% the next day.

Of course, "management not wanting to cut dividends" is true in all markets. But there are three extra reasons why the current market we're in will support dividend growth over the coming years...

No. 1: Companies in the S&P 500 should continue to increase their dividends in the years ahead. They've never had more cash on their balance sheets than right now...

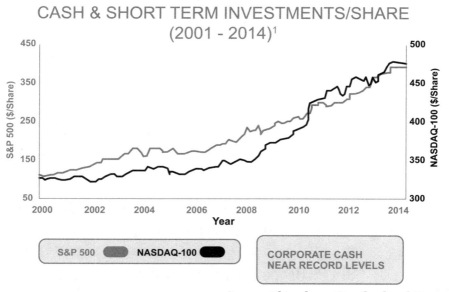

Source: Bloomberg, Standard and Poors

It's from the cash pool that management is able to pay (and increase) dividends.

No. 2: Dividend payout ratios are near historic lows ("payout ratio" is dividends divided by earnings). Low payout ratios tell us the largest U.S. companies have plenty of room to boost their dividends in the years ahead...

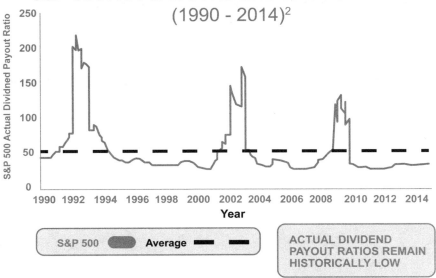

S&P 500 ACTUAL DIVIDEND PAYOUT RATIOS (1990 - 2014)[2]

S&P 500 Actual Dividend Payout Ratio

Year

S&P 500 ⬤ Average ▬ ▬

ACTUAL DIVIDEND PAYOUT RATIOS REMAIN HISTORICALLY LOW

Source: Bloomberg, Standard and Poors

No. 3: Shareholder activism is growing. Assets managed by activist hedge funds have increased 269% in the last five years.

DIVY's Hedge Fund Strategy Is Cheap...

DIVY's expense ratio is 0.85%. In dollar terms, you'll lose $8.50 to expenses with a $1,000 investment.

Sound expensive? It's not...

Hedge funds charge 2% fees and 20% of profits. And the average liquid alternative ETF has an average expense ratio of 1.22%.

And keep in mind, these trades are too expensive to do on your own... would require a high option-level approval... and retail investors can't get the pricing that institutions can get.

Paying 85 basis points for a hedge fund strategy is very reasonable.

Carl Icahn, Bill Ackman, and Dan Loeb are just a few famous activist investors. As shareholders of publicly traded companies, they pressure management for change (new leadership, spending cash: dividends/buybacks, reorganization, etc.). Forcing company management to spend cash on its balance sheet has been an easy activist's prey.

For these reasons, we're betting on continued dividend growth.

Equity-Like Returns of 8-11%, Without the Equity Noise...

Here's how we're going to achieve our returns...

Long-term S&P 500 dividend growth (90% DIVY)...	6-8%
Long-term Nasdaq 100 dividend growth (10% DIVY)...	12-24%
Dividend discount...	2%
Less expenses and transaction costs...	-1%
Return projection...	8-11%

With our *Palm Beach Letter* mentality, these projections are conservative...

As DIVY eventually moves toward its 70% S&P 500/30% Nasdaq 100 allocation, return potential should increase (historically, the Nasdaq 100 has much higher dividend growth than the S&P 500). And recent dividend growth has trended higher for the S&P 500—14% over the last three and five years. Even analysts are predicting double-digit growth (10-12%) for S&P 500 dividends this year.

But we're not factoring in any of this upside potential. Over time, DIVY's returns could easily be higher than our forecasts.

These safe and sizable returns are what excited Mike Rosen (a former portfolio manager of a multibillion-dollar mutual fund company). Eric approached Mike with his DIVY idea in 2011. Here are Mike's own words:

> *Four years ago, I was introduced to Eric to discuss a novel idea for a new ETF. Having built two investment firms myself, I was*

---

not particularly enthused. Most new products I see are neither novel nor value-adds. Over a series of meetings, I became more and more intrigued with the concept. And I decided to help seed a new company to further explore the concept.

Every single investor I know, from the guy who cleans my pool, to friends and former colleagues who manage multibillion-dollar portfolios, all have had their frustrations with separating "fundamentals" from the "noise."

[The "noise" Mike is referring to is any random news—not related to the fundamentals of the stock—that results in price fluctuations.]

Getting the fundamentals correct is a Herculean task by itself. And even under the remote odds that you get that right, you still run the risk of being blindsided by noise. The problem is that you can be right on fundamentals and experience meaningful financial loss because of noise.

DIVY attempts to deliver the fundamentals through isolated dividend growth without the noise. Don't confuse this fund with the 100-plus dividend ETFs or mutual funds that are essentially diversified equity funds. Their $1 of investment delivers $0.02 of dividends. In essence, you are buying a chocolate chip cookie when all you really want are the chocolate chips.

With DIVY, we're buying the chocolate chips instead of the whole cookie... we're investing in the "dark" line, not the "light" line... And we're using the "jelly roll" to gain access to the market's sweet spot—pure dividend growth.

And the best part is our returns will come without the noise, risk, or volatility of the stock market.

Action to Take: Buy Reality Shares DIVS ETF (NYSE: DIVY) up to $24.25.
Stop Loss: 20%

CHAPTER 15

An Investment "Oddity" Preferred by Billionaires

This unusual investment behaves like a stock when markets go up. But it has the safety of a bond when markets go down.

By Grant Wasylik and Tom Dyson

Warren Buffett loves one type of investment so much, he was recently fined $896,000 for misusing it.

But he barely flinched and immediately agreed to pay the fine.

Perhaps he was a bit too enthusiastic about the asset I'll share with you in this chapter...

This asset is so discreet, hardly anyone outside of elite financial circles knows about it. (It makes up less than 0.5% of the entire investment universe.)

You see, the "Oracle of Omaha" didn't get in trouble for buying an illegal security, or insider trading, or anything sinister like that. It seemed like an honest mistake.

Not long ago, his company Berkshire Hathaway violated the Hart-Scott-Rodino Antitrust Act. This obscure 38-year-old law requires investors to notify regulators before they complete transactions of a certain size.

For whatever reason, Buffett didn't report the purchase. And he got nailed for it. *Twice, in fact...*

"We made a mistake when we overlooked the filing requirement," Buffett said.

These stories didn't attract much news. But it's interesting that Buffett committed the same securities infraction twice...

He may have gotten so greedy about buying this favorite "billionaire asset" that he forgot to stay on top of securities laws.

I (Grant) have actually known about this investment for quite some time...

When I worked in private asset management, I studied all kinds of investments. I spoke with hundreds of investment professionals every year.

I researched and vetted the best investment ideas I heard. This rare asset was one of my favorites... precisely because so few (outside of billionaire hedge fund managers and large institutions) know about it.

I learned that Buffett wasn't alone in profiting from this small, niche area of the market. George Soros, Carl Icahn, and David Tepper are a few of the other elite money managers who operate in this space.

Even Benjamin Graham, the father of value investing, was a fan.

Why has this investment vehicle been so favored by great investors and billionaires alike?

Because it provides the upside of a stock... along with the safety of a bond. Specifically, it has three important attributes we love here at *The Palm Beach Letter*:

1. Steady income (higher than most stocks)
2. Significant appreciation potential

3. Safety of principal. No traditional stock or bond provides all three of these attributes. But this investment does.

In this chapter, we'll explain how this investment works... why it's traditionally been reserved for only "elite" investors... and how we can now participate alongside these legendary money managers.

And we'll share what level of income and capital appreciation you can expect.

We'll also show you how to buy it—conveniently and easily—from your own brokerage account.

But first, let's discuss how this particular security type became the "private playground" of billionaires...

It All Started 150 Years Ago With the "Railroad King"

Buffett's darling investment isn't new.

Corporations have been issuing these securities for over 150 years.

The first issues were used to finance the Internet of the late 1800s—railroads. Soon after, telephone companies started issuing them to fuel their growth, as well.

One of the greatest speculators in stock market history, Jacob Little, was the very first user of this security. He traded this security to a $2 million fortune in 1846 (over $52 million today). Little was thus dubbed the "Railroad King."

Little effectively cornered markets. And was able to gain control and manipulate the prices of certain securities.

Unfortunately for him, these maneuvers were so unpopular that the New York Stock Exchange made rules against his techniques. And eventually, they blackballed him.

Just as Little made big profits from these obscure securities... other brilliant investors have continued the tradition.

Ben Graham wrote about them...

In *Security Analysis*, the famous book he co-authored with David Dodd, he referred to convertibles as:

"... The most attractive of all (securities) in point form, since they permit the combination of maximum safety with the chance of unlimited appreciation in value."

Mario Gabelli, who runs $30 billion global investment firm GAMCO Investors, calls them a "win-win proposition."

Even large institutions, pensions, and global asset managers quietly put money into this space.

Why are the world's greatest investors and largest institutions buying this specific asset?

They love it because it's like a convertible car. Investors get to put the top down on warm, sunny days. But they can quickly put the top up when the weather turns stormy.

I'm talking about convertible securities.

Why Most Investors Don't Know About Convertible Securities

I tapped into my financial network and called up three separate portfolio managers who oversee more than $2.5 billion in convertibles... each.

All three are experts on this "yacht club" investment. So, I asked each one point-blank:

"Does the average investor know about convertibles?"

Their responses?

"Absolutely not." "Nope." And, "If they did, they'd own them for sure."

In fact, one manager estimated that mom-and-pop investors own just 1-3% of all convertible assets.

Convertibles are complex. So they fall outside of the "buy stocks you know" scope of the typical investor.

You have to do some serious homework to understand convertibles. This extra work keeps all but the most knowledgeable and experienced investors away.

Most financial writers don't understand them either. Which is why you rarely read about convertibles.

That's a shame, because this shouldn't be an "exotic" investment. It belongs in your portfolio. Let me explain...

Convertibles are actually a standard asset, like bonds and equities.

Remember, companies can raise money three ways:

1. They issue bonds. And pay a stated interest rate to investors who buy them.
2. They issue additional stock. This is "free money" for the company. But it dilutes existing shareholders.
3. Or they issue convertible bonds.

Convertible bonds are an attractive option for companies (especially smaller companies in growth mode) because they usually pay lower interest rates than standard corporate bonds.

Investors are willing to accept a lower rate because they have additional upside potential from stock appreciation.

So, Investors Get the Best of Both Worlds

You can't find another investment that pays a yield—like a bond...

But also gives you the benefit of a "special switch" feature. Letting you buy shares of the issuing company's stock at a predetermined price.

In other words, convertibles are similar to stock options, except they have yield—and almost never lose all your money (unlike speculative options).

Convertibles combine the higher income and safety of fixed income instruments with the capital appreciation of equities.

They present an attractive mix of yield and equity exposure.

One of the portfolio managers I spoke with—who's been running convertible strategies for 30 years—called them "chameleons." Because they adapt to the markets.

If you're worried the market is too frothy, convertibles are tailor-made for you.

Why?

Convertibles can work in good times and bad. And they offer a smoother ride than equities.

You don't have to fret about timing the market with this strategy.

That's because you'll earn income no matter what the underlying stock does...

"Get Paid to Wait"

Convertible securities provide a natural overlay for conservative investors. You earn income while you wait for the underlying stock to rise.

Simply, you "get paid to wait."

Just as with traditional bonds, convertible bonds have stated repayment dates and interest payments.

Even in a market correction or bear market... convertible investors get paid with interest. They essentially get paid to wait for the next market recovery or bull market.

Now, convertibles aren't completely risk-free. Bonds, like stocks, can also decline in value.

But convertibles provide investors with downside protection.

Historically, they've only participated in 30-50% of the downside of their underlying equity... but they've enjoyed 60-70% of the upside during positive moves.

This is why convertibles are considered to be "favorably leveraged."

You probably know "leverage" as debt used to fund instrument. In this case, it's the price movement of one issue relative to another.

For example, a warrant is highly leveraged. Its price rises and falls faster than the price of its underlying stock.

A convertible, on the other hand, moves more slowly than its underlying stock.

It will rise more on a gain in the underlying stock than it will fall on a decline in the stock. These are "asymmetric returns"—which is why superstar investors love them.

And studies show that not only are convertibles "favorably leveraged"—they can even outperform stocks themselves over extended periods of time.

Great Upside for Four Decades

Take a look at the following chart...

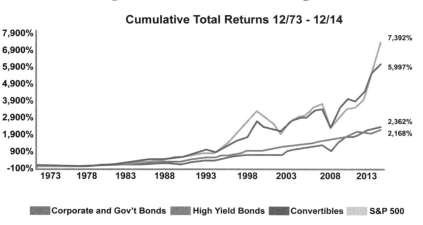

Beating Other Assets Over A Longer Period

Cumulative Total Returns 12/73 - 12/14

Source: Wellesley Investment Advisors

Notice the convertibles index line is above the S&P 500 index line for almost 40 years. Convertibles captured 81% of the upside of the equity market over from 1973 to 2014.

Also, convertibles outperformed high yield by 154%. And they beat corporate and government bonds by 177%.

Here's a real-life example of a convertible's upside one of my investment manager contacts gave me...

> We'll use the Gilead Sciences Inc. 1.625% convertible bond, due 5/1/2016. If you purchased this convertible bond at par ($100) on 7/26/2010, you would have seen a return of 321.1% through 12/31/14.
>
> The stock (GILD) returned 464.4% over the same time.
>
> As a convertible owner, you got 70% of the stock's return.

Even while the stock was bouncing around, you collected four years of interest payments. And had sleep-at-night comfort knowing that you owned a bond at the end of the day.

Lower Volatility

Successful investing has more to do with limiting downside risk than maximizing upside reward.

Convertibles provide strong risk-adjusted returns.

One of the investing mantras we've preached about at *The Palm Beach Letter* is that avoiding and minimizing losses is the key to finding superior long-term investment returns. Put more simply… "The best offense is a good defense."

Large losses during market drops outweigh the benefits of "equal" gains during periods of market upside.

For example, if you lose 33% of your portfolio, a subsequent 33% gain doesn't get you back to even. You'd need a 50% gain to recover your initial loss.

Adding a convertible strategy to your portfolio, not only increases returns… it also reduces volatility…

Look what happens when you add convertibles to the traditional 60% stocks, 40% bonds asset allocation model that Wall Street touts.

Replacing one-third of your stocks with convertible bonds would have boosted your returns a full percentage point, while lowering your volatility (as measured by "standard deviation"—a statistic that defines historical volatility).

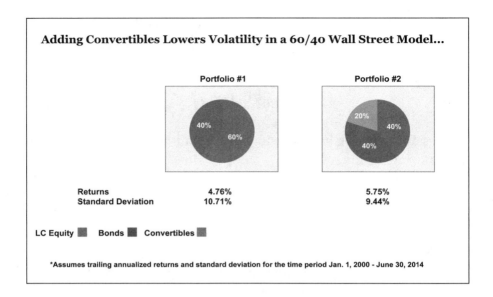

Convertibles also boost returns and lower volatility when added to a
more diversified portfolio of investments...

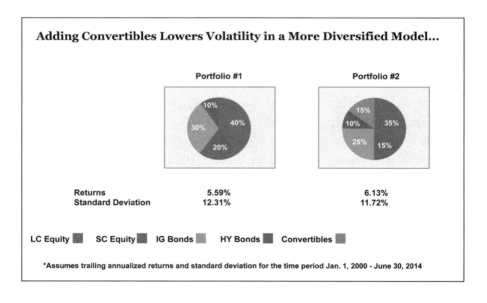

In both cases, convertibles enhance portfolio efficiency and safety.
Here's why...

When assets are correlated, their prices move up and down together. Think about the 2008 financial crash, when most asset prices moved in the same direction—down.

That's not ideal. It's why most investors lost a lot of money.

And it's why you want a portfolio of assets that are uncorrelated.

(Correlation shows how two securities move in relation to another... a score of 0.00 means there's no correlation at all, and a score of 1.00 is perfect correlation.)

So, I pulled a study showing the correlation that convertibles have had with other asset classes...

Convertibles and Their Correlation With Bonds and Stocks (1998-2012)

Index	Correlation
Barclays U.S. Aggregate Bond	0.01
Barclays U.S. Treasury TIPS	0.12
Barclays Global Treasury ex-U.S.	0.12
Russell 3000	0.84

Convertibles have a very low correlation to bonds (between 0.01 and 0.12).

They have a much higher correlation (0.84) to stocks. But the Russell 3000 Index was up 63% over this 15-year period. So the high correlation to stocks is not that surprising.

And convertibles have much lower volatility than stocks...

Convertibles Are Much Less Volatile Than Equities

Index	5-Year Standard Deviation
Russell 3000	13.4%
Barclays U.S. Corp. Inv-Grade Bond	4.1%
Barclays U.S. Convertibles Comp	9.6%

Less volatility generally means less downside...

What's Our Downside?

Conventional wisdom says that most bond investments are doomed when interest rates rise.

But convertibles are less interest-rate sensitive than regular fixed income investments. In fact, <u>convertibles are the best bonds to own when rates rise</u>.

Here are the bond sector returns in rising rate quarters from 1993-2013. *Wall Street Daily* added an annualized return column to the table (right-column)...

Bond Return During Rising-Rate Quarters (1993-2013)

Bond Sector	Average Quarterly Return	Annualized Return
Convertible	3.97%	16.85%
U.S. High Yield	2.50%	10.38%
Emerging Markets	2.33%	9.65%
Preferred Stock Fxed Rate	1.53%	6.26%
Asset-Backed Floating Rate	1.28%	5.22%
U.S. Treasury TIPS	0.62%	2.50%
U.S. Intermediate Corp.	0.53%	2.14%
U.S. Mortgage-Backed	0.40%	1.61%
Municipal (5-10 yrs)	0.19%	0.76%
U.S. Aggregate	0.70%	2.83%
Global Aggregate	-0.05%	-0.20%
U.S. Treasury (3-5 yrs)	-0.21%	-0.84%
U.S. Treasury	-0.48%	-1.91%

As you can see, convertible bonds have averaged 16.85% annual returns during rising-rate periods!

As we mentioned earlier, convertibles generally participate in 30-50% of the downside of their underlying equity. But sometimes, they partake in none of it.

Here's an actual example of a convertible's downside protection from one of my expert contacts...

> Consider the Best Buy Co. 2.25% convertible bond, due 1/15/2022 with a 1/15/2012 put date. A put option allows the owner/buyer of the bond to sell it back to the company at a future date. Let's say you purchased this convertible bond just above par ($100.643) on 5/18/2009. If you exercised the put option and sold the bond back to Best Buy at par ($100), you would have lost 0.64% off your original purchase. But with the interest payments you banked, your total return would have been a positive 5.57%...
>
> The stock (BBY) lost 28.4% over the same time.
>
> As a convertible owner—with the promise of principal repayment—you were able to make a nice return, although the underlying stock lost almost one-third of its value.

Now, let's discuss the best security for us to buy... so that we can actually invest alongside these "yacht club" investors...

The Best Convertible Investment Vehicle

We can't trade convertibles the same way the "filthy rich" do...

Retail investors are penalized with steep transaction costs when they trade individual bonds (including convertible bonds). These opportunities to buy and sell are largely reserved for the larger, more active customers. Especially in the new issue market.

And even if there weren't these barriers, everyday investors don't have the time, resources, or patience to choose and manage their own convertible investments. This is a dealer's market. You have to go and figure out who's got the bonds.

At which point, their lack of liquidity makes them expensive. If our 70,000-plus subscribers tried to buy the same individual convertible bond, it would get marked up.

Fortunately, there's another way for us to do it...

I looked at every possible investment vehicle for us to use. I had one of my Morningstar contacts send me all the available options: 10 closed-end funds and 103 mutual funds (all shares classes).

But the majority of these funds weren't tax efficient—investors were losing more than 2% of their assets to taxes each year. And annual expenses were high—costing an average of 1.35%.

I had a hunch what the best option would be before I started this search. And by vetting all the available options, my research confirmed it...

A convertible securities ETF (exchange traded fund).

No leverage to worry about...

Lower expenses (0.40%) than any closed-end fund or open-end fund...

Half the turnover of actively managed funds (high turnover means high trading fees—if we have the option, we want low turnover)...

The most tax-efficient vehicle in this category...

And performance that's proven itself superior to the alternatives. It's beaten the average fund option over one-, three-, and five-year periods.

That's why we recommend the **SPDR Barclays Convertibles Securities ETF (NYSE: CWB)**.

Launched in 2009, it's the largest registered convertible securities fund available in the U.S. And the only convertible securities ETF listed in the U.S.

What's important when buying an ETF?

The underlying index... You need to know what's under the hood—the index that the ETF is tied to. In this case, the Barclays U.S. Convertibles > $500MM Index measures the U.S. convertibles market with more than $500 million outstanding and at least one month until maturity. The index has 100 constituents. And it provides exposure to the most liquid segment of the convertible securities market.

Tracking error... How close do the ETF's returns come to the index's returns? Remember, the ETF is trying to mimic its index's benchmark. Removing expenses, tracking error for the ETF vs. its index was 0.01% over one year... 0.09% over three years... and 0.40% over five years. A Morgan Stanley annual study in 2012 reported an average tracking error of 0.59% for all ETFs.

Expenses... At 0.40%, this ETF is the cheapest option of any convertibles product.

Tax efficiency... Most ETFs are tax efficient. This ETF's pre-tax returns are within 2% of its after-tax returns. Much better than actively managed funds.

Is the ETF fund family reputable? State Street is the second largest ETF provider in the world. It manages $2.5 trillion in assets. The company has deep relationships with hundreds of dealers across the industry. You can't find this kind of access in many places. State Street's scale gives it easy entry to the dealer community. No convertible manager has the same gateway into the dealer community to locate bonds.

Other characteristics to know about CWB...

The ETF never converts its holdings to equity. Instead, it holds securities until they are called, close to maturity (31 days out), or no longer meet liquidity screens. When a bond gets within 31 days of maturity, it's removed (sold) from the ETF.

This means State Street has no possibility of seeing a fine like Buffett received.

The duration of CWB's underlying bonds is short (2-and-a-half to 3 years). Convertibles are already the best performing bond sector in rising rate periods. But here's an added buffer against rising rates. A portfolio with a lower duration should be less sensitive to interest rate changes than a portfolio with a higher duration.

This ETF's average credit quality breakdown is 32% investment grade, 38% below investment grade, and 30% not rated. While the majority of convertibles are below investment-grade, this ETF is well diversified by credit.

Many issues come from recognizable companies: Wells Fargo, Bank of America, Intel, Anthem, Yahoo, Alcoa, and Tesla Motors make up more than 20% of the weight.

CWB trades like a stock. And you can see its holdings daily.

It pays a monthly dividend. Which means you will see distributions deposited into your account the second week of every month.

And it's never had a default in its portfolio since inception.

Why Buy Convertibles Now?

The answer is straightforward...

While you may **think** a stock will go up, you don't **know** that it will.

No one correctly calls stock market moves 100% of the time. You'd be hard-pressed to find a CNBC analyst, macro expert, or all-star investor who gets more calls right than wrong.

As I write, we're in the midst of an incredible bull run.

Could it continue to chug along and go higher? Sure.

Could we have a correction—or worse? Yes, we could.

Neither is out of the question. And convertibles can work in all market conditions...

We're all about protecting capital here at *The Palm Beach Letter*. When investors think about their need for income and growth, they also need to understand that protecting capital should be a high priority.

Remember, when buying convertibles, you also get paid to wait...

You'll strengthen the risk-reward profile of your portfolio when you add this investment.

We're going to take advantage of all the positive attributes of convertibles:

- Higher yield than equities
- Capital appreciation potential
- Asymmetric returns (more upside than downside)
- History of strong risk-adjusted returns
- Capital preservation
- Best-performing bond sector in rising interest rate periods.

I expect we'll gain around 6.5% for every 10% market rise... and fall just half (maybe less) of what the broad market does during a correction.

Over the long haul, I predict we'll make 6-7% returns owning CWB. After all, stocks have returned an average of 10% per year. If the market turns south, CWB will switch to defense mode. And pay us a 2% yield while we wait out the pullback.

Action to Take: Buy SPDR Barclays Convertible Securities ETF (NYSE:CWB) up to $48.

Stop Loss: 20%

CHAPTER 16

One of the World's Smartest Minds Is on Sale

Collect a "hidden" 10% distribution from this fixed-income prodigy.

By Grant Wasylik and Tom Dyson

This chapter's pick is rather unique. It comes in the form of a superstar investor—he outperforms everyone in his space... the "world bond" sector. But few retail investors know of him.

After more research, I (Grant) knew this investment would be the perfect solution for income-seeking investors. And I knew I could trust it...

You see, I once worked for a billion-dollar wealth management firm that had over $60 million in one of this manager's strategies (a mutual fund). I even own one of his other mutual funds for my own mother. She's 68 years old. As her money manager, I've made it a staple in her IRA for years.

I don't know of a better international fixed-income money manager in the business.

It hadn't come across my radar before because—as I said earlier—we've steered clear of the bond sector. But if our sole goal is to address the income problem—and get more money in your pocket NOW—this is my solution.

With this investment, you'll get an income distribution that's 125% higher than what a five-year U.S. Treasury is paying. And it yields twice as much as an investment in the S&P 500 Index (as I write).

Plus, you don't have to worry how stocks perform. We can sit back and let the best international fixed-income manager in the world pick bonds for us.

In this chapter, I'm going to introduce you to a closed-end fund that will generate 4-9% income. And total distributions north of 10%. (I'll explain what a closed-end fund is in a moment.)

This investment is loaded with more benefits: invisible income, increased diversification for your portfolio, protection from rising rates, and the opportunity to buy at a significant discount—above 10% as I write...

Plus, it's safe. The yield-junkies don't know about it. And the longer you hold it, the safer it gets. I'll prove it to you later.

First, let's cover the main reason behind today's recommendation: income.

Today's Investment Pays Solid Income

This closed-end fund has a monthly distribution policy. We don't have to wait every three months to get paid, like we do with most dividend-paying stocks. And it beats most bonds, which pay semi-annually.

As I write, its last monthly distribution was $0.025 per share. If we receive 12 monthly dividends of that amount, we're clearing a 4% distribution rate.

A distribution rate over 4% in today's ultra-low-rate environment is exceptional.

But that doesn't mean we'll always have to settle for a monthly distribution of $0.025. Going back 15 years, the monthly distribution has ranged from $0.025 to $0.05.

It all depends on the market environment. And on what this manager is finding for us in the bond universe. Lucky for us, he can invest anywhere in the world.

You see, while many companies constrain their bond managers to one specific area (U.S. bonds, high-yield bonds, foreign bonds), this manager gets to buy bonds wherever he sees value.

And he sits at the helm of a great investment opportunity: **Templeton Global Income (NYSE: GIM)**.

Templeton Global Income is the best international bond fund in the closed-end universe. It's a great way to solve today's income problem.

In buying GIM, we'll get a monthly payout that clears a 4% annual yield. But there's a unique situation with this particular closed-end fund—something that occurs every December. And unless you already own it, you would never know about it...

Templeton Global Pays Invisible Income

This fund pays out year-end special distributions. It's done so 10 of the last 11 years.

So there's a hidden yield. I checked some of the most popular websites: CNBC, MarketWatch, and *The Wall Street Journal*. No one shows it.

And this special distribution is a big one. The fund paid out $0.3616 at the end of 2014, $0.29 at the end of 2013, $0.63 in Dec. 2012, $0.67 at year-end 2011, $0.47 in Dec. 2010, and the list goes on. All year-end special distributions.

<u>If you add up all the income distributions (regular and special) from 2010-2014, the fund averaged a 9% "income" yield.</u>

That's more than double the distribution yield that financial sites report.

Who's in charge of producing this great yield? It's an expert money manager directing all the investment decisions. A man by the name of Hasenstab...

A Top Contrarian Investor Who Covers the Globe

Dr. Michael Hasenstab is the chief investment officer for Franklin Templeton's global bond team.

Hasenstab has been with Franklin Templeton since 1995, except for a short hiatus to finish his doctorate and dissertation on China's financial markets. When he first started with the company, he managed $100 million. Today, Hasenstab oversees close to $200 billion worth of fixed-income assets.

He's garnered quite a following over the years. There are three main reasons why institutional investors prefer him to the typical fixed-income manager...

First, he's a true contrarian. When investors are fleeing certain markets because of fright, Hasenstab steps in. He exploits panic. And isn't afraid to make a big bet, either. His argument for investing in risky situations is simple: He and his team have done the research. And they see far more opportunity than risk.

Some of the bonds Hasenstab buys are government-issued bonds from so-called "troubled countries." After extensive research, he buys these bonds because he believes they're "money good" (meaning the bonds are safe and have no risk of default).

For example, in early in 2012, he scooped up Irish debt at $0.50 on the dollar. He was up 70% on those bonds at the end of 2013.

He bought into Hungary during volatile times. That purchase resulted in returns of more than 40% in a two-year span. He's also fared well lending money to Lithuania, Poland, and Mexico.

Second, he's a boots-on-the-ground world traveler. Hasenstab doesn't sit in his San Mateo, Calif., office waiting for the next deal to come across his desk. He treks to numerous overseas countries to see firsthand what's really taking place. Recently, he visited China, South Korea, and even Ukraine.

Here's a picture of the YouTube clip from his Ukraine visit:

The third and most important reason institutional investors love Hasenstab: He outperforms everyone else. Check out the performance of his flagship mutual fund, Templeton Global Bond ($72 billion in assets).

Total Return % (Through 8/31/14)	5-Year	10-Year	15-Year
Templeton Global Bond	7.8	9.3	9.5
Index: Barclays U.S. Agg Bond	4.5	4.7	5.7
Index: Citi WGBI	2.5	4.6	5.2
Category (World Bond)	5.0	5.1	5.8
Rank in Category	10	1	1

Note: The Barclays U.S. Aggregate Bond Index is the global benchmark used for bonds. And Franklin Templeton uses the Citi WGBI for its benchmark.

As you can see, Hasenstab crushes the competition. He took the helm at Templeton Global Bond in 2001. His fund has beaten the Citi World Government Bond Index (WGBI) by 83% since then. And he's beaten his peers by an average of 64% over that timeframe as well. That makes Templeton Global Bond the top-performing fund in its category over that time.

Five- and 10-year returns show similar outperformance. Templeton Global Bond also holds the No. 1 ranking over the last 10 years.

Now, I'm not recommending you invest in Hasenstab's mutual fund today...

I've found a cheaper way to access his strategy... and it will protect us if interest rates start rising in the next few years.

Other Things You Should Know about Michael Hasenstab...

- He's only 40 years old. Chances are he'll be making money for us a lot longer than Warren Buffett (84), Bill Gross (70), and Dan Fuss (80).

- He was named Morningstar's Fixed-Income Manager of the Year in Canada (2013). And Morningstar's Fixed-Income Manager of the Year in the U.S. (2010).

- *InvestmentNews* recognized him as one of the most influential fund managers of 2010.

- *Bloomberg Markets* elected him Top Global Manager in 2010. And Top U.S. and Global Bond Fund Manager in 2009.

- *Investment Week* dubbed him Global Bond Manager of the Year in 2008, 2010, and 2011.

- *BusinessWeek* titled him Best Global Manager.

Hasenstab's Protection Against Rising Interest Rates

We don't have to fret about interest rates rising with this investment. Hasenstab has been worried about this for years.

He believes we're at a turning point in interest rates. For 30 years, rates have been coming down. And he thinks that's over. He's positioning his portfolio to combat the threat of rising rates.

How's he doing it?

He keeps the fund's duration short—about two years. (Duration is a measure of a bond's price sensitivity to interest rate changes. You can expect a portfolio of securities with a lower duration to be less sensitive to interest rate changes than a portfolio with a higher duration.)

By keeping a short duration, Hasenstab's portfolio won't be subject to the negative price effects when rates go higher. In contrast, the Citi WGBI's duration is over seven years. And the duration of the Barclays U.S. Aggregate Bond Index is five-plus years.

A short duration is just one of Hasenstab's safety measures. Another is his broad diversification.

Hasenstab's Diverse Strategy

Hasenstab finds value among currencies, bonds, and interest rates in countries with healthy or improving fundamentals. This often occurs in countries the market dislikes.

He avoids low-yielding bonds from many developed countries. Hasenstab doesn't like countries with large debt balances or poor policymaking—since none of these characteristics are good for bond owners.

One sweet spot he's found is emerging markets. About two-thirds of the fund's debt exposure is in emerging markets. Hasenstab thinks many developing countries have better fiscal policies and prospects.

But he's not about to place money on risky bets. He avoids many of the countries his rivals love, such as the U.S., Japan, and India.

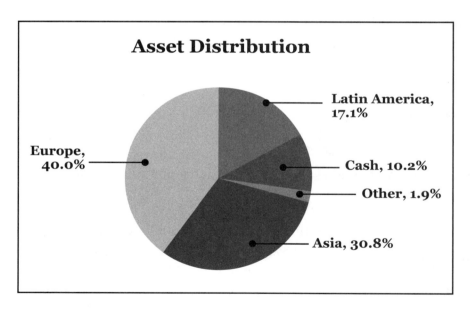

Asset Distribution

Latin America, 17.1%

Europe, 40.0%

Cash, 10.2%

Other, 1.9%

Asia, 30.8%

I could get into the details about more of the tools Hasenstab uses to generate his great returns. But that would get too technical for the scope of this essay.

The takeaway is this: We're covering some new ground with this recommendation—foreign investments, emerging markets, currencies, etc. The important thing to know is that Hasenstab is a seasoned portfolio manager who knows what he's doing. He's achieved stellar returns using these tools in the past—so the bigger his toolkit, the better off we'll be as shareholders.

You'd think we'd have to pay an outrageous fee to access Hasenstab's skills. But that's not the case.

How We're Getting Super-Cheap Expertise

The average closed-end fund has an expense ratio of 1.63% (that's the annual cost you pay). There's a reason the average expense ratio is high: Funds must count borrowing costs (i.e., leverage) in their expense ratios.

The average closed-end fund uses about 30% leverage. This means the fund takes on additional debt to maximize returns. This can be good or bad. While it allows the fund to achieve higher returns, it also increases volatility and market risk.

We don't have to worry about leverage in GIM's case. Hasenstab doesn't use it—he's more conservative. And this helps keep the expense ratio low.

GIM's expense ratio is only 0.72%. It's 56% cheaper than the average closed-end fund.

What does this mean in dollars and cents? With a $1,000 investment, you're paying only $7.20 in expenses per year. Well worth it for Hasenstab's expertise.

So why haven't more investors tapped into his talent... especially since it comes so cheap?

A Relatively Unknown Investment

I called two of my contacts at Franklin Templeton to see what else I could find out about GIM.

To my surprise, they both told me the same thing: We don't market our closed-end funds. Franklin Templeton doesn't even have a department or any employees covering its closed-end funds.

"Sorry, Grant, everything we have is on our website," they said.

I admit: I was a little frustrated with their response. Why was this difficult to get information on the fund?

I checked the website. It was almost bare. I found a few statistics, annual and semi-annual reports, and the transfer agent's contact information.

Then it dawned on me...

How many investors buy, track, or even know of closed-end funds? The answer: not many. Closed-end funds have been around for over a century. But they hold only $286 billion in total assets. Compared to ETFs ($1.7 trillion) and mutual funds ($17-plus trillion), they're tiny.

Now, a closed-end fund is part stock, part mutual fund. Like a mutual fund, a professional manager invests in bonds and/or stocks. And like a stock, it trades on an exchange.

Now, bigger institutions know of closed-end funds. But they have a hard time buying them. With a limited supply of shares, it's difficult to purchase large quantities. Just like at my old wealth management firm, we couldn't buy $60 million-plus of this closed-end fund—about 7.5 million shares at today's price—no matter how attractive it was.

As I kept searching, I started to realize something: This investment is concealed from mom-and-pop investors. The everyday investor buys mutual funds and stocks, not closed-end funds.

This also means the yield chasers would have to go to great lengths to find this fund. And even if they found it, they wouldn't see the hidden income.

That makes Templeton Global Income safe. Let me show you another reason it's safe...

Today's Investment Grows Safer Over Time

Hasenstab has been a terrific performer, as I showed earlier. Remember, he beats the returns of other bond indexes and other international bond managers.

But I wanted to see how safe his fund has been long term. Let's say five years.

So I reached out to one of my Morningstar contacts. I asked him to run rolling five-year returns over the last decade. That means, starting in 2004, I wanted to look at what would happen if you bought GIM at any month-end where you could achieve a five-year return (basically anytime up until Aug. 2009).

The numbers were even better than I expected.

The spreadsheet showed 61 data points. Each point marked a full five-year period. For example, 08/01/2004 to 07/31/2009... 09/01/2004 to 08/31/2009... and so on... for 61 data points.

The results: GIM averaged a 13% return for the 61 intervals.

But here's the proof that the fund gets safer the longer you hold it...

GIM didn't have a single five-year rolling period where it finished down.

In fact, its lowest five-year return since 2005 was a positive 7.4%.

Now, I'm not saying this fund is never down. It's had down months, quarters, and years. But that's just short-term volatility. Hold the fund for the long term, and the data doesn't lie: Chances are good you will achieve solid returns.

Hasenstab says:

> *It's not always going to be a smooth line. One does have to have a little bit of a longer-term horizon and expect some volatility along the way. With an eye on a multiyear horizon, there are good opportunities to exploit volatility and position for the long term.*

Not only is it safe over a longer holding period, but we can improve our returns another way: via a discounted price...

The Time to Buy Is Now

In buying Templeton Global Income today, we'll get combined income of 9%.

And this closed-end fund is safe... at least 75% of the portfolio is rated at BBB (investment grade) or higher.

It's under the radar because closed-end funds don't get the attention of stocks, bonds, and mutual funds... Its manager protects against rising rates with a short-duration, diversified portfolio... And the fund's superior performance over the long term is unmatched.

We'll hold GIM for at least five years. And there's no reason we can't hold this fund for a lot longer. Here's what you need to do...

Action to Take: Buy Templeton Global Income (NYSE: GIM) up to $8.50. We're not using a stop loss. Do not invest more than 5% of your portfolio in Templeton Global Income.

Editor's Note: If you have the option, buy GIM in your retirement account. Not only does it pay steady income, it can pay out short- and long-term capital gains.

PART 5:

Bet on Yourself

CHAPTER 17

How to Get Rich as an Employee

By Mark Morgan Ford

I was three months into my new job as managing editor for a startup newsletter business in South Florida, and I was nervous. With good reason. I was 32, and most of the writers reporting to me were at least twice my age. I needed to quickly develop my management skills, so I enrolled in an executive training program at a local chapter of the Dale Carnegie Institute.

It was a 14-week program. Each week, we'd read a chapter of Carnegie's famous book, *How to Win Friends and Influence People.* Then we'd come to class prepared to stand before our classmates and tell them, in five minutes or less, just how we're incorporating that information into our business lives.

The first week was about remembering names. I was never good at that, but Carnegie had some useful techniques that I remember to this day.

The second week was about setting goals. Carnegie said that most people fail to accomplish much in life because they don't set goals.

But, he said, there are also some people who fail to achieve success because they have *too many* goals.

Our instructor warned us that anyone with that problem would have trouble with our next challenge: list all our goals, narrow them down to 10, narrow them further to three, and then finally select one—and one only—as the sole goal we would focus on for the next 12 weeks.

I had no trouble listing dozens of goals, and relatively little trouble narrowing that long list down to 10. Narrowing it down to three, though, was tough. It took me six days of arguing with myself. The three goals I ended up with were to be a writer, to be a teacher, and to be a rich guy.

But then I had to select one of them as my primary goal, and I just couldn't do it. It was crazy. I knew that if I focused on just one goal, I would achieve it—but I didn't want to give any of them up!

I was still stymied when I stepped up to the podium the next evening. I was prepared to tell my classmates that I had failed the challenge.

But as I picked up the microphone, I knew what I had to do. "I'm going for the money!" I said to myself. Because I realized that once I achieved that goal, I would have the freedom to pursue all of my other goals.

So that's what I did. I told my classmates that the goal I would be focusing on was to get rich. And what a difference that made!

I didn't stop to ask myself, "How are you going to get rich?" Knowing what my goal was, I woke up the next day raring to go. I couldn't wait to get to the office. In fact, I arrived an hour earlier than I normally did. And from that moment on, I looked at almost everything I did in terms of how it would affect my chances of getting rich.

I realized almost immediately, for example, that the time I'd been spending on trying to improve the literary quality of our newsletters had been foolishly spent. If I wanted to get big salary increases, I would have to figure out how to make our newsletters more profitable. So my interest in grammar and punctuation took a nosedive, while my interest in sales and marketing soared.

Having one goal to guide me made everything easier. Questions that would have puzzled me before were suddenly easy to answer. Decisions that would have taken days or weeks to make were made in minutes. Problems that used to be vexing had simple solutions.

From Ordinary to Extraordinary

Within weeks, I went from being a modestly good employee to a rising star. I revamped our editorial products, making them easier to read and easier to sell. I fired two writers that I should have fired weeks earlier and replaced them with up-and-comers. I spent a lot of time reading our company marketing materials and trying to understand how newsletters were sold. I even tried my hand at writing advertising copy.

A few months later, my boss called me into his office to tell me how happy he was with what I had been doing—and announced that he was doubling my salary.

It was an extremely generous offer. But I told him that, as much as I appreciated it, it wasn't enough.

He was flabbergasted. "Not enough?" he shouted. "I just doubled your salary!"

"You see," I told him, "I've decided to become rich. And I have an idea I've been working on that I think will convince you to give me even more money."

I then handed him a package. It contained my idea for a new investment advisory product—all the details—including a sales letter.

He stared at the package.

"And how, exactly, is this going to make you rich?" he asked.

"It's a great product," I said. "It will make money for you. And if you cut me in on the profits..."

He shoved the package into a drawer and kicked me out of his office.

The next day, he called me back in.

"You're right," he said. "You've come up with a great idea." He told me he thought what I had come up with was worth about $250,000!

"And if you want a stake in it," he continued, "I'll cut you in at 10%..."

I smiled.

"But... You have to come up with $25,000—10% of the capitalization."

I frowned.

I wasn't quite sure what that meant. It seemed odd to me that he would value my idea so highly and then ask me to pay for 10% of it. But this was a take-it-or-leave-it offer, so I agreed.

And then I realized I didn't have any money. So I did something I would have never done before. I asked him to lend me the $25,000. And he agreed.

(Later, after I'd learned something about business and investing, I realized he was teaching me a necessary lesson about the value of money. Ideas are wonderful, but capital is invaluable.)

So that's how my journey from being an ordinary employee to a valuable employee to an invaluable employee began.

I was $25,000 in debt, but I had a chance—a reasonable chance—to change my fortunes for good.

From Money Earner to Money Maker

My idea was to create a service for people who wanted to become rich. It would provide stock tips, but it would also provide tax saving and avoidance strategies, international investment opportunities, and a whole lot more.

It wasn't an especially clever idea, but it hadn't been done before. My boss/partner and I worked together, adding extra benefits and refining the sales copy. Finally, after several months, it was ready. We printed up 50,000 pieces and put them in the mail.

It was a huge success!

It was also the beginning of my very intense, 10-year apprenticeship in the world of making money.

We expanded into specialized financial publications, then into consumer magazines, and finally into marketing a wide range of merchandise, including televisions, radios, luggage, watches, and jewelry.

My boss/partner also introduced me to the idea of investing in businesses that supported our primary business—a typesetting company, a letter shop, a printing operation, and an advertising agency.

What I Learned on the Road to Riches

If you are an employee now and are wondering about the feasibility of getting rich... you can do it. But as an employee, there is really only one way to get rich...

You must first make your boss richer. And if he has a boss, you must make him richer, as well. Your ultimate goal is to make the owner of the company much richer—and the only way to do that is to make the company much more profitable.

So how do you do that?

You start from where you are and take small, sensible steps in the right direction. You begin with the skills and knowledge you currently have and add the skills and knowledge you lack.

In other words, you begin as an ordinary employee and become an extraordinary employee. And after you've accomplished that, you become an invaluable employee.

But there is a caveat: You must be working for the right kind of company—a company that is ready and able to give you the opportunity to help it grow.

Put another way, the road to riches as an employee is a journey of three legs.

1. First, you must find a job with the right company.
2. Then, you must become a valuable employee.
3. And finally, you must become an invaluable employee.

Finding the Right Company

There are three kinds of businesses that can provide the environment you are looking for:

Big corporations

Big corporations will pay you serious money if you are at the top of their food chain. A senior vice president of a billion-dollar business can easily make $350,000-750,000 per year.

But if you like the idea of working for a big company, be prepared. You will be competing with hundreds of very smart, very well connected, hardworking people. You will have to be not just extremely good at your job, but also politically shrewd. Because all big companies suffer from some amount of corporate politics. And even if you have what it takes to rise to the top, doing so will likely take 10-20 years.

* Financial service businesses

Brokerages, banks, and insurance companies are happy to pay their best people $250,000-1 million or more—if they can perform. Career paths at this level include portfolio managers, marketers, and salespeople.

But becoming a top-notch portfolio manager is not easy. It takes years of hard work and a degree of luck. The same can be said for the very best marketers, the people responsible for devising strategies to bring in new customers. And to become a top salesperson, you have to be very good and very aggressive. You may even have to put aside your scruples about treating your customers right.

* Small companies with big potential

This was my choice as a young man, and I don't regret it. Starting out with a small company, especially if you are young, gives you a fast track to big money that you won't get in a big corporate environment. It also gives you several ways to become a big moneymaker without sacrificing your principles.

Becoming a Valuable Employee

Whatever type of company you choose, your journey to wealth begins by establishing yourself as a valuable employee.

Most employees go through their lives working for businesses they care nothing much about, dealing with problems they'd rather not face, and getting paid very ordinary wages. They would like to earn more. They may even be willing to do more. But their ambitions are sporadic and fleeting. Most of the time, they are simply showing up.

Such employees are never going to get substantial raises. They can expect their salary to rise very slowly and very gradually. From 1984-2014, for example, the average salary rose by around 3.5%, according to the Average Wage Index.

But a valuable employee could easily get twice that. And at 7% per year, a $50,000 salary turns into about $98,000 in 10 years, $193,000 in 20 years, and $380,000 in 30 years.

There are four ways to distinguish yourself as an employee and see your compensation accelerate at a faster pace:

1. Work longer hours.

Don't fall for that goofy idea that good employees get their work done between nine and five. If you want your bosses to notice you as someone who is willing to do more, begin by working longer hours.

How many extra hours?

An hour per day is good. Two hours is better. If you can do a little work at home on weekends, that's not bad either.

If at all possible, put in your extra hours at the beginning of the day. Getting to work early is a common virtue of almost all successful people. There is something about getting in earlier than everyone else that seems nobler, smarter, or just plain more industrious than working late.

In *How to Become CEO*, Jeffrey J. Fox puts it this way: "Arriving to work late signals you don't like your job very much. Even if you prefer to come in late and stay late, staying late sends the signal that you can't keep up or your personal life is poor."

You are working more hours for three reasons. You want to do more than your peers. You want to learn more than your peers. And you want to be sure that your bosses—the people who will eventually promote you—know how extraordinary you are.

2. Develop a distinctly positive and infectiously enthusiastic attitude.

Nobody likes a sourpuss—even if the sourpuss is a genius. Become the person who arrives at work with energy, greets his coworkers warmly, volunteers for assignments enthusiastically, and seems very happy with his career.

3. Say "Yes!"

Much has been written about the virtues of saying no. But if you want your boss to support your efforts to move up in the company, you have to support him by making his job easier. You do this by saying yes. By saying yes if he asks you for a favor... by saying yes to taking on that extra project... and even by saying yes when you mean no.

4. Advertise your accomplishments.

It's not enough to be positive, to say yes, and to work more hours. In order to make sure the extra efforts you're making are noticed, you have to advertise them. Doing a good job of self-promotion (without coming off as a braggart) means that you always give others some of the credit for your accomplishments.

Becoming an Invaluable Employee

Valuable employees earn good salaries. But *invaluable* employees earn great salaries.

You become an invaluable employee by embracing a simple truth: The lifeblood of a business is profits. So if you can help increase your company's profits, you will be rewarded.

There are only a limited number of ways to make a business more profitable. You can help create or improve your company's products.

You can help market those products to new and existing customers. You can help manage profits by decreasing costs and raising margins.

How do you get yourself into sales, marketing, product creation, or profit management?

Identify the people in your company who are already doing those jobs. (They are almost certainly the ones who make the most money.) Tell them you're interested in learning more about their end of the business, and offer to help them out in your free time.

As you learn more, you will be able to do more. And your contributions to the business can gradually shift in the direction of creating profits.

CHAPTER 18

How to Start a Million-Dollar Business for $25,000

By Mark Morgan Ford

I've got it pretty darn good. I work only when I want to work. I can work anywhere in the world. I work only with people I like. I do only the kind of work I want to do. And I make a lot of money.

If that isn't the definition of having it good, what is?

I travel about three months out of every year. This past year, I was in England, France, Germany, Belgium, Spain, Nicaragua, and Argentina—not to mention New York, Washington, D.C., San Francisco, and Yellowstone National Park. When I travel, I take my computer with me. I spend half of my waking hours visiting parks, shops, and museums... and going to concerts, dance performances, and the theater. I spend the other half working on my computer.

And because my business interests are international, travel is largely first-class and paid for by one of the companies I consult for.

My office is more a grown-up version of a boy's tree house than it is a workplace, complete with a personal gym, jujitsu room, billiard table, movie-screening room, and art studio. It is located 1.1 miles (a ten-minute jog) from my main home, which is in one of America's best cities, on the Atlantic Ocean in South Florida.

I take off early when I want to and come in late anytime I wish. I have eliminated all of the stress that used to characterize most of my workday.

And if I want to, I can do no work at all for six months or a year or forever.

In short, I am living the dream.

The purpose of all of this self-congratulatory talk is to tempt you to heed my advice. The reason I have this great life is due to one thing and one thing only: About 30 years ago, I decided to become an entrepreneur.

The most profitable thing I have ever done in my entire career of building wealth has been to invest in start-up businesses. Last time I checked, the returns I have enjoyed as an investor in small businesses have exceeded 25% per year.

There was a time when people thought they could earn that kind of ROI in the stock market. That was a very stupid and very costly notion.

If you are a great investor, you can make 10-15% in the stock market. But you can make 10 percentage points more than that, on average, by starting and/or funding small businesses that you understand.

Start-up businesses have given me so much—a steady growth of income, a base of wealth that has doubled every three years, the opportunity to get involved in so many other, interesting investments, and a rich and stimulating business life.

Although I sometimes grouse about working too hard, the truth is that I *love* starting new businesses. It's challenging, but it's also a great deal of fun. And when the business starts to work and the money starts flowing... well, it feels pretty damn good.

Thirty years ago, my track record at starting new businesses was a very mixed bag. But these days, I am usually confident that the businesses will work. This kind of confidence comes from 25 years of accumulated experiences, good and bad, and learning from them.

So if you were to ask me, "What is the absolute fastest way to become rich?" I'd have to answer: by starting a small business.

That's *my* answer. It doesn't mean it has to be *your* answer. You may not want to invest the time and energy that it takes to be a successful entrepreneur. You may be too timid. You may be too tired. You may lack the self-confidence to launch your own thing. But I'm hoping I can persuade you to consider this path.

If you are willing to become an entrepreneur—even a part-time entrepreneur—you will be amply rewarded. Not only can you double (or even triple) your money every three years, you can also enjoy the many other benefits of being your own boss:

- The freedom to choose your own schedule
- The power to create your own products
- The excitement of being fully challenged
- The knowledge that you are providing an income for your employees.

My friend Anna W. asked me to help her start a business based on her love of music. She'd been looking over her current retirement plan and figured out that if she keeps her present job and continues to increase her responsibility and her income, she will be able to have a comfortable retirement in 14 years (at age 67).

That's not bad. Most people in her age bracket won't do that well.

But if she puts her energy and resources into creating a successful business of her own, she can look forward to a much better return on her "investment."

Anna is going to start her new business on the side, working evenings and weekends. She's going to find a partner to back her, develop her product, and take it to market. When we went over the numbers, it became clear to Anna that this secondary business—if it is successful (and I'm pretty sure it will be)—will allow her to achieve her retirement goals in five years instead of 14, while she is still relatively young.

At that point, she can do whatever she wants to do with the rest of her life

That's what a business can do for you.

Think about your own financial situation. Are you okay as you are—or would it be helpful to triple your money every three years?

If you need that kind of way-above-average ROI in your life, you simply have to consider starting your own business. Don't quit your day job. Just get something going on the side. You don't have to invest a ton of money or work endless hours. You can do well starting small.

Here are five proven (and absolutely true, in my experience) secrets of highly successful entrepreneurs that will help turn you into a business-building genius. These are very general principles. I am just touching on them here.

Secret No. 1: Don't Spend Too Much Time Planning

When you are entering a market, you don't know (and couldn't possibly understand) the hidden problems and challenges you will face. You won't understand those problems until you make a few mistakes. And you won't solve them (and go on to making a success of your new business) unless you are capable of changing directions quickly.

Most successful new businesses (probably 90% of them) end up following practices that are different than anticipated. That's why it doesn't pay to spend too much time and money planning. Do a reasonable amount of noodling. Figure out the big strokes and give yourself a bailout option. Then go for it. He who can adapt wins.

Secret No. 2: Don't Spend Too Much Money

The vast majority of business start-ups that succeed do so on limited budgets. Almost none of them have the benefit of venture capital funding.

The great majority of new businesses are hampered (and enhanced) by flying on empty. People involved in businesses that have limited funds must think harder, work harder, and (most importantly) sell harder. Their primary initial effort is to bring in the cash. And that's how it should be. There is only one thing that will surely stop any business in its tracks: a lack of cash flow. Ironically, limited capital usually means a quicker and stronger cash flow.

Secret No. 3: Get Operational Fast

The most common reason for new product/project failures is wasting time *getting ready*. Between making overlong and expensive business plans, endlessly tinkering with the product, fooling around with focus groups, and second-guessing yourself, it's easy to let a good product/project lose its steam.

Bootstrappers don't mind starting with a copycat idea targeted to a small market. Imitation saves the cost of market research—and the start-up entering a small market is unlikely to face competition from large, established companies.

Secret No. 4: Go for the Quick Cash First

Contrary to what some business books may say, successful entrepreneurs are almost always those who take the fastest route to cash when launching a new venture. They do so because they don't have a choice. (See Secret No. 2.) After the cash starts coming in, they have the time and funds to improve the product, enhance customer service, and refine operations.

Keep in mind that the best-laid plans are often arrogant. You don't know for sure how to best serve the market. When launching a new business or product, figure out how you can get to breakeven fastest. This kind of thinking will *force* you to pay closer attention to the market. And the market is your master.

Secret No. 5: Forget About the Crack Team—You Are It

Successful entrepreneurs don't hire experts to run their businesses. They figure it out for themselves. When it comes to making your new product/project work, rely on nobody but yourself to make sure it gets done right. It may be stressful and time-consuming to do a lot of extra work, but it will pay off in the long run. You will understand the project in an intimate, extremely valuable way.

You should want to learn about how your business works from the bottom up. You should want to know how to buy the products and services you learn. You should want to understand how to hire the best people. And most of all, you should want to understand how to bring in new customers at an acceptable cost. This is the key to every successful start-up.

Having started hundreds of successful small businesses in my career, I am bold enough to think that I understand how the start-up and development process works. I outlined it all in my book *Ready, Fire, Aim*. In my humble opinion, it is the best book ever written about starting and growing an entrepreneurial business.

Take Action Now

If you listen to what I tell you and make it a point to keep yourself informed and educated, I have to believe you will come out a big winner.

There are dozens, if not hundreds, of small businesses you could start this year. With the advent of the Internet market, there is virtually nothing you like to do that can't be turned into a business.

My success rate in business is probably 80-90% these days. The main reason is not that I know so much more than I used to (although I do) but that I'm much more reluctant to get into something I don't understand.

Make yourself a promise to devote a good part of your time this year to creating and/or developing a second stream of income. Allocate learning time every week. Develop a three-page business plan. Make at least one new contact every month—and use those contacts to start your business.

No matter what type of side business you decide to start, assign to it a specific financial target each year, and reach that target by figuring out how much you have to accomplish every month to get there. Break those monthly targets down to weekly objectives and the weekly objectives down to daily tasks.

But don't feel overwhelmed. I do not want you to quit your job and risk your life savings. I will show you how you can start slowly, from your home, investing only modest sums, working weekends or evenings, and build your little business slowly until you can figure out the best products and how to sell them. Much of this you can get from reading my book *The Reluctant Entrepreneur*.

When that's done—and that should take about a year (maybe less)— you'll be ready to hop onto that 25% train.

The Art of Chicken Entrepreneurship

When Mary Kay Ash retired from her job in 1963, she took her life savings, $5,000, and opened her own business. Boy, did it pay off! Mary Kay Cosmetics is now a billion-dollar company.

Or take Hugh Hefner. He financed *Playboy* with $8,000 in loans from 45 family members, friends, and other investors. Today, he's a mega-millionaire. (His famous mansion alone appraises at more than $45 million.)

Successful entrepreneurs like Ash and Hefner who risked all their money (and sometimes their family's money) to pursue dreams that others considered foolish get lots of press. And with good reason. Their stories are exciting and inspirational. But they are also misleading.

These risk-taking entrepreneurs are the exception. Most business builders succeed by taking a far more conservative approach.

In *The Leap*, Rick Smith uses Bill Gates as an example. Contrary to popular belief, Gates didn't drop out of Harvard, says Smith. He took a leave of absence—and relied on his parents' financial support—while he developed his programming skills and made the contacts that led to Microsoft. If it hadn't worked out, he could have gone back to finish school.

Look at Ben and Jerry. The two budding moguls started by selling their ice cream from a converted Vermont gas station. They had thought about opening a bagel shop. But they decided the equipment would be too expensive. It was only after two years in business that they expanded into wholesaling their products to local stores.

Google was a side project of two Stanford grad students. Michael Dell started what would become Dell Inc. in a University of Texas dorm room for just $1,000. Apple's first computers were hand-built in a garage and sold to local computer geeks. Wayne Huizenga started Waste Management with just one garbage truck. And he drove it himself!

Read the biographies of successful people and you will discover the truth. Most of them started small and took modest, calculated risks.

They were not reckless and brave, as the business magazines would have you believe.

Yes, starting your own business is the fastest and surest way to grow wealthy. But you don't have to—in fact, you shouldn't—risk everything to claim your slice of the entrepreneurial pie.

I have started dozens of multimillion-dollar businesses. But I have never been willing to "bet the farm" on one.

I want all the benefits that come from owning a business. But I refuse to risk my hard-earned money or time on an unproven idea. I want my cake. And I want to eat it too.

That's why I call myself a "chicken entrepreneur."

A chicken entrepreneur is somebody who keeps his day job while he gets his ideal career going in the evenings and on weekends. He is an entrepreneur because he is taking the initiative to start his own business. He is chicken because he's not willing to quit his day job and lose the income.

I have done my best to promote this concept in all of the business and self-help books I have written, including my most recent book, *The Reluctant Entrepreneur*. My primary point has always been, "You don't have to be a wild and crazy risk-taker when starting a business."

Let me tell you about "Alan Silver." (I profiled him in *Seven Years to Seven Figures*.) Alan has a multimillion-dollar health supplement business. He does what he wants when he wants. He spends much of the winter skiing from his vacation home in Park City, Utah. And when he's back home in Florida, you can often find him on the golf course after doing a couple of hours of work in the morning.

He started as a chicken entrepreneur.

A friend of his, a newsletter publisher, was starting a publication on natural health. One day he mentioned to Alan, quite casually, that he was looking for someone to sell vitamins to his subscribers.

Alan, who had been selling office supplies for 15 years, stepped up. With his friend's help and mentorship, he started his own company with a very small initial investment. Mostly, he invested time and energy.

The going was rough at the beginning. He didn't know anything about marketing, supplements, or the health industry. But he was willing to learn. Keeping his sales job while working on the new business meant 10-hour days. But it was worth it.

Within six months, this side business had brought in more than $250,000 in sales. Alan reinvested most of the profits back into the business at first. But soon he was making enough to quit selling office supplies. And within a few years, he was bringing in $10 million annually.

And Alan isn't the only one. These are just some of the people I've personally mentored:

- CF built her specialized physical-therapy business from zero to $90,000 in 15 months.

- JF's financial teaching program for children is paying him close to $100,000 per year after less than three years.

- WC made $250,000 in less than 18 months—on top of his regular salary—by running a mail-order business I helped him with.

- PR built his health-product business to more than $20 million in six years (and became a multimillionaire doing so).

- KY's business pays her a very nice salary—plus, she shares $500,000 in profits from a career-counseling program that's less than 10 years old.

It's Definitely Worth a Small Investment of Money
and a Large Investment of Time

Having your own business is not the only way to get rich, but it is—far and away—the way that most people do it. Statistically speaking, it is your most likely road to success. It also gives you a chance to eventually become super-rich—to join the $50-million-plus club.

Maybe you think that a small business built from your kitchen table won't amount to much. You'd be wrong.

For example, with less than $10,000 each, I helped friends start American Writers and Artists Inc. (AWAI) and *Early to Rise*—now both multimillion-dollar publishing businesses.

Every business, from your local landscaper to General Electric, started with that first sale.

With each passing year, your business will grow—and that will give you greater cash flow and the potential for a bigger payout when you're ready to retire.

In two or three years, your side business should be big enough to hire you as the CEO. Then, and only then, can you quit your current job.

Once you become CEO, things should really skyrocket. You'll be able to devote all your time and energy to this one single enterprise, and the benefits of all of that concentration will pay off.

But maybe you don't want to be a multimillionaire business owner. Maybe you just want to work for yourself.

If you are retired or unemployed, you can choose to do the work—and that way, you'll be both the owner of a microbusiness and its only employee. But you could also get a friend or relative to do the work, pay them a good salary, and still have a good second income.

Either way, you earn a good living, enjoy a great deal of independence, and—if you follow the advice we're going to give you—you can even get rich.

Chicken entrepreneurs who start microbusinesses do it because they want to give up the routine of commuting to a 9-to-5 job and take on the fun of managing and growing their own little service enterprise. They can make decent money working on their own—often as much as they'd earn elsewhere as an employee—and they can choose their own hours, customers, work clothes, etc.

But some of them find that there's also a way to make a microbusiness into a gold mine.

Basically, here's how you do it...

After investing a few years as the main employee of your microbusiness, you hire someone to replace you and pay him roughly 50-70% of what you were making. Now, instead of earning, say, $80,000 per year, you'll earn $30,000—but you'll be working only 10 hours per week.

By adding other people to your pool... selling franchises, as it were... you can double, triple, or even quadruple your take-home pay without appreciably increasing your workload.

So, you can turn a small amount of money into a lot.

However, it's going to require a large investment of your time. You will essentially be working two jobs, dedicating 50 hours or more to your day job, plus another 20 hours or more to your business. But it's worth it.

For one thing, there is tremendous satisfaction in charting your own course and seeing it through. And when you begin to employ other people, and you will, you create wealth not just for yourself but for them, as well.

Types of Business

Whatever type of business you intend to start—whether it's landscaping or selling landscapes—all businesses fall into one of four categories:

1. Retail
2. Service
3. Wholesale
4. Manufacturing.

You could call this an oversimplification, but the world of business does fall into these four categories. Each has its own pluses and minuses.

What About Retail?

Retail is usually the first thing most people think of when they think of business. They think of restaurants and supermarkets, bookstores and movie theaters. The retail business often seems fun and easy. For that reason, it is very attractive. But the reality of working in the retail sector is usually very different.

There are several distinguishing features of retail that set it apart from the other business sectors in terms of how you might enjoy (or detest) the work experience:

First, generally speaking, the retail business requires you to be in one place for regular periods of time. It does not allow for a great deal of flexibility in terms of hours or travel.

Being in the retail business in a serious way (serious enough to make a good living from it) means tethering yourself to a ball and chain. The ball is the store. The chain is your obligation to keep it running properly.

The most common problem retailers have is finding good people to sell the product and protect their merchandise. Finding, training, and managing retail workers is not something that can be done here and there on a hit-or-miss basis.

Second, the retail business is heavily dependent on location. If the city you are in decides to do six months' worth of roadwork right in front of your store, you may go bankrupt waiting for them to finish. Your customers can find somewhere else to go, but you can't. You're chained to that location.

While this is going on, you still have to pay all of your bills, including rent, utilities, and employee expenses. You can boost sales with good marketing and sales strategies in the retail business (just as you can with any business), but you can't work miracles. The lion's share of your success will depend on walk-by traffic.

Finally, it's tough to get rich with retail. You can make a living, maybe even a good living, and you can enjoy yourself. But you can't get rich. The only retailers who are rich have thousands of retail operations. But they are not retailers themselves—they are marketers of retail operations. There is a big difference.

So if you (a) don't really like to spend time talking to people, (b) like to travel a lot, and (c) want to get super-rich, then retail is probably a bad choice.

The Service Industry

The service industry is also something that quickly comes to mind when we think about business. Maybe you can start a lawn care service. Or maybe you can hire a bunch of plumbers and have them work for you.

How much you can make depends on what service you provide. But the services that seem the most fun or glamorous usually pay the least. Why? Because of supply and demand. Plenty of bright people vying for a limited number of good positions.

Service businesses include everything from blue-collar hole digging... to mid-level technical work... to white-collar executive work... and, finally, the professions.

Yes, accountants and lawyers are service providers. So are plastic surgeons, speechwriters, and most entertainers. I include entertainers in this category, because they share the essential characteristic of the service sector: At the end of the day, they charge for their time.

Ask people who are undecided about a career what kind of work they want to do. You'll often hear "something that involves working with people."

And that's what is good about the service business. You will, indeed, spend most of your time interacting with people.

Much of that time will be a lot of fun, in which your affability and social skills will come in handy. But some of that time will be stressful. Some of it will be downright disagreeable.

No matter how much of a "people person" you may be, it's hard to enjoy yourself when some rich slob screams at you because he isn't happy with the color of the trampoline your event-planning service provided for his five-year-old's birthday party.

The lower ranks of the service sector are replete with high-stress, low-paying jobs. And the upper echelons don't pay as well as you might think. The average physician, for example, makes about $145,000, and the average dentist makes about $116,000 per year. The average attorney makes a measly $108,000.

As you can see, I'm not too hot on service-sector businesses. It seems to me that they offer a layer of fun and/or glamour... but deliver lots of stressful hours at relatively modest pay.

Service is a great entry-level business opportunity, because it's an easy industry to get into. If you make up your mind to do a great (not just good) job at a fair or cheaper-than-average rate, meet your deadlines, and keep your promises, you'll find yourself climbing to the top of the ladder in no time flat.

As your business grows, you can gradually increase your fees. If you work hard to find good workers and offer them the chance to develop in their own right, your business will grow. Eventually, you won't be doing any of the actual service work yourself. You'll just develop new client relationships and renew old ones.

Of course, the problem with the service industry goes hand-in-hand with its main advantage. It's so easy to get into that you will have lots of competition as your business grows. That competition will squeeze your prices, making profits tough to get and salaries low. This is especially true of service industries such as travel and anything to do with the media.

The Wholesale Business

Wholesale is a pretty good business, although it takes a while to develop. ("Wholesale" relates to the sale of goods in large quantities, as for resale by a retailer.)

Today, the opportunity for wholesale is in China and Indonesia. Those countries can make anything that's made in the U.S., but at a fraction of the cost.

But getting good, inexpensive products is only the beginning.

The tough part of wholesale is developing a customer list of retailers. And, unfortunately, your customers will eventually figure out that they can probably cut you out and buy directly from the manufacturer.

The secret is to develop unique products that others cannot

duplicate. You won't be able to do this right off the bat. But over time, it's the way to go.

Once you've developed your unique product, you'll need to sell it to retailers. This will involve going to trade shows, which can be expensive and time-consuming.

The top trade shows, for example, can cost thousands of dollars to attend. You will spend a lot of time talking with retailers and displaying your product, and you may end up with no cash—just a pile of orders to fill later.

Discouraging as it may seem, this is where you have the potential to make the big money. You could possibly take orders worth tens of thousands of dollars. (Remember, though, that you won't see the cash up front. You'll receive payment for those orders over a long period of time.)

My Favorite Type of Business

My favorite type of business is what I'm calling "manufacturing." And in that general category, I include all sorts of things that you would not normally consider. I include, for example, publishing and the selling of natural products, nutritional products, and so on.

Manufacturing, to me, is any industry in which you create the product and sell it directly to the end user.

I love this type of business... It gives you complete control over the entire selling process—from inventing the product to closing the sale and even going back to the customer for more sales.

In this age of the Internet and globalization, manufacturing is a great business to be in. To create your product, you can use anyone the world over. And you can sell to the entire world.

So if you don't know what you want to do but want to get wealthy while you figure things out, get into a business like manufacturing.

Are You Ready?

Right now, you're an employee, working for someone else. You have the security of a job with a predictable salary and benefits. But you want more. You want to be an entrepreneur, but you're afraid. You're not a risk taker.

It's your vision and action that will start you on the road to entrepreneurship.

Are you ready?

CHAPTER 19

How to Become a Freelance Advertising Copywriter

By Mark Morgan Ford

If you're like the rest of us, you want to improve your financial future. The surest and fastest way to grow your net worth is to increase your income and then direct all of that income toward one of your other investments.

There are infinite income opportunities in the world, but this one is one of the best I know of. I am referring to making extra money as a freelance direct-response copywriter.

What Is a Freelance Direct-Response Copywriter?

It is someone who works from home (or just about anywhere), writing sales messages for companies that sell products *directly* to consumers.

Take Paul H., for example. Paul was stocking shelves in a supermarket when I met him. Now he's making $300,000 per year as a copywriter. This is how Paul describes his life now:

> *I spend most of my time in a little historic town in the Vermont countryside and one week per month a short walk from the beach in South Florida.*

I have no bosses, no commute.

I write from an extra room I set up in my home. Some days, I'll head to the local coffee shop, just for a change of scenery.

For a break, I'll walk over to the old Equinox Resort for lunch—or take our dogs, Yukon and Betty, over to Hildene Meadows for a run.

I absolutely love the freedom of it!

My neighbors think I've taken early retirement—probably because they never see me working.

In many ways, I have retired. Because, for the first time in my life, I decide how my days will be spent. Some days, I'll feel like working for a few hours (typically in the morning). Other days, I'll play some golf, tennis, ski—or just hang out with my 13-year-old son.

But what surprises people most (and may surprise you, too) is the income my "retirement" lifestyle gives me: around $300,000 per year.

The income potential from copywriting is significant. If Paul wanted to work fewer hours, he could do so at the drop of a hat. He could work just two hours per day and make $60,000. Or half days and make $150,000.

You can see why direct-response copywriting is so high on my list. It's da money!

But it's not just the money that makes being a freelance copywriter so appealing. It's the freedom it gives you to create your "ideal" career.

That's what Krista J. did. After 18 years as an engineer, Krista was ready to find a less stressful, more satisfying career. "It was easy for me to walk away from my career after I [learned the skill of copywriting]. I had all of the work I could handle. I feel like I'm finally leading the life I was meant to live."

Paul began copywriting as a 30-year-old. Krista was also in her 30s. But you can get into the game at any age. Take Starr D., who became a copywriter at 58 after she was laid off from her job as a quality control coordinator.

Starr describes her transition into copywriting:

> I realized I was living the copywriter's life when I became glad I had lost my corporate job. Believe me, I was terribly insulted when it happened, and it was a huge blow to my confidence. But now I know I have the skill and determination to depend on myself—not someone else, and especially not a corporation that viewed me as a statistic rather than a real person. Now I don't worry about the company's bottom line—I take care of my own.

Starr has been a copywriter for several years now, and she says, "The freedom factor just keeps getting better. I can take a two-hour lunch and go for a swim. I can run to the school and pick up a sick grandchild. And I can work from anywhere I like—home, the bookstore, while traveling. Absolutely nothing beats being your own boss!"

And importantly, you don't have to commit yourself to working full time to enjoy the benefits of copywriting. Many people work part time as freelance copywriters to supplement their current incomes.

Let's take a closer look at this income opportunity.

What Is Direct-Response Marketing?

Companies use direct response to sell everything from mattresses to financial newsletters... from health supplements to fruit baskets. Nonprofits—from political candidates to environmental

---

organizations to children's aid groups—raise billions using direct-response techniques, as well.

And let's not forget the multibillion-dollar business-to-business market, one of the most lucrative and in-demand niches of the direct-response industry for copywriters.

All of them use direct response, because a well-written letter can bring in millions of dollars—for a fraction of the cost of opening a storefront or selling wholesale to retailers.

Direct-response marketing allows companies to reach the people and businesses most likely to buy their products... simply by sending letters and emails to those who have shown an interest in similar products in the past.

But a direct-response promotion is nothing without the right words. It needs to convey the right message... say the right things... be structured in the right way... and be written to make the prospective buyer take action.

And these days, more and more selling is done online. Through websites, emails, landing pages, discussion boards, and forums— even through the pages of well-known social media sites like LinkedIn, Facebook, and Twitter... and lesser-known ones like Friendster, MyLife, Ning, Plaxo, XING, and others.

That's where the copywriter comes in.

Income Potential

Advertising copywriters typically make from $50-500 per hour. (That's $100,000-1 million per year, working 40 hours per week.) How much you can make per hour depends on two factors: how good you are and what kind of businesses you work for.

Competent copywriters can find plenty of work writing sales

brochures and letters for local businesses. Writing copy for a six-page brochure, for example, will take between two and five hours—depending on the skill of the copywriter. At the local level, businesses would be happy to pay $500 for a brochure.

Good copywriters tend to work for larger companies with national or international reach. Such companies spend millions of dollars on advertising every year, so their budgets for copywriting are much larger.

Writing a sales package for a new product might take the copywriter 40-60 hours. The compensation for such a package would typically range between $4,000-10,000.

The best copywriters (and there are hundreds of them) charge $10,000-50,000 per package and then demand royalties on sales that their letters generate which can easily double or triple their base fees.

Sometimes royalties can bring them hundreds of thousands of dollars in commissions while the advertisement is running.

I know this chapter seems like sales copy. But I can tell you from having spent more than 30 years teaching ordinary people how to write sales letters that copywriting is a seriously good way to earn extra income.

When Monica D. first heard about the income potential of copywriting about 10 years ago, she was skeptical. But she was "desperate" and "broke," so she decided to give it a try. Three years after making the decision to become a copywriter, she claimed $134,408 on her income tax return. And it was all from copywriting!

Make $206,000 Writing One Letter per Month!

Get paid $206,000 to write 12 letters? It can (and does) happen.

A writer with an established track record can command $8,000 per letter. So 12 letters pays $96,000 in writing fees alone.

Now let's say six of those letters become "controls"—which means they bring in the most money and keep mailing time after time. If, over the course of a year, each of those six letters mails five or six times, your royalties can add up to another $120,000.

That's over $206,000 per year, writing one letter per month!

More letters equal more writing fees. More controls equal more royalties!

The Size of the Opportunity

One of the best-kept secrets in the advertising world is how large the direct-response industry is. When you think of advertising, you typically think of Madison Avenue executives designing magazine ads and television commercials. But the big market for copywriters is the direct-response industry—with yearly sales of $2.3 trillion worldwide.

In fact, direct-response advertising is larger than magazines, television, and radio advertising put together. And it is fast becoming the dominant form of advertising on the Internet, as well.

The leading industry organization, the Direct Marketing Association, cites that there are 1.4 million employees working with direct-marketing companies in the U.S. Because of its immense size, the direct-response advertising industry employs hundreds of thousands of freelance copywriters and is always looking for more.

That means plenty of opportunities for new writers—and the ability for copywriters to pick and choose where they work.

Copywriting Is a Great Transitional Income Opportunity

Most beginning copywriters have part- or full-time jobs. They need to continue making money while they learn their new trade.

Copywriting offers you the chance to do just that. You can learn the skills you need in the evenings, on your lunch breaks, after dinner, or on the weekends. And you can begin your own freelance career working odd hours.

As Ed G. says:

> In 2003, I had advanced to a point in my sales career where weekly travel was inevitable. I was at the top of my field, earning a great living. But as a new dad, I didn't want to be away from home all the time. Plus, I was getting tired of continually rising quotas—an inevitable reality when you're in sales. Eleven years of chasing numbers had worn me out. I was ready for a change. Yet I didn't want to sacrifice my high income and my family's financial future.
>
> Copywriting allowed me to develop the skills I needed to transition away from a six-figure sales career and into a six-figure copywriting business. In my first full year as a freelance copywriter, I earned $163,481.

Copywriting Is a Great Part-Time Retirement Business

If you are retired and dread going back to work full time, copywriting can offer you the opportunity to enjoy a good secondary income without working 40 hours per week. Many copywriters do that, especially after they have achieved their financial goals. They keep writing because they love to and because it brings in extra income—which is always welcome.

Take Kelly R. for example. He wrote to me a while back to thank me for introducing him to the copywriting opportunity. He says, "Working VERY part time (I'm still a full-time high school English teacher), I've just cleared over $40,000 in project fees in the past year."

Fringe Benefits

I've said that direct-response copywriting is one of my favorite extra income opportunities because of the flexibility it offers and also because of the extraordinary income potential. But there are many other benefits, as well.

For example:

You don't have to dress in business clothes. You can work in your underwear. By working at home, communicating with your clients by phone or email, nobody will ever know the difference.

"I don't even have to get out of my PJs," says Penny T., who discovered copywriting after being laid off from her investment-banking job right before Christmas 2002.

You don't have to work with people you don't like. Once you develop expertise in some market, it won't be hard to find as much work as you want. With more potential clients wanting you than you can afford to service, you'll be able to "fire" those who don't value your services (i.e., pay you enough) or are disagreeable in any way.

By learning the skill of copywriting, you can derive all sorts of "fringe" benefits.

You will find that you are a more persuasive thinker and talker. You will better understand advertising as a consumer. And you will become a better thinker simply through the practice of writing copy every day.

Another benefit of being a freelance direct-response copywriter is travel. Since you can write from anywhere, you can work and travel anywhere—while getting paid.

As Paul H. says:

> *I've been on dozens of trips over the years: Barbados, France, Spain, and beautiful five-star resorts throughout Canada and the States. My last trip was a seven-day cruise aboard a Crystal Cruise ship. And since I actually worked on these trips, I paid for none of them.*

If you like to write fiction or essays, learning copywriting can only improve your skills. As Steve Sjuggerud, editor of the investment newsletter *True Wealth*, says, "My success in investing has come from learning and applying the secrets of the investment masters— Soros, Buffett, Templeton, etc. My success as a writer has come from learning and applying the secrets of [copywriting]."

Perhaps the greatest benefit is peace of mind. As Cheryl Malcham, a "retired" freelance copywriter from Mercer Island, Washington, says, "The ability to pay my bills no longer worries me, even in these rough times. I know I can always market my skills to an endless list of clients and keep enough copywriting projects rolling in."

Do You Need a Talent for Writing?

When most people think of writing professionally, they assume that it takes a great deal of natural talent to succeed. And some professional copywriters like to keep this idea alive because it is flattering to them. (I make six figures as a writer. Therefore, I am a creative genius.)

The truth is that having a natural talent for writing, though helpful, is not at all necessary. Some of the best writers in the business have no formal writing background at all. They just like to write and have learned the skill of copywriting.

If you can write a simple letter or tell a simple story, you have the fundamental writing skills you need.

How could this be? Writing novels and poems and essays requires skill and creativity. But writing sales copy is simpler. The reason for that is the most basic principle of the sales process: At the emotional level, most people are the same.

We all tend to respond the same way to exciting stories, to big promises, to hidden secrets, to personal invitations, etc., in a predictable way. Successful salespeople understand those patterns. As a student of direct-response advertising, you can learn those patterns and employ them to write letters that sell.

In my experience, it takes about six months of guided practice to attain competency as a copywriter. At that point, you should be able to begin soliciting clients at the $50-per-hour range. If you continue to practice your trade diligently, you can become relatively expert at copywriting in another 18-24 months.

By that time, you should be able to take on larger clients who will be happy to pay you $100-500 per hour. (You normally don't charge by the hour. You charge by the job. These hourly figures are estimates based on average productivity.)

Josh B. was $200,000 in debt when he discovered copywriting. Within a few years, his life, and that of his family, had completely turned around.

> *This year, we took a 16-day vacation, touring the Southern states. We toured old Southern mansions and plantations, visited a couple of amusement parks, chartered a private boat, and went snorkeling down in the Florida Keys, spent a day touring the mangrove forests and swamps, hunting down alligators, dolphins, and gigantic spiders, and relaxed, talked, learned, experienced, and built incredible memories together.*

My income grew while on the trip. I picked up a couple of more clients. I did very little writing. It was magical and wonderful.

When you consider that we could afford doing this with 10 children, it's a wonder we have any money or sanity left! But actually, we have both in spades and mountains of joy to go with it.

The Process

In a minute I'll tell you how you can get—for free—a really terrific 123-page book that will get you going. But right now I want to go over some of the realities of making this income opportunity work for you.

We all want success to come quickly and easily. But we also know that it usually takes work and time. Let's talk about that.

How Much Time Is Required to Learn the Skill of Copywriting?

First and most importantly, you must recognize that copywriting is a complex skill. It is not nearly as complex as brain surgery but it's more complex than cutting a lawn. I've studied and written about the time it takes to develop a complex skill. My conclusion, in a nutshell, is that it takes about 1,000 hours to achieve competency and five times that time to become a "master."

You don't have to be a master copywriter to earn an income. You can do quite well by being competent. The reason for this I've already explained. The demand is huge. And the supply is limited.

So get that in your head right now. You will have to study and practice for 1,000 hours.

You can cut that down by about a third with instruction. At the end of this chapter, I'll make a few recommendations.

Six hundred and sixty hours is just a bit over four months if you are working full time on it. If you can devote only six hours per week to developing your copywriting chops, it will take just over two years.

I'd like to tell you that you can do it quicker than that, but I'd be lying to you if I did. Not that I haven't had students that beat that record. I have. But they had extraordinary natural talent. For planning purposes, you have to plan for 1,000 hours or 660 hours with instruction and help.

Two Key Skills You Must Learn

The skill of writing advertising copy is really two skills. One is the skill of salesmanship. The other is the skill of writing simply and clearly.

You don't need to be a wordsmith to be a good copywriter. But you do need to know what sort of things to say in what order.

So you must learn how selling works. You should do that it two ways. First you need to read books and articles about advertising. There are thousands of them available online—dozens of which are very good.

Copywriting genius John Forde suggests the following:

- *Scientific Advertising* by Claude Hopkin
- *Ogilvy on Advertising* by David Ogilvy
- *Tested Advertising Methods* by John Caples
- *The Copywriter's Handbook* by Bob Bly.

The second skill you must learn is how to structure a sales presentation. There is a shortcut for that. When I train copywriters, I insist that they read one good advertisement per day. In fact, I recommend that they actually hand-write their ads word for word for the first several weeks. This is an entirely different way of learning. I won't explain it here, but I can promise you that it will do you a great deal of good.

You can begin this process tomorrow. Spend 15 minutes per day reading about advertising (trying to learn the principles) and another fifteen minutes studying (by writing or reading aloud) a successful advertisement. You will be surprised at how quickly you can learn the basics following this protocol.

Start Writing Before You Are Ready

The most important trick I have used to accomplish what I've accomplished is encapsulated in the title of one of my books: *Ready, Fire, Aim*. (You'll notice it is not ready, aim, fire.) The idea, in a nutshell, is to begin doing what you want to do even if you don't think you're good at it. By practicing your goal, you not only learn it, but you mute the subconscious voices telling you that you can't do it.

After you have finished reading the free book, you should start writing. In the beginning, write only very short ads—50-100 words is enough. Write ads for anything—toothpaste, spaghetti, anything. The main purpose of this early writing is not to produce good copy but to break down whatever mental obstacles you may have about how hard it is to write.

Just keep writing one ad per day. Again, the length of it doesn't matter. Just keep at it until you feel like it's starting to flow.

Your First Full Advertisement

Once you have overcome your fear of writing, you should raise the bar a little. Give yourself the challenge of writing a longer ad—at least 1,000 words—once per week. You should find products that you like in industries you'd like to write for. Read an ad for a product and then write one of your own.

When You Can Begin to Earn Money

After you have completed 10 ads, you may be ready to test yourself. You will know. When you are ready, you will have a sort of semi-confident, semi-giddy feeling. "I think I'm getting this," you'll think. Will you be ready then? Probably not quite, but it is still the right time to try. Remember, it's always ready, fire, aim.

Find a business that you'd like to work for. Write the best ad you can for their business. No, don't write one ad, write three.

Then call that company and find out who is the director of marketing. Send that person a letter (buy email or post) that explains why you admire his company and his product and explain that you'd like to write an ad for him for free.

Include your samples. Admit that you are a beginner. Tell him you are willing to lose. Do this not once but as many times as it takes to get a positive response. You might get a trial gig the first time out. Or it may take you fifty times.

Don't worry about rejections. Becoming a professional freelance copywriter is just a matter of finding the right client—someone who sees potential in you.

Generating That Good Extra Income

When you get someone who is willing to work for you, don't blow the opportunity by pretending you are more experienced than you are. Recognize that this person is giving you the break of a lifetime. Be grateful for the criticism he gives you. Respond quickly and affirmatively to all of his suggestions. Be a happy slave.

The relationship with your first mentor may not work out. He may decide he doesn't have the time to bring you up to speed. That doesn't matter. Find a second. And, if needed, a third. Keep going until someone asks you to write a second advertisement. Now you have a customer.

Once you have your first client, getting others is much easier. Just remember to stay humble and keep learning. Until you have 5,000 hours under your belt you are not a master. But since you will be getting paid, you should be happy to earn while you learn.

How to Accelerate Your Progress

American Artists and Writers, Inc. (AWAI) offers excellent resources for both beginning and advanced copywriters. I have consulted for this organization for many years, and I believe it is the most comprehensive resource for copywriters. You can learn all about them at their website, www.awaionline.com.

In particular, AWAI publishes a book called *Copywriting 101: Secrets for Launching Your Million-Dollar Writing Career.* This will explain in greater depth what I've described here, including how the industry works, why copywriters are in demand, how much you can expect to earn, and what steps to take.

It also teaches you the most important copywriting secrets I've discovered. These are the same secrets I teach the young men and women I have mentored for more than 30 years.

They also have an extensive job board where they post gigs to which you can apply.

If you have questions about whether copywriting is a good fit for you, call Cameron, Debbie, or Pat at AWAI directly at 866-879-2924. They'd be happy to speak to you.

I recommend AWAI's course enthusiastically. It was based on my original teachings and has been revised and improved a dozen times in the past 15-odd years with the help of the insights of many of today's best copywriters. If you want to learn this amazingly valuable skill at home, there is no better way than to enroll in this program.

Special Offer for Members of the
Palm Beach Wealth Builders Club

If you're interested in learning more about any of the unique income opportunities I mentioned, the Palm Beach Research Group team and I offer additional guidance and support to members of our Palm Beach Wealth Builders Club.

I hold PBWC close to my heart. In fact, I created it myself after learning that many of our readers were struggling financially.

The Club provides in-depth guidance on everything I did to create wealth... and more. If you like any of the ideas mentioned here—whether it's rental real estate, entrepreneurship, or extra income opportunities—we explore these in much greater detail in the Club.

Anyone interested in learning more can contact PBRG at (888) 501-2598 or visit: www.palmbeachwealthclub.com. As soon as you sign up, you can start receiving our many perks, such as:

> *Existing members of the Club can enroll in AWAI's program for a discounted price. They can also receive a free 58-page report from AWAI detailing secrets to launching a successful copywriting career. For details, just give us a call.*

CHAPTER 20

Make Money Importing Goods From China

By Mark Morgan Ford

Would you like a simple formula for earning extra income?

Here it is: Find a popular product that is selling for $100. Find someone in China to knock it off and sell it to you for $10. Then sell it to the market at half price.

This is the formula the Walton family used to make Wal-Mart the biggest retailer in the world. It is also the formula that Target, Macy's, Rooms to Go, Amazon, Best Buy, and just about every other major retailer in the U.S. has used. And they account for just a fraction of the billions of dollars' worth of Chinese products imported into the U.S. every year.

Nobody can resist a bargain. And that's how these retailers stay in business. By selling in-demand goods at discount prices.

Import/export is a great opportunity for spare income. You don't need a lot of money to get started. (I'd like to say that a reasonable minimum investment is probably in the $2,000-3,000 range but that you can actually "test the waters" for as little as $50.) And you don't need official office space or a fulfillment center.

In fact, Amazon.com has made selling and shipping the products you import so easy, you don't even have to store inventory at home. With the right account, they'll accept your merchandise straight from your overseas supplier, take orders online, charge the customer's credit card, and ship them the product. All for a fraction of the sale price.

What's more, this is something you can do in your spare time. By limiting the number of products you buy and sell (and by using websites like Amazon to handle your fulfillment and order management), you can limit your involvement in the business.

Getting the cash flow started may take some effort and persistence. But once it's flowing, it generally keeps flowing without much additional work on your part.

Another thing I like about this business is that it has the international dimension. Some people enjoy getting to know other countries and cultures. If you do, this may be good for you.

I have a friend named Bernard. He came to the U.S. from England about 25 years ago and started a business selling furniture shortly after he arrived. He made a pretty good living for a while because he was a great salesman. But when he started importing Chinese knock-offs of popular furniture lines, he became rich.

I have another friend, George, who made more than $1 million in less than a year by simply brokering wholesale health products that he purchased in China. Once he found a Chinese manufacturer that could provide the products he needed, he phoned up the CEOs of several dozen health-supplement businesses.

When they heard how cheap his products were, many of them gave him orders. Before long, he was making more money than he ever expected to make. And it was easy!

Bernard and George experienced the immense wealth-building advantage of being able to sell a popular product for a fraction of the market price.

I have talked about this strategy for years, and now, I can finally recommend a specific way to do it.

In the old days, you had to have big bucks and/or big balls to get into the Chinese knock-off business. You had to travel to China, meet with dozens of suppliers, select one you thought you could trust, and then pay him a large sum of money to meet his minimum manufacturing requirements.

But all that has changed, thanks to the Internet.

In fact, there is one site—a mega-site—that can give you pretty much anything you could possibly want. You can say what you want and how much of it you want, and it will give it to you at the price you need... almost instantly.

You can use this site—and some support services that are tied into it—to set up your own international trading business, acting as a highly commissioned broker, hooking up U.S. buyers with Chinese manufacturers.

This is a very exciting situation. For the first time in history, individuals can compete with the world's largest retailers. They can buy modest quantities of popular products extremely cheaply... and have them delivered to the States in a matter of days.

America is a country of entrepreneurs. There are tens of millions of us who are constantly looking for ways to start new businesses to increase our wealth. Most people have no idea how easy it is to start up a Chinese import trading company... but word is getting out. The time to get into this, if you are interested, is right now.

A Program You Can Do From Home

If you can identify a ready market and deliver products at half price, it makes the selling process much easier. And later on, after you have developed a relationship with your customers (after they trust you), you can sell them other goods at higher margins.

I did this myself many years ago. My partner and I had a contest and sweepstakes business that needed thousands of little gifts— such as bracelets and cutlery—as "consolation" prizes. We made a connection with a merchant in New York who was able to supply us with all sorts of inexpensive Chinese tchotchkes (as he called them) for pennies on the dollar.

Recognizing the opportunity, we began selling somewhat more expensive goods—watches, jewelry, radios, and even small TVs—for crazy-low prices. We were eventually selling more than 30,000 items every month.

Selling inexpensive knock-offs from China is hardly a new industry. The experience I just told you took place in the '80s. Since then, Chinese goods have become a mainstay of consumption in the U.S. and the rest of the Western world.

What's new is that Internet access to Chinese distributors will permit you to buy in small quantities. This allows you to test various offers and markets while you are still in the first stage of your business development.

Another big change is the move to online shopping. Sales on Amazon.com in 2005 were $8.49 billion. By 2011, they climbed to $48.08 billion. And by 2014, $88.99 billion!

The combination of bargain and online shopping gives this business opportunity a powerful advantage. It spells opportunity for the individual entrepreneur who wants to follow in the footsteps of the Walton family and get into this wonderful business of selling Chinese goods to the still-huge U.S. market.

The simplest way to enter this business is to identify products that are already in demand and buy them from China. But you can also create your own product if you have a good idea.

Make Money With Your Own Good Ideas

An example is Valerie, a housewife who wanted to earn extra money to help pay for her kids' college education. Several years ago, there was a popular trend in children's wear called "footie" pajamas. These were soft, very comfortable one-piece items with covered feet built in.

Valerie had the idea that adults might want to have their own footie pajamas. She had no experience in the textile business and knew *nothing* about product sourcing or how to run an online business.

Yet, using very little money, she was able to create a home-based business that eventually grew to seven figures. These days, she works according to her own schedule and answers to nobody but herself.

She is very happy with her new life. She attributes her success to finding a source that allowed her to import the pajamas exactly the way she wanted them, for pennies on the dollar, from China.

There are plenty of others like Valerie. For example:

- A woman, pregnant with her first child, started her business back in 2004. She needed some maternity wear but didn't like what was available at the stores she shopped in. The clothes were bland and unflattering.

  She was looking for something a little sexier and more exciting, but the only places that carried what she wanted were very expensive boutiques. She figured there were a lot of other pregnant women in the same boat.

  So she found a source in China for the kind of maternity clothes she wanted to wear and went into business. Today, her company brings in more than $1 million per year.

- A married couple started importing flags from China in 2001 and reselling them on the Internet. Their business took off right away, so they expanded their offerings. Now they are generating revenues of more than $25 million per year!

The Opportunity Is Yours for the Taking

You can start your own business by importing Chinese goods and selling them online. You can get exactly what you want and have it made so cheaply you probably won't believe it at first.

You can also have the manufacturer deliver it wherever you want—to a distribution warehouse, to a wholesaler, or to the end customer. It's as easy as pushing a few buttons. That's how sophisticated this "underground" market has become.

What you need first, though, is just a little bit of education. You need to know how to:

- Research all the ready markets that are hot right now

- Locate reliable manufacturers

- Create purchase agreements that ensure your full satisfaction

- Find buyers eager to take your products at big discounts.

Here are eight reasons why you should consider getting into this market right now:

1. You can start out small. Many an empire has been started from a spare bedroom or the kitchen table. You don't need a huge office or a lot of overhead.

2. You will be your own boss. No more stupid memos and dress codes and meetings! You have the chance to do everything the way YOU want to.

3. You can make your own hours. You can work two hours in the morning and go golfing the rest of the day, if you feel like it.

4. You have unlimited profit potential. You can make as much money as you can spend. Want to make an extra $2,000 per month? Okay. Need to make an extra $10,000? No problem. It's all up to you. The sky's the limit.

5. You don't need any employees. (If you've ever had employees, you know what I'm talking about.)

6. You can run your empire from anywhere. All you need is a computer and an Internet connection. Go ahead, work from the side of the pool. It'll be our little secret.

7. You can learn everything you need to know in under an hour.

But I saved the best for last...

8. You don't need to have a ton of money to get started. You'll actually learn methods that can get you started for less than a couple of hundred dollars.

Import/export is a multibillion-dollar industry. And the fastest growing portion of it, I predict, will be small-time entrepreneurs, just like you, who are taking advantage of the new Internet technology.

CHAPTER 21

Earn up to $1,500 for Capturing a Simple "Story" on Camera

By Mark Morgan Ford

Can you take a photo like this?

Every time I see photos by Richard Avedon, Diane Arbus, or like the one above by Walker Evans, I tell myself I should take up photography as a hobby. What I admire about their work is that these single images deliver beautiful little stories straight to the heart. But what inspires me is that they are so simple. They look like something I could do.

I have many friends whose hobby is taking pictures. Some of them are quite good, as you can see here:

Photo Courtesy Gwen Gove

Photo Courtesy Trish Irish

When I first had this fantasy many years ago, photography was a challenging pastime. One needed expensive SLR cameras, various attachments, access to a developing lab, and a good deal of technical knowledge.

["SLR," short for "single-lens reflex," is a term associated with both film and digital cameras. SLR cameras use a mirror between the lens and the film (or image sensor) to provide a focus screen. This means the image you see in the viewfinder (or LCD screen) will be the same as what appears on film or as your digital image.]

Nowadays, the barrier to entry is much lower. You can buy amazing digital cameras for a fraction of the cost of the old SLRs. Even the cameras on iPhones and iPads produce great photos.

And developing and editing photos is now an easy task. Dozens of online photo services that make sizing, cropping, framing, and color correcting easy are available.

In short, creating beautiful photos is easier than ever. And that is why millions of people all over the world are becoming amateur photographers every year.

But this chapter is not just about becoming a skilled photographer. I also want to talk about how you can make money by taking photographs—money that can serve as a nice second income if you put your mind to it.

I wouldn't have believed it was possible to earn income as a part-time freelance photographer had it not been for a friend of mine who started a newsletter on the subject several years ago.

For about 10 years now, Lori Allen, the director of Great Escape Publishing, and her team have been teaching people how get paid to travel.

Focusing first on making money through travel writing, Lori realized that her team was overlooking a big opportunity. They realized that more and more, the folks who took their travel-writing program were writing in to say they were having success selling not only articles, but especially articles with photos.

They looked into it and discovered that magazine editors love it when writers submit photos with articles because it makes their jobs easier. Otherwise, the editors would have to commission photographers to take the pictures they need.

Typically, these editors pay from a couple of hundred to more than a thousand dollars per photo. But they won't accept just any photo. They have very specific requirements that most amateur photographers simply don't understand.

That's when Lori decided to develop a program to teach the trade of professional freelance photography to amateurs—people with simple cameras. The program went public in spring 2005 and has been a huge success ever since.

You can learn more about this program at www.thephotographerslife.com.

Can You Really Make Money Taking Photos?

I asked Lori about the income potential of taking and selling photos—and I asked her to be realistic. She said, "If you can get past the idea that it's only pretty pictures that sell... and you can learn how to spot what it is that photo buyers really want, it's possible to make $50-500 per photo as an amateur. That's fantastic money for something most of us do anyway—taking pictures."

I asked for examples.

Stock photography, travel photography, and local photography are the three biggest markets Lori talks about in her programs.

When you sell your photos as stock ("microstock" is what it's called when you do it online—the only kind of stock photography really open to amateurs), you send your photos to an online warehouse (a microstock agency).

Shelly Perry, Photo courtesy of Great Escape Publishing

The agency reviews the photos and decides if it will accept or reject them. And then it makes them available in an online catalog for buyers to search and buy. Shelly Perry, a photographer who sells her images as microstock, said she "earns, on average, $0.87 per photo per month from sales through online stock agencies."

As of this writing, she has more than 3,366 photos on file with one agency, which amounts to more than $2,800 per month in passive income. She doesn't have to lift another finger and she'll continue to earn $2,800 per month.

Think about that. If Shelly stopped taking photos today, she'd still earn enough money every month to cover two car payments, a weekend getaway, and a mortgage payment and still be left with money to save.

The Million Dollars in Three Years

LookStat.com published an article about the math of stock photography titled "How to Make a Million Dollars in Microstock."

It crunched some numbers and found that if you make $4 per image, and you add 400 new images to your portfolio per month, you'll be a millionaire in fewer than three years.

Hard to believe?

I'd say so. This is the trouble with abstractions. They can look great on paper, but they don't work in reality. There are two problems with this equation. First, you'd have to work full time to develop 400 good shots every month. Second, you wouldn't get paid for every one of them. Just some.

So let's look at some more realistic numbers...

Let's say you start now with zero images in your portfolio. And instead of uploading your photos to only one agency, you upload to four different agencies.

If you upload 20 photos per week to four different agencies, that's 320 new images for sale per month.

Assuming you'll earn around $1 per image per month (a much more realistic goal), by this time next year, you'll have made over $23,000.

Keep uploading 20 new photos to four agencies per week, and your monthly income will continue to grow...

In your second year, you'll make $69,120.

In your third year, you'll make $115,200.

It keeps going up from there.

Of course, this is assuming you can upload 20 new photos per week, that they're all accepted, and that you maintain an average income of $1 per image per month.

To do that, you'll need to consistently take good photos that sell. And you need to reserve some time at night or on weekends to learn how to edit your images in a program like Adobe Photoshop or Lightroom, as it's an absolute necessity that your images get processed before you submit them.

Local photos are a different market. Photographer Rich Wagner sells his local photographs as fine art, postcards, greeting cards, and even to magazines featuring articles about his hometown.

"My best-selling image is one I took just 15 miles from my house," he said.

"I waited for fall when the leaves were just right and the sky was clear blue. There's a tower in the distance—one everyone who lives here has to pass on their way to work, school, or the airport, so it's iconic.

"That image has earned me over $20,000 in the last five years.

Others sell for between $45 and $800 per piece. Photography is not my day job. It's a hobby that has now put all five of my daughters through college."

You Can Earn Big Bucks from Your Vacation Photos

Travel photos also sell. These are pictures you take while on vacation or out doing touristy things in your hometown.

Travel photos sell best to magazines, newspapers, websites, and guidebooks. But they also sell locally and to microstock agencies.

Lori told me this about selling travel photographs: "Our members have the most success selling their travel images with a travel article. For both a small 300- to 500-word article and one to two photos, they might earn $500-1,500. Some publications pay more. Others pay less."

Patrick Stevens, whose wife is a travel writer, says he sometimes gets more for his photos than his wife gets for her articles. Together, they can turn a vacation with the kids into nearly $3,000. She writes the travel stories. He takes the pictures. The kids step in as models when needed.

Here's one of their more recent magazine spreads about Colorado Springs, Colo. This one appeared in an airline in-flight magazine...

How Big Is the Market for Photography?

Every year in the U.S., print media alone publish more than six million photographs. That's more than 16,000 per day.

Worldwide, more than 15 million photographs are published each year. That's more than 40,000 per day.

That's big. But what is more important for our purposes is this: Freelance photographers produce the great majority of published (and paid-for) photos.

Stock photo agencies are constantly on the lookout for new talent. As are magazine editors. And in the past few years, the Web has become a huge market of its own.

That means there are plenty of opportunities for you to sell your photos... once you know how to take salable photos.

Where Can You Sell Your Photos?

Photo opportunities exist everywhere. On the roadside... at work... while talking with friends... in your backyard... a nearby zoo... special events... festivals... sporting events... pie-eating contests... and more...

Just take a look around you—at magazines, newspapers, books, trade journals, technical manuals, and almost any published material. Look at the cover and flip through the pages. What do you see? Photographs.

Someone has to take those pictures. Why not you?

Amateurs Become Professionals

Meet Tim O'Rielly, a San Diego resident. Tim has long enjoyed taking pictures of his home city. On walks and even at work, he finds time to snap photos of people and places and things that catch his eye. But unlike tens of thousands of amateur photographers in his area, Tim sells his photos for cash. He recently netted $2,000 for just 10 shots.

Tim also sells photos that he takes on vacation. He recently traveled with his family to Kauai and had his expenses paid, just for taking pictures.

And take a look at this photo:

Photo by Shelly Perry

This is Lori and her husband at their wedding. It sells online as microstock and has sold more than 200 times like this and in black and white. On iStockphoto.com, the smallest one sells for $19 and the largest for $70.

Buyers have included photo editors, graphic designers, and small businesses.

Here's how some of them have used the image...

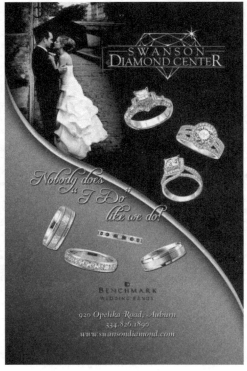

Tim, Shelly, Rich, and Patrick aren't doing anything you can't learn to do. You don't need expensive equipment or technical knowledge. All you need is a short education on how to identify and take salable photos—something I'm going to talk about in this chapter.

Imagine traveling to Tahiti for a vacation but treating it like a self-assignment. You shoot plenty of pictures that you can sell when you return home.

Or finding yourself in the Bahamas touring a local zoo and swimming with dolphins on a nearby island, all for free.

Or whisking your spouse away on a three-day weekend to Vancouver Island at someone else's expense...

These particular trips did not come from my imagination. They came from my research. They are the stories of ordinary people who decided to make extra money taking photos. Two of them, in fact, were brand-new to photography!

If you've been looking for a fun and creative opportunity to earn some extra income, this could be it. I'm going to outline a plan that can help you get started.

Here's What You Need to Get Started

- A decent camera (see box for recommendations)

- A willingness to learn a few things that set your photos apart

- A computer to edit your photos (this makes a big difference in how much you can earn from your photos).

How to Buy the Right Camera

By Lori Allen

 Don't get too wrapped up in buying the latest and greatest equipment.

The best equipment is made of metal and not plastic. Great for durability. But it's heavy, and if you're just starting out, you'll find yourself less likely to take it out of your bag because of its weight and sophistication.

Not only that, but when your pictures turn out blurry, too light, or too dark, you'll have a dozen bells and whistles to check before you find the culprit.

You'll spend your first days frustrated with the equipment before you even get a chance to shoot.

Photography should be fun. The more fun it is, the more pictures you'll take. The more pictures you take, the better you'll get at it.

Each market requires a different level of picture quality. Local photographs and some travel photographs can be created with simple point-and-shoot cameras. Microstock agencies are tougher, and the ones that pay the best no longer accept photos from a point-and-shoot.

Regardless of which market you choose, there's a new mirrorless camera technology that's all the rage. Both Panasonic and Olympus are recognized leaders in this Micro Four Thirds market, and each makes first-rate equipment.

Here's a good place to start for an under-$500 camera. If you find you want something more down the road, these will become great backup bodies:

- The Panasonic Lumix DMC-GF6 Mirrorless Micro Four Thirds Digital Camera with 14-42mm f/3.5-5.6 II Lens

- The Olympus E-PM2 Mirrorless Micro Four Thirds Digital Camera with 14-42mm and 40-150mm Lenses Kit

Can Anybody Do This?

Anyone *could* do this. As I've explained, the barriers to entry are low. The market is huge. And the demand is only getting bigger.

You don't need to take exotic pictures to make money. The subjects that are most in-demand are very simple to take. For example, here are a few of the subjects that are high in demand in microstock agencies right now:

- Products like a peanut butter and jelly smoothie
- A man or woman walking a dog with a collar
- Doctors examining patients
- Beach and travel shots
- People in business suits
- Multiethnic groups
- Seasonal photos—Halloween, Thanksgiving, Christmas, etc.
- Hobbies—golf, knitting, swimming, biking, scrapbooking, fishing, reading, sunbathing.

As with any new income opportunity, photography isn't hard—but most people will convince themselves that it's "not for them." They will tell themselves that they don't have the time to learn, don't have the little extra money it takes to get set up, or don't have the creativity to succeed.

The truth is, Lori's group has trained people from all walks of life to do this—teachers, retirees, boat captains, flight attendants, retired military, TV producers, politicians, real estate agents, event planners, software consultants, massage therapists, doctors, nurses, small business owners, retired CEOs, firemen, technical writers... you name it.

How to Get Started

You can get started immediately by buying or renting a camera, joining a local photo club, reading a few books, and just getting out there and taking pictures.

Composition and exposure are the two most critical elements behind a good photograph. Learn them by practicing and asking friends for feedback. You can also learn specific techniques through several resources online (simply Google "photo composition").

Next, Lori advises, "Practice first by putting your camera in 'Program' mode.

"This will keep the flash from popping up, but will otherwise put your camera in automatic mode. Cameras have come so far, they're right about 90% of the time. You should override what your camera suggests only when you know enough to know it's making the wrong choice.

"Put it in 'Program' mode (or 'P') and focus on composition. After that, you can learn how to manipulate your camera's aperture, shutter speed, and ISO to get the creative effects you want."

Lori has free videos online for explaining these more advanced settings, but warns not to get too bogged down with the technical specifics before you learn good composition and what it takes to create an appealing photograph.

"It doesn't matter how technically perfect your photograph is if no one likes to look at it," Lori says. Take things one step at a time.

You can access Lori's videos and lots of other free and useful information at www.thephotographerslife.com.

Additionally, here are some recommended books about photography:

- Bryan Peterson's *Understanding Composition Field Guide: How to See and Photograph Images with Impact*
- Bryan Peterson's *Learning to See Creatively: Design, Color and Composition in Photography*
- Michael Freeman's *The Photographer's Mind: Creative Thinking for Better Digital Photos*
- Bruce Barnbaum's *The Art of Photography: An Approach to Personal Expression*

I've looked into courses online about selling your photographs, but none are as good as the course that Lori produces.

I've watched Lori's and her team's progress from the beginning, and I've been very impressed with not just the quality of the teaching but also the success their students have enjoyed.

I asked Lori to put together a list of places where you can sell your photos with details about the types of photos that sell best in each market. You'll find it here...

Where to Sell Your Photos

Market No. 1: Magazines, Newspapers, and Websites

Large publications like *The New York Times*, *Travel + Leisure*, and *National Geographic* don't usually work with amateur photographers. But small publications, local papers, and limited-budget websites do.

To get a good idea of what sells, pick up a few publications around town and flip through them. Before you contact the editors, get a sense for the kinds of articles and photos they like to run. These are the types of images that will sell best to them.

Market No. 2: Fine Art

The unofficial definition of a fine-art photograph: A photo that someone buys to hang on their wall at home, in their office, or at a business they own.

Rich Wagner, the photographer I told you about earlier, says, "People buy fine-art photos that 'mean' something to them. If you live in Paris, your photos of the Eiffel Tower could prove quite lucrative. But if you live in Connecticut, the likelihood of selling your Paris pictures as fine art is pretty slim.

"If you want to sell photographs locally as fine art," he explains, "you've got to take local photographs. Among my best-selling photographs are pictures of the cows in the field next to our local airport, pictures of our local bakery, pictures of the town hall, and pictures of the local high school baseball field."

Market No. 3: Stock Agencies

Online stock photo agencies, such as iStockphoto or Shutterstock, are, in general, happy to work with amateurs. But they do expect near-perfect photographs, so you've got to have a good digital camera and an eye for composition.

It doesn't cost you anything to upload your pictures, and buyers can download whichever pictures they choose for anywhere between $1 and $20 or more, depending on the size of the image they want.

In exchange, you get a royalty for each image. Anywhere from 20-40% of the photo sale.

I recommend you invest in Lori's program. There's no better way to get up to speed on taking salable photographs. Here is a bit of what you will learn:

- The difference between a snapshot and a $5,000 photograph: five tricks you can use to bump up sales

- The tips you need for shooting in a variety of locations and situations—beach scenes, night photography, snow, rain, sunsets and sunrises, waterfalls, landscapes, pets, fireworks, sports, street photography, and more

- Why the most important asset is not your camera but your eyes. Learn classic principles of composition from great artists, painters, sculptors, and architects… and you'll never take an average photo again

- How to use your camera's built-in features to ensure you get great lighting in every image. The average Joe doesn't even know these exist!

- Why your camera's automatic mode will work for some pictures but will leave others looking washed out or too dark—and what you can do about it

- Eleven things I bet you didn't know your little camera could do

- How to use natural light—and window lighting—to snap salable product photos of everyday household items

- The press photographer's trick to taking sharp photos—even among a crowd of pushing fans (it's real easy and will help you snap perfectly focused pictures in crowded situations)

- Advice on buying the right equipment (if and when you upgrade)… how to set your fees and present your work professionally

- How to encourage editors to buy more than one photo at a time: Master the secret to writing great photo captions.

These are tricks that will set you apart from the amateurs, giving you a much-better-than-average chance of selling your photos.

Your Next Step: What to Do, Starting Today

1) If you already have a camera (point-and-shoot or otherwise), program it to shoot with the best quality, largest size possible.

If you don't know how to do this, look it up in your camera manual (or look online). Camera companies sometimes set the default on their cameras to the smallest settings so you can fit more images on your memory card.

This is fine if you're only creating photos for a photo album. But if you want to make money from your photos, change your settings to record the largest amount of data possible and buy an extra memory card. It's an investment that will pay off in spades and save you frustration.

2) Learn to take better-than-average shots. Watch online videos, read books on photography, flip through magazines, and look at the photos that are getting published. What do you like about them? Can you create photos like that? Invest in a class or Lori's program to improve your skills.

3) Take lots and lots of pictures. When you get home, you can weed out the best shots; the more you take, the better the possibility of good shots you have to work with. Keep in mind that not every shot is a winner or salable, and that's all right. That's why you want to take a lot while you're there.

Try, of course, to make each shot interesting. Looking at your subject from a variety of angles might give you a new idea or a fresh perspective... taking several shots will help ensure you get the right one.

Two More Stories to Inspire You

1) **Efrain Padro**

Efrain Padro spent nearly 20 years practicing law before pursuing photography. Like 95% of Lori's members, he didn't go to school to become a photographer—but he knew that it was his true passion. So he left the briefcase behind and picked up his camera.

Now he's selling pictures to a wide variety of clients who pay him anywhere from $100-500 a pop for the use of his images.

And on top of the income his photos generate, he's able to use his photography to bag all-expenses-paid trips like a six-week trip to a beautiful Caribbean island. There, he took pictures similar to the types of things that you'd probably photograph on vacation—the beaches, sandcastles, and rainforests.

The only difference is that he later sells his photos for a profit, while yours likely get buried on your computer.

2) **Terry Robinson**

Before Terry Robinson attended one of Lori's programs a few years ago, he had sold a handful of images to family and friends for $25-50. But when he finished the program, he immediately put to use the secrets and tricks he picked up. In his spare time, he set up a photo shoot in his hometown (you don't necessarily have to travel beyond your back yard to make this work)...

And he made $275 on his first set of images.

Today, he "works" only part-time. When he wants extra spending money, he breaks out the camera and knows he can make $500-1,000 in a single weekend.

The point: Neither of these guys had formal training as

photographers. They took classes, watched videos, and practiced, sure. But if you can learn how to create good photographs and whom to sell them to, you can turn a fun photo hobby into a viable income stream. An income you can take with you anywhere in the world— whether you do it full time, part time, or even just on vacation.

CHAPTER 22

Turn Your Skills Into Cash With e-Lancing

By Mark Morgan Ford

There are many ways to earn extra money, and one of the most interesting is through a method called e-lancing. E-lancing sounds fancy, but it simply means working as a freelance professional through the Web. It means selling a skill you have to people looking for that skill on the Internet. As an e-lancer, you find your clients online and you also—usually—service them online.

There are three big advantages e-lancing gives you.

First, the market for your services is huge. You don't have to limit your advertising to your local town or your Rolodex, as freelancers did in the past. With a little know-how, you can reach hundreds, thousands—even hundreds of thousands—of potential customers with a modest advertising budget.

Second, since you will be working online, you don't have to spend a lot of time traveling. For the normal freelance professional, traveling is a huge and costly part of his expenses.

Third, because you'll deliver your work electronically, you can copy and replicate it easily and thus serve many of the same customers with much of the same information and advice. This allows you to leverage the value of your time and make more than you could ever make in the old days.

I did a bit of research on e-lancing and discovered that it is a big, growing business. When I first wrote this chapter, the website Elance.com reported more than 92,500 posted jobs in only the last 30 days.

Even more impressive, Elance reports that the total value of work done to-date through its site alone is over $657 million. That's staggering! And Elance isn't even the biggest of this type of website.

It gets better.

According to a study released on Bitrebels.com, the average hourly rate of e-lancers with fewer than five years of experience is between $44.87 and $49.96! For freelancers with five or more years, that number skyrockets to between $59.15 and $84.55!

The upside, in my opinion, is much greater than $84.55. Remember, this is a figure based on people doing it now—thousands of people with no particular knowledge of how to increase their fees. That is something we'll be talking about in this chapter.

As a consultant to the publishing industry, I've seen how many of my clients have turned to the Internet to find the researchers, writers, and analysts they need.

And I have friends in the insurance, brokerage, and accounting industries who rely heavily on e-lancers for all sorts of jobs. There's demand for data entry, computer model development, customer service, and more.

There's a prestigious architectural firm in Boca Raton, Florida, that uses e-lancers to do design work for its hotel and restaurant clients. I know doctors who use e-lancers to review and write précises on medical journals to help them keep up with developments in their fields.

I know dozens of direct marketers who routinely turn to the Internet to find the copywriters and graphic artists they need.

Yes, it is a big and growing industry.

Actually, I take that back. It's not really an industry at all. It's more like an enormous marketplace, bustling with eager employers searching out people with the skills, availability, and desire to do almost every conceivable kind of job.

Peggy's Story

In my research, I came across a story about a Midwest homemaker named Peggy who was able to turn her many hobbies into cash flow. Peggy is one of those people with boundless energy. Besides taking care of her family, she helps friends plan weddings and parties and creates handmade greeting cards. She even assists her husband in writing business reports.

One of her friends asked Peggy why she did all of these things. Her answer? "Because I like to." The friend suggested that Peggy advertise her services on the Internet. Why not make money doing all of these things she likes to do anyway?

Peggy was skeptical. Especially when she failed to get the first several jobs she applied for. But on either the sixth or seventh try, she landed her first job.

The second came quicker. The third, even faster than the second. Since she did great work, her clients kept returning. Before Peggy knew it, she had more paid work than she had time for.

With all of this demand for her services, Peggy gradually increased her fees. Eventually, she was making more money per hour than her husband. And since she loved what she was doing, it wasn't truly "work"!

What Our Researchers Discovered

E-lancing, you see, is not a single opportunity, but a thousand opportunities rolled into one.

Here are some facts about e-lancing you should be aware of:

Data entry and customer service jobs used to dominate e-lancing. Most people have experience calling what they presume to be a local number only to find themselves talking to someone half-way across the globe. But this is rapidly changing in two ways.

First, many of the large companies that were using Indian companies because of the low costs have turned back to employing e-lancers in their home countries. Why? The large companies realized that the e-lancers produced better-quality and more cost-efficient work.

Second, the kinds of jobs advertised on an e-lance basis today are rapidly expanding. Data entry and customer service are still very much in demand, but employers are now seeking e-lancers for hundreds of other skills. These include:

- Photography
- Graphic arts
- Translation
- Dictation services
- Marketing analysis
- Stock analysis
- Copywriting
- Property management services.

As you can see from just glancing at this list, these types of e-lance services will demand higher rates than $50-85 per hour. I fully expect to see the data on e-lance income continue to expand as these programs expand. In a few years' time, they should be well into the $50-500 per hour range that I like.

There are far too many types to list them all here. Just visit any number of the e-lance websites and browse for yourself! You're going to be amazed at the volume of opportunities in the most obscure fields or niches.

Consider this: According to Elance.com, the fastest-growing jobs are now in legal services (176%), bookkeeping (75%), and accounting (88%).

Why the growth? In part, books or philosophies like Tim Ferriss' *The 4-Hour Work Week* have alerted working people to the possibility of making a good income from working part-time on the Internet.

Why e-Lancing Will Last

When you see a market expanding like this one is, the natural question is: Will it last?

My answer? Absolutely! Here's why. The growth of the e-lance marketplace is largely due to the fact that small business owners have begun to recognize the economics of hiring e-lancers. Many small- and medium-sized companies can't afford to hire full-time researchers, writers, marketers, bookkeepers, accountants, programmers, and salespeople.

But they can afford to hire people to work part-time from home... or possibly from the beach. Part-time e-lancers are more economical for entrepreneurial businesses because e-lancers can be employed only when they are needed and they don't need to be given office space, utilities, tools, and other things that full-time employees require.

Plus, they don't receive full-time financial benefits such as medical insurance and retirement plans.

As one expert put it, "Freelance workers give employers the skills they need on a fractional and affordable basis."

To outsiders, being an e-lancer may sound like a risky proposition. But once you have an established clientele, you are actually much safer and more independent than you would be as a full-time employee.

Think of it this way: E-lancing thrives when economies are bad. It's basically recession-proof, because hiring online is how companies save money when times are tough. This is great news for anyone who is dependent on a business for his paycheck.

But companies aren't just turning to e-lancers because of cost savings, either. Increasingly, managers are looking online to find top talent.

Gary Swart, CEO of the online marketplace oDesk.com, writes:

> *Thanks to the growing adoption of online work, businesses can increasingly access talent on an on-demand basis, hiring online contractors from around the world so they can stay nimble and reduce overhead.*
>
> *Businesses are using online workers to extend their existing staff (often with talent they can't find locally) to launch resource-strapped microbusinesses, and even to create companies that are entirely virtual.*

Consider this statistic provided by Swart:

> *According to 82% of the millennials surveyed, within 10 years, many businesses will be built completely with virtual teams of online workers.*

So where do you find these jobs?

There are countless websites that match employers with e-lancers. Two of the biggest and best we've found are oDesk.com and Elance.com.

Toward the beginning of this chapter, I detailed a few statistics from Elance. Let me revisit those and add to them. It will help show you just how big of an opportunity this is.

- In 2015, there were more than two million contractors on Elance.

- The value of work done through Elance, as of 2015, was $1,092,538,510.

- Some companies have paid rates on Elance as high as $150 per hour... You string together 20 of those hours in a week, and you have an income of $150,000 working half-time!

And remember: Elance is just one of these online marketplaces. Hundreds more jobs are added every week on competing sites such as FreelanceSwitch.com, oDesk.com, or even Craigslist.org.

How to Get Started With e-Lancing

So if you're interested in e-lancing, let's talk about the action steps to take to get started...

1. Ask yourself: What skill or talent do I have that I can offer online to employers?

2. Get online and visit the following websites:

    a. Elance.com

    b. oDesk.com

    c. Guru.com

    d. Freelancer.com

    e. Project4hire.com

3. Post your services.

4. If you're unclear what service you think you're good at, browse job postings to see if anything sounds like something for you.

I also recommend that you read *The Freelancer's Bible* by Sarah Horowitz. It will help answer questions you may have.

The bottom line: E-lancing is an amazing opportunity to turn your skills into cash. Even better, you decide how much time to invest.